Fine Lines
from the Box

Fine Lines from the Box

further thoughts about our country

Njabulo S Ndebele

Compiled by Sam Raditlhalo

UMUZI

Published by Umuzi,
P.O. Box 6810, Roggebaai 8012
an imprint of
Random House (Pty) Ltd,
Isle of Houghton, Corner Boundary Road &
Carse O'Gowrie, Houghton 2198, South Africa
www.umuzi-randomhouse.co.za

First edition, first printing 2007
ISBN: 978-1-4152-0037-7

Cover design by Sally Swart
Design and layout by Abdul Amien
Set in 10.3pt on 14pt Minion
Printed and bound by Paarl Print
Oosterland Street, Paarl, South Africa

Contents

Abbreviations

AIDS	Acquired Immune Deficiency Syndrome
ANC	African National Congress
AUETSA	Association of University English Teachers of South Africa
AZAPO	Azanian People's Organisation
DP	Democratic Party
HIV	Human Immunodeficiency Virus
MDM	Mass Democratic Movement
MRC	Medical Research Council
NEDLAC	National Economic Development and Labour Council
PAC	Pan Africanist Council
SABC	South African Broadcasting Corporation
SAHRC	South African Human Rights Commission
SSA	Statistics South Africa
TRC	Truth and Reconciliation Commission
UCT	University of Cape Town
UDF	United Democratic Front

Preface

A turning point in my life occurred when I discovered a treasure trove of banned books in my father's garage. One day, alone at home and bored during school holidays in the mid-1960s, I began to explore my home. There was that wooden crate at the front right corner of the garage against which the silver bumper of my father's Ford Zephyr 6 sometimes rested. That crate had been there for many years. An assortment of garden tools was often positioned around it. On top of it was a heavy layer of unused floor tiles; old copies of *Huisgenoot*, *Zonk*, and *Drum* magazines; and two bulging cardboard boxes laden with old shoes, empty oil cans, old Chinese Checkers, Ludo and Snakes and Ladders game boards, abandoned toys, and other odds and ends associated with various members of the family. All these would not encourage anyone of casual interest to open the crate.

Once I had removed everything from the top of the box, I opened it. Inside were many books on music, art, and poetry, and others that I thought my father must have used for his degree studies at the University of the Witwatersrand. But as I got closer to the bottom of the box, my heart leapt with disbelief! Here was *Down Second Avenue* by Ezekiel Mphahlele; and *Road to Ghana* by Alfred Hutchinson; and *Blame Me on History* by Bloke Modisane; and *Naught for Your Comfort* by Trevor Huddleston; and *Tell Freedom* by Peter Abrahams; and *Splendid Sunday* by James Ambrose Brown; and *Transvaal Episode* by Harry Bloom; *Chocolates for My Wife*, by Todd Matshikiza; *South Africa: The Struggle for a Birthright* by Mary Benson; *The Ochre People* by Noni Javabu; *Ghana: The Autobiography of Kwame Nkrumah*; *Let My People Go* by Albert Luthuli; *Go Well, Stay Well* by Hannah Stanton, copies of *Africa South* magazine, and other lesser known books that I do not remember now. Banned books!

After putting the books back, dangerously placing the banned books at the top of the box for easy access, I went back into the house and began to read *Down Second Avenue*. Two days later, I read *Blame Me on History*. I still remember clearly the thrill of reading these two books and beginning to discuss them with myself. How different they were from each other, conveying different aspects of the same overriding political and social reality! It struck me then that no matter how much black people suffered under apartheid, they did not experience oppression in the same way. They did not evoke the pain of oppression in the same way. It struck me then that oppressed people were far more complex than the collective suffering that sought to reduce them to a single state of pain. This has been a consistent interest of mine: thinking about South Africa.

Beyond that, these books spoke to me with a directness I had not encountered in many school books about South Africa. For the first time I began to read books that spoke directly to me about the forbidden subject of white people's oppression of blacks and the latter's resistance to it. I had heard about these books and knew it was dangerous to possess them, but despite that I felt privileged that they were right there in my home and that I was going to read them in secret.

My experience with these books directly linked my preoccupation with South Africa, particularly in exile in Lesotho, with my attempts to reflect on that preoccupation through writing. It was these books that started me on a reading and writing journey that has not ended. As I read more and wrote more and got to experience increasingly the beauty of reading and writing, it struck me that reading and writing are two sides of a coin I wish to call *the art of the fine line*. Writing is the one art that compels the writer to explore and express complex feelings and thoughts through an attempt at simplicity and concreteness that are yet able to preserve the complexity. Otherwise, mere simplicity to achieve clarity of expression may diminish the subject.

This is not an effect that one always achieves. But the ability to achieve it develops over time. The more one writes, and the more one's range of experience expands, the more insight into writing grows alongside and deepens. That process achieves a point of maturation when the writer learns to be suspicious of extremes of expression and chooses rather to work with the tension between extremes. In the best writing, I have come to understand, there is nothing to condemn or elevate without a concomitant sense of doubt. Achieving this balance has been the ultimate struggle of my writing. It is an unending process of pinning down words to express insight and to increase and deepen understanding. It is always a demanding exercise to work with thoughtfulness to express the fine line.

This kind of experience with discursive prose brought home to me a close relationship between the speculative essay and the short story. Both make an attempt at brevity but of the kind that resonates and invites several readings. The effect comes from an intriguing interplay between brevity, clarity and depth.

One more element completes the scene with regard to social commentary. It is that social commentary, through the device of the speculative essay, has to work with polemic. This is when the writing uses insight to mount a challenge, to entreat, to cajole and prod the reader towards an activist understanding. It is this kind of understanding, I believe, that should be at the heart of a democracy such as ours which was intended, among other things, to thrive on thoughtful intervention. This would be an antidote to orthodoxy and the comfort zones of populism.

So, starting from my father's box of banned books, I have sought to cultivate in my writing the art of the fine line. In this regard, I like to think that a consistent feature of the essays in this book, taken together with the essays in the earlier *Rediscovery of the Ordinary*, is the attempt to capture the essence of issues through a thoughtful engagement with them. I hope that goal is achieved most of the time.

This collection of thoughts brings together a range of issues that I explored between 1987 and 2006. The span of eighteen years may seem at once a moment and a lifetime, depending on whether we run fast through history or slowly ponder it. Much has happened in between, from pain to deliverance. Now we struggle with the challenge of the future and face the necessity of hope. In this collection, I have refrained from commenting on the range of issues covered, preferring to point the reader towards the overall effect intended: pushing the boundaries of thought in our democracy and deepening intellectual engagement. In that, I have been concerned as much with the issues as with the means of engaging with them. We have been far more concerned in the new democracy with what to do than with how to do it. Many disasters have occurred, such as when we offered retirement packages to thousands of teachers, thinking we were pursuing transformation. We lost many of the best ones. Our schooling system has never recovered. A little more thought could have saved us.

This book is a tribute to my father's banned books: imprisoned thought now freely available, challenging us to build on the legacy.

Good morning, South Africa

whose universities, whose standards?

1987

South African English-speaking universities have long proclaimed themselves the custodians of the liberal tradition. Over the years, they have succeeded in convincing the bulk of the population that the proclamation is valid. This proclamation needs to be re-examined. I focus on these universities in the belief that history has established them, thanks to their liberal posture, as the major terrain of battle for the intellectual future of this country. Since the historical exclusion of blacks from the democratic process has meant the absence of real opposition, what was left of legitimate opposition was taken over by the English-speaking political interest. The resulting relationship between the general black opposition and liberal English nationalism has been that of allies as well as contestants.

For example, it is reasonable to assert that the general black opposition has, over the years, supported the stand of these universities on such issues as academic freedom and university autonomy. But then, such support should be seen in its proper perspective. The stand of these universities was seen as a function of tolerable opposition within the confined compass of white democracy. Black support for such a stand was restricted largely to the form rather than to the content of opposition. It cannot be doubted that the stand served the interests of English cultural nationalism while allowing the tantalising possibility of black participation within that liberal universe. The content of opposition, therefore, has remained contested terrain. That is why there may be no agreement over the meaning of the two concepts of academic freedom and university autonomy, and their implications for the role of the universities in a truly democratic South Africa.

The problem is that white South African culture, highly developed in its

---

Senate Lecture Series, University of the Witwatersrand, 1987 technical features, is unlikely ever to reach maturity. This is because it is unlikely by itself to accommodate the full creativity of all the people of this country in a way that would reflect the specific creativity and dynamism of our nation. The conceit that they are representative torchbearers of Western civilisation in the southern corner of South Africa has prevented white South Africans from coming to terms with the full implications of the realities around them.

The result is that they have developed an essentially derivative culture that sought to reproduce the metropolitan centre as the measure of their self-image. Accentuating their difference from Africans was part of their civilising mission. This tendency expresses itself in various forms, but its academic version was reiterated recently by the chairman of the council of the University of the Witwatersrand when, in response to Eric Molobi and Mluleki George, two of this year's Richard Feetham Memorial Lecture speakers, he asserted in *Frontline* that the need for universities in South Africa to maintain high academic standards 'has nothing to do with apartheid, or politics for that matter; it relates to the *internationally accepted standards of teaching and research* [my italics].'

The hegemony of apartheid culture is extensive and complex: even those who would otherwise disavow it become its unwitting servants. For how can we fail to notice that part of the psycho-social justification for apartheid is the need to maintain the illusion of metropolitan purity precisely where it is impossible ever to achieve such purity without the genocidal extermination of black people? Consequently, in proportion to the considerable measure of this impossibility is the number of drastic measures required to maintain the illusion. Perhaps one of the most tragically infantile expressions of this illusion is how every morning the entire nation is subjected to the insufferable chit-chat of TV announcers desperately trying to emulate their American counterparts on the morning shows, and in the process wasting thousands of miles of potentially valuable film footage. 'Good Morning America' has spawned an intolerable local version: 'Good Morning South Africa'. This has become a daily replay of sterility.

What this illustrates is that the technical capability of a modern state to achieve universal social progress is available, but it is a capability without vital content.

Certainly, the cultural reproduction of Europe in South Africa has been particularly beneficial to the settlers during the period of rampant capital accumulation. Unfortunately, periods of capital accumulation have been characterised by a general lack of scruples over the methods of accumulation. By the time the period of accumulation reached its highest point of fruition for the settlers, now habituated to the material advantages of imported metropolitan technology, uncritical emulation had become an entrenched behavioural trait. It is eminently understandable why, now wielding considerable political and economic power, the white settlers of South Africa have insisted on being the human point of reference for all the people of this country.

It is for these reasons that many of them who want change, even those who hate apartheid with all their hearts, insist that the need for the maintenance of European culture in South Africa is not negotiable. Instead, change means drawing the oppressed into this culture and making its benefits available to all – to some extent. While apartheid insisted that the oppressed would develop better alone, liberals insisted they would develop better within the prescriptions of European standards. They insist on wanting to draw the oppressed into an already sterile, derivative cultural environment that could expose the oppressed to its forms only by law. By definition, such a situation would not allow them to bring in 'the baggage' of their African experience.

At this juncture, one of the most significant realities of contemporary South Africa needs to be borne in mind. As a starting point, there is a need for us to recognise and accept the historical fact of the rise of the black South African masses. The reality of the black mass is pervasive: the mines, one of the most grotesquely visible symbols of mass oppression, bring together hundreds of thousands of workers; the state, under various resettlement schemes, has undertaken the removals of millions of people; Bantu Education was designed to produce and reproduce mass ignorance; millions of people commute to work from the township everyday; it is not enough that millions of people are unemployed, newspapers these days are constantly reporting how thousands of people are being fired from work. Everywhere we come across the mass, that crowning achievement of South African capitalism. For is it not so that at the centre of the history of South African capitalism is the mobilising of millions of people for the exploitation of their labour? Such a history will certainly have its consequences.

Surely we should expect that at some point the mass will make some massive demands on behalf of the mass interest?

Surely the children of the masses are destined to invade the universities. To recognise this fact is to appreciate that at this historical juncture the issue is not academic standards, nor is it university autonomy, or freedom of speech: we waste our time when we debate these issues outside an appropriate historical and social context. They are not fundamental. The fundamental issue is the education of the mass. The issue is the democratisation of education and the process by which knowledge is acquired and disseminated, such that millions of those who were deprived of the opportunity to know can have access to knowledge.

Once we recognise this need we will realise that any society will tend towards the 'highest standards' in the promotion and protection of its interests. We assert this with the full knowledge that even apartheid society can boast of its best minds, some of whom, having graduated from institutions of higher learning espousing the highest academic standards 'according to internationally accepted standards of teaching and research', were responsible for engineering the sufferings of millions of people.

For high standards are matters of societal efficiency and are not prerogatives of any ideology. All civilisations, anywhere in the world, at any moment in their history, have or have had traditions of efficiency built into their functioning to ensure their survival. That is why American universities will insist on high standards in the same way that Soviet universities do. It is the socio-political context in which high standards are applied that distinguishes universities.

On this basis, we distinguish between universities that, on the one hand, proclaim high standards as a function of their active involvement in combating oppression and injustice through the manner in which they articulate and organise their intellectual commitments and, on the other hand, those that proclaim high standards as a subtle principle of exclusion, thereby effectively asserting the status quo. With this understanding, 'people's education', for example, is not necessarily antithetical to efficiency and high standards. To think so is to reveal a lack of understanding, or even ideological prejudice. The starting point is to define a vision. Once we have that vision we will devise the most efficient methods, proclaim the highest standards in the pursuit of it.

How can liberal universities respond to this situation?

For a start, they need to recognise the extent to which the liberal posture may itself be a subtle justification for the status quo.

Secondly, they must realise that opening the doors of learning to the mass is not an ethical or moral issue dependent on the conscience of decision makers. Instead, it is inherent in the mass struggle for liberation; it is a logical outcome of the history of struggle. This is not to suggest that we cannot intervene and shape that outcome. We have to. But we can only properly do so once we have clearly defined our allegiances in the light of our understanding of the historical forces at play.

The aim is to situate the universities within the general ambience of the mass-based democratic movement. But the question is: can they do so by themselves or should they be made to? At the centre of the question is how change will ultimately come about in South Africa; for whites themselves are not the oppressed, yet they control the universities which may have to re-orientate their academic activities to reflect the emergent predominant interest.

Recognising the rise of the masses, the universities must try to find ways of consulting with the mass-based democratic movements on policy issues. This is premised on the recognition that the oppressed will steadfastly refuse to be turned into consumers of the pre-packed activity of knowledge production.

I am reminded of the words of Richard Lichtman in an essay 'The Universities: Mask for Privilege' published in *The Campus in the Modern World*. His words seem particularly apposite to our situation in which the responsibilities of the universities and organised intellectual pursuits need to be redefined in the light of the magnitude of changes underway in South Africa:

> The University is at this moment an ideological institution, a mask for systematic dominance and privilege. But as Marx noted: 'The call for men to abandon their illusions about their condition is a call for men to abandon a condition which requires illusion.' A free and human community of scholars can flourish only when the multitudinous communities of the exploited, the wretched, and the brutalised peoples of the earth have broken the bonds of their sub-

17

servience and established themselves as men of full stature. To participate in the projection and the making of that world is the responsibility of the intellectual.

I would add that it is the responsibility of the university, as an influential institution, to redefine its priorities in such a way that the committed intellectual, the student, and the community, all hungry for knowledge and a sense of direction promising a redeemed world, can function with maximum creativity.

The Brilliant Trick

apartheid's fireworks display

1988

The fireworks display is one of the oldest forms of public celebration. Its impact lies in the momentary effect of the most brilliant, yet fleeting, intensity. It is not meant to last long. Indeed, the brevity of the display enhances the significance of what is being celebrated; for the celebrated event really does not depend on the display. It has its own significance. The display can never substitute for it in any fundamental way.

That is why the display should not last too long. Too much of it may begin to overwhelm viewers, easily resulting in numbing, if unintended, impression of banality. It may even draw attention away from the commemorated event, stand in its place, and become an end in itself, more so if the event being celebrated has itself lost some of its significance. At that point the display begins to degenerate and becomes an empty gesture 'signifying nothing' beyond its brilliance. It becomes a grand deception.

The prolonged fireworks display is the aim of apartheid today. The display points to a dead past and memories of past glory, rather than to something alive that feeds the unfolding future. That is why government in South Africa may be seen to have become the sum total of spectacular tricks performed according to the rules of political gamesmanship. But this massive effort underscores nothing more than apartheid's futile grand endeavour to change its colours in a brilliant display of shrewd resourcefulness.

When seen against the visible and irreversible hunger for freedom in South Africa; against the selfless determination of black youth all over the country; against the consolidation of the trade union movement; against the rising crisis of confidence in the white population, and much more – we have clear evidence of the end of an era. Apartheid has lost its vitality, even

Leadership, Vol 8, No 1, March 1989

among whites. It can no longer inspire confidence. Suddenly the earth is no longer the centre of the universe. Suddenly the world has become the most insecure place to live in. To maintain the illusion of security, let's have a fireworks display.

There is an unforgettable scene in Karel Schoeman's novel *Promised Land* in which the aspirant poet Raubenheimer recites his poetry before a gathering of neighbourhood celebrants during a party that painfully and devastatingly lays bare the tragic emptiness of a culture that, no longer engendering the real sense of a vital present, induces belief in a dead past through heroic recall. In few novels has an author so succeeded in creating a scene in which words uttered by characters are repudiated by the physical and social context in which they are uttered:

> Civilisation's torch, with brave and steady hand
> They bore across the void and darkling land ...

As the voice of Raubenheimer booms, my mind is forced to recall the numerous ox-drawn wagons doggedly blazing trails across the country in celebration of 'The Great Trek'. At that instant in Schoeman's novel, while Raubenheimer is reciting his poetry, an accordion squeaks and the daughters of the accordion player giggle at this rude, albeit brief, intrusion into a weighty poetic moment, while his wife, Aunt Loekie, 'who wasn't even pretending to listen', calls for more drink.

> Heroes were all – man, woman,
> child alike,
> No sacrifice withheld, no gift
> refused ...

Raubenheimer plods on, in celebration of heroism, as we realise just how much of it is actually gone.

Minister of Defence Magnus Malan recently 'unveiled' a new weapon in South Africa's store of armaments. He called it South Africa's 'insurance policy'. I have tried to figure out the implication of the metaphor. What does this weapon insure the country against? Does it insure it against war? Political change? The outbreak of disease? Collapse of the education system?

Inflation? Unemployment? Drought? The relationship between such problems and a weapon of war is hard to fathom, under the circumstances. Clearly, the minister's imagination seems to have been carried away by the ruggedness and speed of a metal monster careering across the plains, running over mines only to emerge out of the blast of smoke and dust remarkably unscathed. Surely such a spectacle calls for dramatic metaphors!

No doubt the minister must have had a hand in the decision to build this weapon, following an elaborate exercise involving project proposals and evaluations, and other serious rituals of governance, all suggesting an admirable application to duty. So his sense of personal fulfilment and unguarded exuberance can well be understood. The weapon must be seen as a culmination of administrative and technical effort; it may even be a remarkable technical achievement. But the minister's metaphor bears a chilling dimension.

With the best will in the world, it is difficult to see any meaningful social dimension to this military development. Supposing the weapon is a bestseller – where will the money go? The scientists who produced it – what connection do they have with the hundreds of thousands of South Africa's schoolchildren who may wish to become scientists? The soldiers who will fight in it – what will they be fighting for? As a scientific and military achievement, its impact has little bearing on the social reality around it. Its real meaning can only be in its capacity to intimidate. It is meant to defy the world through a display of technological independence at the same time as it is designed to intimidate a restive black population and offer solace to an insecure white population. It is the ultimate symbol of a hardened and doggedly indifferent sensibility. Proof of technical achievement has less to do with the search for solutions to human problems than with demonstrating 'successful' ideological recalcitrance. The momentum of recalcitrance no longer has anything to do with the noble pursuit of a social vision.

What has become a sensationalist approach to politics is reflected and marked in the newspapers. 'Beware of the rooikat', goes a headline in one Sunday paper. Who, we may ask, must watch out? Is it the militarily weak neighbouring states; the black population in South Africa; the white right; the rest of the world and the Cubans in particular? Objectively, the dimension of significant meaning to the threat is extremely narrow. What we are left with, therefore, is a dramatic metaphor underscoring the absence of real drama.

One is commonly told that the will of Afrikaners to survive should never be underestimated; that they are capable of fighting back in a most devastating manner. That impression can only come from someone who believes in the fireworks display; who believes that the Afrikaner today is still the Afrikaner of yesterday and remains unmoved by the success of the high commodity consumption culture in South Africa, bequeathed by colonialism and apartheid.

That culture has attacked the moral fibre of heroic resolve and replaced it with business cosmopolitanism. The display of militarism is no longer proof of the will to fight to the bitter end. The urge to fight may well be there, but it is no longer connected to a strong belief in what is to be fought for. Many will be perfectly content to replay the Great Trek, attend the military parade, and express satisfaction with new military hardware 'made in South Africa', and feel good about the new image of the modern, sophisticated, and cosmopolitan white South Africa being marketed on SATV today. But when they do so, they are merely visiting a museum, except that they may be willing to believe that the museum is real life.

There are many other features of South Africa's official, contemporary political culture that lend themselves to a similar understanding. But in no other area is the drama more evident than in the field of foreign policy, where the aim seems to be to give to the world the impression of normality where there is none.

President P W Botha's expeditions in 1987 into Mozambique, Malawi, Zaire, and the Ivory Coast have been hailed as a significant step towards ending the isolation of South Africa. Declarations were made to the effect that white South Africans are, after all, Africans. These 'new Africans', of course, understand Africa better than any European or North American power. Consequently, the 'new Africans' will rescue the continent from the mire of ignorance, poverty and disease. When these declarations are made, the ignorance, poverty and disease engendered by apartheid is conveniently forgotten.

What qualitative difference is there between this activity and former Prime Minister John Vorster's erstwhile 'outward looking policy'? Perhaps there is one dramatic difference: the present effort features a young foreign affairs minister who studiously reflects the image of accomplished diplomatic flair, and who embodies the dilemmas of his generation.

Pik Botha is without doubt one of the most fascinating of contemporary South African politicians. He appears to symbolise two interesting tendencies in the contemporary Afrikaner approach to the world: to defy the world while needing its acceptance as an equal in the affairs of the modern world. This calls for a display of confidence, flair, sophistication, wit, and calculated toughness. Somewhere there, also, is to be found an intriguing innocence. I have an unforgettable image of Pik Botha when he debated with Archbishop Desmond Tutu on American TV a few years ago. I thought I saw a man simmering inside, struggling to contain himself; a man decidedly angry, not with his opponent, the archbishop, but perhaps with himself; a man fully conscious of being forced into a position in which he had to defend what he knew to be untenable. He was a man who respected truth and logic, but was compelled to defend an illogical situation, taking refuge in rationalisations; an enlightened man who was compelled to be somewhat crude in his defence of a difficult position. I felt it must have hurt him inside.

A year or so later, he was to be publicly rebuked by his president for daring to suggest that a black president was a very real possibility in South Africa today. Since then, Botha has settled down to his fate: he has allowed the past to deprive him of the right to exercise visionary choice. For Botha, I am convinced, belongs to the same ilk as Frederik van Zyl Slabbert; he possesses the same quality of drive, intelligence, enlightened compassion, and charisma. But he may well be remembered as one who, having read accurately the need for change, failed to take the decisive leap. He had to reconcile himself to remaining within the form of traditional politics despite his intuition of the ultimate futility of it all.

The crisis of Afrikanerdom today lies in its rather inadequate capability to address change and all its implications. It is the tragic denial or postponement of growth precisely at that moment when there is recognition of its need. The need to chart a new course. Afrikanerdom seems trapped by an inability to embrace a new kind of heroism. That heroism may consist in the ultimate recognition that the goals of the mass movement in South Africa have a human thrust to them that has implications for all of us.

Until that moment comes, sensitive and intelligent people have to continue to live with the fact of detention and imprisonment of countless intelligent and responsible South Africans; have accommodated themselves to the moral outrage of detained children; of rent evictions; of vigilante squads; of the onslaught against a press driven by a contemporary and humane radicalism. They seek to do the right thing but seem to have limited choices before them since history has habituated them to a futile politics of single-mindedness and self-centredness.

Recently, I revisited Aristotle's *Nicomachean Ethics* and was struck not so much by what Aristotle was saying as by the matter-of-fact tone of his writing. It reflects the confidence of an intellectual explorer attempting to shape the world into some order by asking simple yet fundamental questions. His was a time of definitions, of the patient slotting of things into place. Perhaps we need to recall that time in history, for it is surely relevant to ask white South Africans a seemingly trivial question: what is the purpose of government in South Africa today? Is it the fireworks display of the National Party? The Hitlerite fury of the Afrikaner Weerstandsbeweging? The anachronistic revival of the Conservative Party? The insipidity of the Tricameral Parliament? The violence and intimidation of Inkatha? Events appear to have outstripped the thinking represented by all these organisations.

The challenge of the future in South Africa is nation building: no more, no less. It is the massive task of creating one nation out of the institutionalised divisions that currently beset it. The National Party, possessing no transcendent social vision, is ill-equipped for such a task. On the other hand, the conceptualisation of the problem by what are called the mass-based democratic movements, whatever their current organisational problems, offers a promising alternative. The call for a unitary state is not a mere political trick, but an historical necessity in the evolution of South African culture. It is the necessary antithesis to the constricting strife of engineered division. It is simply a more advanced social envisioning, potentially superior to anything apartheid culture can ever offer. Even more fundamentally, the issue does not have much to do with whether one supports these organisations or not. They are merely an organised collective agent for what will certainly come to pass. They personify an inevitable historical movement. Hence the futility of an array of government actions through mass bannings and detentions and torture, all deployed to delay the imperative to face the future.

As we watch the fireworks display brightening the anxious night, we sense that very few watchers are fascinated. Neither the black majority nor the white right. They stare into the sky with tired necks knowing what it is they actually see: a tragic fantasy. But how many are aware of the irony that this display is almost historically unavoidable? It suggests the emergence of something beyond itself, something calling for a new and urgent sense of inventiveness. While the white right may hanker after the past, the black majority asserts its belief in the future.

The organisers of the display, in planning it and executing it with spin-drama, paradoxically know the truth. That is why they may be credited somewhat with having seen the light without being able to determine who shall use it and what shall really be done with it. For this reason, they appear to believe in neither the past nor the future. In this ambiguous position, they can reassure without comforting. They represent the dance of transition, temporary agents of history who seem destined to open gates but never to walk through them.

Living with Disagreement

a lesson from Lesotho

1988

It is an interesting phenomenon that, following their overthrow, many political leaders, whose rule was characterised by the routine abuse of power, appeal to the courts of law for fairness and justice. By so doing they seem totally unaware of the irony that they appeal to the very institution the authority of which, during their rule, they did all they could to undermine.

The latest example is none other than George Matanzima in the Transkei who has been battling to have the courts declare illegal the government restrictions imposed on him. Apparently never having considered that his own security measures would one day be used against him, he appears to see no irony in challenging the legality of his own restrictions. In his day, he may even have ordered the detention of lawyers representing people who found themselves in the same position that he now finds himself. What is it that suddenly makes him respect what he would previously have done everything in his power to undermine?

Another example will suffice. I note with interest how, these days, various representatives of the minority white government in South Africa, faced with the prospect of inevitable change, are heard to express reservations about the future of the rule of law and 'civilised standards' in the event that the oppressed should take over the reins of government. Somehow, they are unable to appreciate fully the extent to which the rule of law has actually been eroded in the last forty years by the harsh, repressive policies and actions of successive Nationalist governments in their efforts to deal with African opposition. At this very moment, the state of emergency has made total nonsense of the very concept of due process. Clearly, the

Index on Censorship, 5/88

South African government has done its best to ensure that it is not a very good model, unless emulators seek to institutionalise hypocrisy.

Examples of this phenomenon, I believe, abound in human society. It is a phenomenon that stretches right back into the dawn of history. At the root of this problem, it would seem, is how political authority has sought ways of dealing with the inevitability of human disagreement.

A few months before the fall of the government of Chief Leabua Jonathan of Lesotho on 20 January 1986, his government had tolerated a particularly disagreeable method by which its supporters dealt with fellow citizens who disagreed with the government's views. Respectable members of the community were dragged out of offices and public bars and paraded through the streets of Maseru in a most humiliating manner. I cannot say to what extent this kind of behaviour was repeated in other parts of the country.

The question is: why was it found necessary by some supporters of the government, with its tacit approval, to exact this kind of retribution? What does this tell us of the times out of which Lesotho has so recently emerged?

Firstly, it suggests that so confident was the government of its impregnable political position that it ceased to be ashamed of the possible exposure of its worst excesses. No longer embarrassed by the revelation and public viewing of what could go on under cover of the institutionalised secrecy of the prison cell, the government tolerated repulsive acts of public harassment of people who did not agree with it. This form of punishment represented the death of whatever public conscience was vested in the presumably responsible authority of government.

Secondly, from the point of view of both the government and its supporters, this development may have reflected the granting of legitimacy to some notion of political loyalty, something that may have made the rampaging mobs *feel justified*. Simply stated, the principle is: openly declare your support for the government, and be prepared to accept without question whatever is demanded of you; then the kingdom of earth is yours.

I have since met a few of the members of the terrible mobs whose actions were guided by this principle. On each occasion I was struck by how unlikely it was that such people could have perpetrated such terrible acts. I was struck by their intelligence, their easy friendliness, warmth and sensitivity, and their normal sense of decency. I was certain that if they were to see themselves on film at that particularly unthinking moment in their lives they would recoil with shame and a sense of wounded decency. What went wrong?

It is highly probable that many of these people were caught in something they little understood. It could be said that they were victims of the same agency that used them to humiliate people in the streets. They were victims of a political culture that had officialised a strong correlation between political support and the day-to-day survival needs of its supporters. Clearly, in a situation of scarce resources, support for the dominant political power may mean, for its supporters, the easy availability of jobs, scholarships, promotion, food aid, village development schemes, and a host of other benefits.

For these conveniences to be available, no more human effort would be required than mere expression of support. That is to say, the supporters were assured of survival without the need to exert and distinguish themselves in any area of human endeavour other than the expression and demonstration of political support. Thus, they were assured of the means of livelihood without the kind of struggle that would most likely bring out the best in them. Clearly, to officialise this situation is to signal the end of progress and the death of culture.

Furthermore, while it is comforting for people in this situation to know they belong, it is even more comforting to know that others have been effectively excluded. Those excluded become legitimate targets for whatever can be hurled at them to keep them at bay and deny them similar opportunities. Carried away by this comforting feeling, the majority of the supporters become convinced that nobody but themselves has rights. It could be said then that such people most probably supported the government less from belief and conviction than from the promised advantages of patronage, on the one hand, and the fear of exclusion and its possible dire consequences, on the other.

Finally, there is another consequence of this kind of political culture: it is what we might call the socialisation of fear. To illustrate this, let us return to the victims of public humiliation and attempt to understand further the form of punishment meted out to them. What may have been intended by it?

Looked at closely, this kind of 'punishment' began as a concerted assault on the person of the victim. But this assault on his body was actually a gateway to something else, the ultimate prize: his mind. By rolling him in the mud in such a way that he becomes an undignified, whimpering piece of flesh, completely shamed, his self-esteem is destroyed. It was a form of public torture in which the public was called upon to witness the spectacle of retribution so that all would learn, through the social fear induced in this manner, *how dangerous it could be to disagree with authority.* Indeed, it was a spectacle calling for the end of all thinking. For isn't it true that when the mob has got its victim it is totally consumed by the smell of blood? That when the victim finds himself in this untenable situation he is totally consumed by fear, disbelief, and utter bewilderment? And that the public, when they see the spectacle, are totally consumed by the horror of it? So the collective social mind is bludgeoned into apathy. Nothing much can be expected of a terrified mind.

It is worth noting that many governments in Africa have stridently called for development, yet have gone on to contradict the clarion call by assailing the one resource that would ensure development: the human mind. Witness the current concerted onslaught on intellectuals in Kenya. Recently, Wole Soyinka has had to come out on behalf of an internationally acknowledged, brilliant Kenyan intellectual by the name of Maina wa Kinyatti, who is languishing in jail and going blind from an eye disease contracted there 'among certified lunatics'. Why?

Because he disagreed.

To come back to Lesotho, it should be emphasised that I'm trying to understand a tragic phenomenon in the recent history of that beautiful land. And beyond that, I hope that out of the trauma resulting from the shocking realisation that no political situation is permanent, the last government and its supporters acquired a humbling knowledge of the potentially devastating consequences of too much power wielded at the expense of those who were forcefully consigned to silence. I wish to hazard a guess that Lesotho, since 20 January 1986, has more people, hundreds of thousands of them, who ought to have no vested interest in the politics of retribution. One consequence of this is the high likelihood that any future government that can be perceived by the public to follow that kind of politics will encounter opposition potentially much vaster than that encountered by the last government.

So the mob of yesterday should understand that if they feel, or have a definite perception, that they are today being deprived of the means of livelihood simply because of their past association, *without at the same time being given the opportunity to account for their past actions*, there will be many people who sympathise with their plight *in the very same way* that those people sympathised with the victims of mob action under the last government. The obvious lesson is that justice, fairness, and compassion are indivisible, they cannot be applied selectively. Once people have arrived at that kind of understanding, they can then all agree, as a nation, to bury altogether an unfortunate past *without ever forgetting its lessons*. The nation can then move forward in the unshakeable conviction that every Mosotho has a contribution to make, and must be given the opportunity to make it, without fear of victimisation. *That* would be a more lasting basis for reconciliation.

The one crucial lesson to be learned from this unfortunate past is that we have to find a way, in Lesotho, of living with disagreement. We should begin from the unavoidable truth that conflict, misunderstanding, and disagreement are an inseparable part of the human condition. Indeed, at the centre of political history has been the human effort to find ways of dealing with the phenomenon of disagreement; unfortunately, the vast majority of methods devised have sought to *eradicate* disagreement rather than *live with it*. We have seen, as a result, much violence and brutality within nations, and violent conquests between nations. Since the Second World War the world, through the United Nations, has searched for negotiated solutions to disagreement. In the age of nuclear armament – and the proliferation of non-nuclear but devastating instruments of death and destruction – the violent option, consistently used as an instrument of policy, or as a substitute for the absence of ideas, threatens the very survival of human beings. Besides, evidence is abundant of the brutalising effects of violence on the humanity of both the agent of violence and its victim.

It is instructive to cast a cursory glance at the especially well documented history of how the many countries in Europe punished people for offences resulting from disagreement. Particularly interesting are some of the early forms of burning at the stake; the dismembering of a person (called 'quartering') by tying his hands and legs to horses and then having the horses tear him apart; the hanging scaffold; the guillotine, and the public firing squad. (For a most fascinating discussion of the history of punishment in the Western world, see *Discipline and Punish: the Birth of the Prison,* by Michel Foucault, the late, distinguished French intellectual.)

Indeed, the West has come a long way in this matter. This, of course, is not to suggest that the Western world has eliminated violence and brutality. It is only to suggest that it has become a lot more sensitive to and socially embarrassed by it. Over time, public conscience solidified around the issue, thus substantially reducing the tendency for constituted authority to use violence as a standard method of ensuring people's compliance. Of course, there have been many times when such constraints simply did not work, with the result that the world has witnessed the terrible and brutal history of colonialism and the two world wars. Nevertheless, a stormy history of legal, constitutional, political and philosophical disputation has ensured a high level of social consensus against violent solutions. Historically then, a climate was gradually created for a less stressful social debate of controversy, for greater tolerance for uncomfortable research findings, for press freedom, etc. In other words, the human mind was given more leeway to express its genius. Such can be the rewards of developing the art of living with disagreement.

What does all this mean for Lesotho, twelve years before the twenty-first century? One thing is clear: the country's contemporary history has shown without a shadow of doubt that political violence has failed to achieve its objectives and is unlikely to succeed in future. It has largely resulted in social fear, cynicism, pessimism, and people's general disengagement from the arena of creative political participation. I have heard expressed with alarming frequency, by people in buses, taxis, and in casual conversations in public bars and private homes, the perception that Lesotho has been going down over the years; that things can only get worse before they can get better. This is testimony to the pervasive sense of pessimism. How should the nation deal with this debilitating situation?

It does seem as if in one way or another, Lesotho has to engage in a serious dialogue with its contemporary history, particularly in those aspects of that history that pertain to economics, politics, law, security and defence, religion, education, and the modern culture of mass communication and its resultant heavy flow of information. This dialogue should take place in the schools, churches, in Parliament, etc. Such a dialogue can be a much needed social therapy, helping to release deep-rooted fears and anxieties.

A healthy sense of perspective with regard to national history is crucial. History requires to be understood for it constitutes actual experience whether pleasurable or painful. It may be necessary for Basotho to accept that the last government suffered from the tragedy of limited vision and flawed means.

In the contentious field of foreign policy, for example, there is one lesson the government of Leabua Jonathan may have left his people. It is that in its relationship with its infinitely more powerful neighbour, South Africa, Lesotho must begin from a strategic acceptance of its geo-political disadvantage on condition that this neighbour – with whom friendship can never be entirely free of the context of its pariah status in the international community – will have to work extremely hard to win Lesotho's capitulation. There, Jonathan showed, lies some semblance of honour and self-respect: never to give in without a struggle.

Another lesson is that evidence in other parts of Africa and in the developing world indicates that too much centralisation of power in the capital city can lead to various degrees of national paralysis. For this reason, one fervently hopes that the experiment with municipal councils, currently being conducted in Lesotho, will succeed and spread throughout the country.

The point is: what history is there if not of a people's national life as they actually live it, as they talk and argue about it openly and honestly? Such is history as development. There can be no other more meaningful contemporary history for all of Africa.

Of course, all is not gloomy. There is enormous and undeniable, highly literate, and extremely cosmopolitan human potential in Lesotho. As in the rest of the continent, that potential is waiting to flourish. All it requires is the freedom to express itself. Around that potential is the beauty of the land: its rivers, mountains, plants, birds, and animals. Lesotho produced the literary genius of Thomas Mofolo, JJ Machobane and others; the musical genius of JP Mohapeloa and of countless travelling poets of the *lifela*, a poetry developed out of the adventures and experiences of the miners of Lesotho whose voices undulate like the hills and the mountains, and the longer history of the *lithoko* that express so movingly the cadences of the

Sesotho language itself, conveying a message of deep longing for some profound meaning in the lives of the people.

I look forward to the day, in the not too distant future, when Basotho can say, together with all the millions of Africa's hopeful peoples: NEVER AGAIN!

Recovering Childhood

a reminder of innocence

1992

Early this century, Thomas Mofolo, Lesotho's most famous writer, published a book (part fact, part fiction) about the life of one of the central figures in southern Africa: Chaka, king of the Zulus. What fascinated me as a young reader of this book, something that has fascinated many other readers with whom I have discussed the book, is how Chaka, an illegitimate child cruelly treated in his early years, flees with his mother to seek refuge under a sympathetic chief. Years later he returns with a vengeance to claim his right to the throne. I felt that there was something satisfyingly just about his triumphant return. Indeed, he proceeded to build one of the most powerful kingdoms in Africa.

Unfortunately, it is not long before the justice of his return is tragically undercut by his excessive ruthlessness which negates the earlier sense of moral triumph. At the end of the novel, I was left disturbed by how something potentially glorious, in which there was the real possibility that the kind of cruelty shown towards Chaka as a child would be a thing of the past, finally degenerated into physical and moral ruin. One closes the book wistfully, disappointed by the failure of potential.

Stories of this kind, I believe, are many the world over. Taking various kinds of narrative permutations, they reveal one major strand: how the hero or heroine, highly vulnerable as a child, is ill-treated, subjected to all kinds of indignities, and is finally spurned by a society that should have known better. The child protagonist has no means of physical or intellectual self-defence. The child depends on the protection of society through its laws and its conscience, which are encoded in its primary instinct to survive.

Edited version of a paper presented at the Children at Risk Conference in Bergen, Norway, 1992, published in the *Southern African Review of Books* September/October 1992

Underscoring the moral thrust of these stories are the kinds of depriva-
tions visited upon the children. The children are denied human contact and
become lonely; they are starved; they are spoken to harshly; they are
exposed to illness and disease; they are made to work under extremely
dangerous and, sometimes, slave conditions; they are deprived of education,
and may even have been turned away from the gates of churches and hospi-
tals. What we see are the workings and the effects of the invisible hand of an
unjust and insensitive society. The travails of children are presented as
reminders, probing the slumbering conscience of society, particularly in
societies that may have experienced extensive social disorder. Should the
child victims grow up to wreak vengeance upon us, we should understand
that we may be receiving our just rewards. The images of the travails of
children become and remain powerful metaphors of indictment, calling for
social redemption.

However, no matter how compelling the metaphors, there is a threshold
that is seldom crossed. We are generally spared the ultimate horror: the sight
of the blood of children. Seldom are we shown the dashing of little heads
against the wall, or their splitting with pangas which are withdrawn drip-
ping with the gore of blood and brains; seldom if ever are little children
thrown into burning furnaces. Such images involving children are 'too
ghastly to contemplate' as a South African prime minister (John Vorster)
once said. But should they appear, they would most likely indicate the ultimate degeneration of society. They would indicate that there are few horrors
left in society; for, horror that has become the norm profoundly ceases to be
horror. If such a point is ever reached, it would surely require much introspection for society to rediscover its conscience.

South African literature has generally handled the images of childhood
as social criticism in the conventional manner I have described. Two images
in particular became archetypal. The first is the image of an infant abandoned by its mother. In the early 1950s, Es'kia Mphahlele published a story
in which a man lands up with a suitcase with a dead child in it. At least we
are spared the details of how the death actually came about. By the time we
see the infant, it is already dead.

The second image concerns the tragedy of bad race relations. In the late
1950s, Arthur Maimane published a story called 'Just Another Tsotsi' in
which two boys, one white and the other black, grow up together on a farm,

far out in the remote rural areas of South Africa. They become so close that they enter into an oath, committing themselves to lifelong brotherhood. Ritualistically cutting themselves, they join their wounds in a clasp of brotherhood through the mingling of their blood. Unfortunately when they grow up, they go their separate ways, only to be thrown together by fate many years later. One day, the white boy, now a grown man in the police force, chases away a suspected black criminal and shoots him dead, only to notice the ritual mark of his connection to the one he has just killed. The death of a young adult may not be so horrifying; it is common enough. What is horrifying in the context of the story is the tragic breach of a bond made in the innocence of childhood.

Some twenty years after Mphahlele published his story, Oswald Mtshali was to publish 'An Abandoned Bundle' in his collection of 1971, *Sounds of a Cowhide Drum*:

The morning mist
and chimney smoke
of White City Jabavu
flowed thick yellow
as pus oozing
from a gigantic sore.

It smothered our little houses
like fish caught in a net.

Scavenging dogs
draped in red bandannas of blood
fought fiercely
for a squirming bundle.

I threw a brick;
they bared fangs
flicked velvet tongues of scarlet
and scurried away,
leaving a mutilated corpse –
an infant dumped on a rubbish heap –

'Oh! Baby in the Manger
sleep well
on human dung.'

Its mother
had melted into the rays of the rising sun,
her face glittering with innocence
her heart as pure as untrampled dew.

Here we are shown 'a squirming bundle', an infant dumped on a rubbish heap, being set upon by the hungry dogs of the ghetto. The environment in which this takes place is bleak. People are trapped in it, with no avenue of escape. It is hell on earth. In this hell, and in a tremendous daring of the imagination, Mtshali actually shows us the sacrificial blood of a child. However, we are still spared the ultimate horror. It is, after all, dogs that tear apart the child, and not the hand of a human being. Nevertheless, this poet was like a seer, foreseeing the on-coming tragedy of a nation that would soon begin to slaughter its children. The killing began in earnest in June 1976. It is still with us.

❏

On the morning of 16 June 1976, the schoolchildren of Soweto in their school uniforms took to the streets in protest against the imposition of the Afrikaans language as a medium of instruction in black schools. This development, the children reasoned, was the final act in the attempt by the racist government to complete the subjugation of black people. But what the children had not bargained on was that so determined was the State to have its way that it would not allow even children to take refuge behind their childhood. For the first time, the government purposefully pointed its guns at children and opened fire. Many children were killed that day, and from that moment onwards, no one, no matter what age, would be spared the wrath of the government: men, women, and children.

And so we began to hear of the arrest, detention, torture and disappearance of even those as young as eight years old. The military occupation of the black townships became a regular feature of the times. An irony in this occupation is that the soldiers were young white conscripts sent to kill their black peers. Of course, you will immediately notice in this drama the replay of Arthur Maimane's archetypal relationship. These events have found their way into our literature. Mbulelo Mzamane published a book called *The Children of Soweto* which is based on those incredible years. And so, the children of South Africa effectively entered national politics as active participants.

This dramatic entrance of young people into national politics should be seen in perspective. When the major political organisations (the African National Congress and the Pan Africanist Congress) were banned in 1961, the entire political leadership of these organisations were either imprisoned, or in exile, leaving a political void that had to be filled sooner or later. This void was indeed filled towards the end of the 1960s by the advent of the Black Consciousness Movement which organised mainly university students. It was this movement that drew its inspiration from Steve Biko. On average, the participants would have been between twenty-four and twenty-six years old. In 1976, in the year immediately after the banning of all the major organisations of the Black Consciousness Movement, the average age of the participants went down to between sixteen and eighteen. As many of the student activists in this age group fled into exile, even younger ones filled the vacuum created. And if the targets of the government could be eight-year-olds, then the phenomenon of childhood in my country was dangerously at an end.

Nowhere was the impact of the entrance of the young into national politics more visible than in education. The notorious system of education designed especially for black people to prepare them for certain kinds of jobs reserved for them in the racial hierarchy, and beyond which they could not advance further, was under concerted attack. This attack was why young people decided to stay away from school. A new slogan was proclaimed: 'Liberation now, education later'. What has now come to be called 'the culture of learning' was effectively dead.

Many of the demands the students made were valid. A repressive education system was the product of a repressive political one. Schools were run like army barracks with principals expected to play the role of a major-general. Corporal punishment was rife; the professional conduct of many teachers does not bear scrutiny. Many of them were unqualified; books and school facilities were more often than not unavailable. To crown it all, the

government spent a highly disproportionate amount on a white as compared with a black child. Even the curriculum was not entirely relevant to
the needs of the black community, who had no say in designing it. It was not
long after the youth entered the political arena that an already discredited
education system was finally reduced to dust.

After many decades of apartheid, South Africa is finally trying to become
a nation of people who, at this most challenging moment in our history, find
that they know very little about one another. The divisions, purposefully
cultivated over time have taken their toll. The removal of much of the
repressive legislation, however, has only made it possible for previously
repressed tensions to emerge more fully. Having relatively little experience
in managing these tensions without recourse to force and repression, we are
only just discovering the full force of the depth and range of human issues
with which a new democratic order will have to contend.

❑

At the root of the problem is the near total devastation of the social fabric
of the vast majority of the South African population. As we face the reality
of the implications of this understanding, something is rearing its head to
further undermine our capability to heal our wounds. I am referring to the
current rampant violence in many parts of the country in which even children are not spared. The threshold of tolerable and metaphorical violence
against children has been decisively passed.

Consider a recent report in the *Weekly Mail*. The report has the general
headline 'Children in the war zone' but specific reference is made to an article entitled 'Playing games among the ruins'. It is about children in a squatter community that was attacked by an unknown group of people. Such
attacks are common all over the country now:

> All that's left alongside the flattened shacks of families wiped out in
> an attack on Crossroads, a predominantly Zulu squatter camp next
> to Katlehong on the East Rand, are the trampled remnants of once-
> thriving vegetable gardens. Now, children who survived the
> onslaught, and are on holiday from school, play among the ruins.
> At first sight, they appear unaffected by the brutality of the attack –
> which was a rare example of children joining their parents as

specific targets of townships violence ... After the early morning attack last Friday, mothers, fathers and children were left for dead in the smouldering ruins of their corrugated-iron shacks.

One mother, identified only as 'Khampane' by a neighbour, was asleep with her husband and two children when, shortly after 1 a.m., a group of men armed with knives, knobkerries and pangas barged into their shack demanding money.

They said they had none, hoping the attackers would leave, but the men rained blows on them mercilessly beating them, the neighbour told the *Weekly Mail*. While trying to ward off the blows, Khampane tried to protect her one-month-old daughter, holding the child close to her body. But she could not defend it from the blows, and the baby was struck on the head by a panga, leaving a gaping hack wound across her tiny forehead. She was lucky: she survived.

All the while her terrified four-year-old brother stood hugging his father around the legs, crying hysterically as he watched him being hacked to death. His 'interference' by holding on to his father so angered the attackers that they hit him repeatedly, slashing his forearms and wrists before killing his father.

The boy is also in hospital, fighting for his life.

This family was the first to be attacked, but they were not the last.

Thus ends the first segment of the report. The next segment reads:

Vera Ndlela (19) was also asleep when the men barged into her shack. They immediately began beating her, and demanded money from her. She said she was a student, and had no money. On hearing this, they told her that they wanted her 18-month-old baby, to remove parts of his body. She tried to hold on to the boy, but repeated blows from knives and knobkerries forced her to let go. As the men took the boy, she broke away and ran. They flung him into the ruins and chased Vera among the dense reeds of a nearby stream. For three days Vera lay in the smelly, marshy stream running alongside the squatter camp. Unable to move after her severe beating, she remained stuck on the stream bank until she heard people nearby and let out a weak scream. Residents found her and took her to the Natalspruit Hospital.

Her son is missing, and police do not know whether he is one of the injured in hospital, or a body in a morgue.

By Wednesday, five days after the attack, the police could not confirm the names or number of children injured or killed. The only incidents they were able to give details of were the cases of two children, both believed to be younger than one year, whose bodies are at the Germiston mortuary. Both suffered 'excessive burn wounds' and are thought to have died as a result of their burns.

It may be in order to ponder briefly on the newspaper report itself. There are some social facts referred to that have become part and parcel of the political knowledge of South African society. They have become reference points crucial to the construction of understanding. For example, there is the almost casual reference to Zulus and Xhosas. The average South African is highly likely to conclude that there is an underlying ethnic conflict. There is the suggestion that for some reason, as long as there are different people, speaking different languages, with different customs, such inter-ethnic violence will follow. It is a law that governs inter-ethnic relations. There may be no possibility of probing further beyond this basic understanding; no suggestion that there could be other causes. This grammar of political understanding is the legacy of our immediate past, bedevilling every effort to think anew.

In a slightly different category are some graphic details of the incident. They underscore the irrationality and unspeakable horror of the events. They are described to elicit horror and outrage, showing us how brute male strength is pitted against the vulnerability of women and children. They enable us to ask some important questions about children and society. Beyond the horror and the outrage, what is there to be salvaged? What ought to be salvaged? How can such violence be prevented? On what basis can agreement be reached on such prevention? What value system can be created to prevent such a tragedy? But these questions are soon rendered impotent when we notice how easy it is for the perpetrators of the violence to simply melt away undiscovered to continue somewhere else with their carnage.

These problems, however, are not inherent in the report itself; they are part of the way society is made to understand violence. The newspaper article, seeking to report and perhaps shed some light on a newsworthy phenomenon, becomes trapped in its own society and cannot transcend the limits of its own information and reporting. It becomes itself another social feature of the violence. From this report, all of us and the children can conclude: things are the way they are.

Overall, the situation is bizarre. A government that has been responsible for the horror of the past is still in power. To create legitimacy for itself, it has endeavoured to appropriate the vocabulary and rhetoric of those it has previously hounded into prison, exile, or to the grave. It has demonstrated no vision besides the skills of staying in power, developed over forty years of continuous rule. In this regard, many governments all over the world have mistaken the change of rhetoric for the real thing. They have rushed head-long to recognise the government in a bizarre festival of blindness. Many foreign powers have seen only what they wanted to see. Insisting on a speedy normalisation, they have been prepared to put the victim and his persecutor on the same moral level.

I recall these horrible stories not with the intention of shocking, but rather with the wish to use them as an occasion for some painful reflection on the state of affairs in our country. That children are at the centre of these events, sometimes as victim, sometimes as perpetrator, is at the root of the problem. For isn't our goal nation building? What can we expect of children who have witnessed the death of parents; who have seen people being stoned, hacked with pangas and burnt to death; who have themselves been the direct targets and victims of this violence; who have sometimes participated in these gruesome events?

I look at our country caught in this grip of violence and see nothing less than what in some situations has been called the breakdown of culture. Notwithstanding the impressive infrastructure of roads, railways, and harbours; the punctuality of airline schedules; the ups and downs of the stock exchange; the flurry of diplomatic initiatives and the opening of new embassies; trade agreements and investments; the technical sophistication of assembly line production; the abundance of electronic goods and other commodities, the fact is that we have an industrial and political infrastructure anchored in an over-privileged minority which, in spite of a presence of more than three hundred years, has never shed the mentality of being visitors. Consequently, the fruits of their achievements have no organic connection with the realities of the larger human environment in which they occurred. We have a culture of technical achievement that is merely drifting forwards by sheer momentum. Where are we going? We have to do something to rediscover some human direction towards being a nation of the future.

Where can we locate the metaphors of hope? No longer in children, for not only do we kill them; they themselves have killed. Let's have a look at what has happened in some of our schools. The young have taken over, hiring and firing teachers and principals. But how long can such a thing go on? Ultimately, they cannot run schools or the education system; they cannot run banks or businesses, not even churches. They cannot run nations. Yet they have attempted to do so when, being on the firing line, they began to feel responsible for bringing in the future. Ultimately, in a society without children there can be no concept of innocence. We have lost it. It can no longer carry much strength as a metaphor for redemption. So we have to rediscover the child and childhood.

Nor can it be easy for children, heroically transformed into adults overnight, to be their own redemptive metaphor because the experience of compassion and the nurturing of conscience have not been a consistently informing aspect of their growth in recent times. Can they succeed in effecting a strategic distance from themselves for the purpose of moral reflection? That we need their energy is beyond dispute. And so do we need their fearlessness and questioning attitude, which, under the circumstances, are strange gifts of these terrible times. But where will the visionary authority come from that will harness that energy and assign a proper role to it in a new and infinitely challenging society?

Beginning with the recovery of childhood and innocence, there are so many other things to be recovered and even redefined: the family; the sense of autonomous and secure neighbourhoods rebuilding the concept of a community; the sense of nationhood and, beyond that, the sense of being part of a larger world. It is a task of enormous proportions. But we have to locate the process of rediscovery in the child and genuinely believe in the newness that will emerge from there.

A Call to Fellow Citizens

freeing the white community

1992

The University of Cape Town is one of the major institutions of higher learning in South Africa and enjoys a reputation that goes far beyond our borders. It has over the decades built solid traditions in teaching and research. The achievement of graduates assumes even greater significance against this background of a distinguished history. They have become part of these traditions and have in turn helped to keep them alive and even to extend them.

I make this observation with the full understanding that traditions have become extremely fragile in this country. Our movement away from our infamous history has made many of us unsure of the value of much of what we may have inherited. Although the university long ago took the heroic step of opening its doors to black people, it was difficult for it to go against the strong socio-political currents of our history. Many significant strides have been taken, but the obstacles, long entrenched in our history, remain formidable. Although the obstacles are largely located in the wider society, we find them also inside our universities. But whether they are inside or outside, they remain different aspects of the same larger problem. Graduations are often an appropriate occasion at which to raise important matters of public concern. I take this opportunity with all humility to address my fellow white citizens, whom I knew would still be a majority in this hall.

A terrible spectre is stalking the land: it is the spectre of violence, corruption, and mismanagement of national affairs by the government of the day. Evidence keeps mounting that the South African government, in spite of assurances to the contrary, is busy supplying weapons to the rebel movement Unita in Angola in defiance of the government of that nation's choice.

Graduation address, University of Cape Town, December 1992

In whose name does the government continue to do this? Probably in your name, fellow citizens, rather than mine. After all, you have come a long way with this government. Can we trust these people to lead us towards democracy at the very moment that they are destroying it in another country? I cannot. Perhaps some of you do, not because you want to, but because you may think you have no viable alternatives.

I believe that while the terrible past out of which we are emerging resulted in an efficient and convenient system of managing the exploitation of both human and natural resources, it also exacted a high toll on the collective morality of its beneficiaries. We are used to discussing the horrible effects of apartheid by focusing on the easily observable plight of its victims, and how these victims may now be helped. That is as it should be. But is the helper in a position to help? To answer this question, we must increasingly turn our attention towards some of the experiences of white South Africa, not for the sheer fun of it but to increase our understanding of the enormous human problem before us. In doing so, we may be forced to retrace some historical steps, not to induce guilt or open up wounds but to attempt to bring about a more mature and more honest society.

Let us take stock of some of the things that have happened. Recently, the president of the Nationalist Party, FW de Klerk, railed at the ANC, saying, among other things, that South Africans were 'sick and tired' of the ANC and its mass action. He was cheered by his audience of 'South Africans'. This left me wondering: who are de Klerk's South Africans? Who are these 'sick and tired' South Africans? I recognised something familiar: an old habit. It was the 'South African' habit of associating the attribute 'South African' with one segment of the population. The rest of the people, to whom this special attribute did not adhere, then become a faceless mass to be kept at bay at all costs. That is why I conclude that Mr de Klerk was thinking of white South Africans rather than of me. If I am correct, do you accept this membership which excludes me?

Secondly, it is my impression that the revelations of massive corruption in the government service have not elicited large-scale outrage from the general white public. Why? I have asked myself. Why is there no indignant call for the resignation of the government? When the General Indemnity Act was passed and imposed on us, there was no noticeable expression of outrage. Why? Is this the government that was given such overwhelming support in the historic white referendum early this year? Is it that when it does these things it feels certain that white South Africa approves of them? I have a feeling that the white community is aware that something is wrong. But why does it seem so powerless? I want to ask.

Is it that history has inured this community from all shock? After all, the current revelations are really nothing compared to the massive resettlement schemes and land appropriation; nothing compared to the scale of suffering produced by the migratory labour system, and influx control laws; nothing compared to the virtual slavery that flourished in the remote farms of South Africa; nothing compared to the unlimited power of the police and the defence force. This community has witnessed all this throughout the decades without a serious moral whimper or historically noticeable agonies or crises of conscience, except for one or two voices which irritated the white government. Is it that this community has learned to note these things and that, in spite of them, it chose simply to get on with life? How can you go on like this?

I understand the anxieties brought about by change. Such anxieties may easily make this community prefer, in an instinctive sort of way, the reassurance of old habits in which the National Party is perceived as still being in a position generally to take care of things. That it is better to have them and all the corruption and the violence, and the continued destabilisation of neighbouring countries, than to have a new and untested black government.

I believe that this community now has to make the most important decision in the history of three centuries of its presence in this country. The referendum did not represent such a decision; it was a shallow, technical solution, not a great human awakening. The white community cannot take comfort in the referendum. It has to do no less than engage in a human transformation of historic proportions. This may mean no less than a clean break with historic corruption. By corruption I mean something more than moral failure: I refer to a historic state of being in which political power, wealth and privilege nurtured an essentially self-indulgent, uncreative, and uncaring attitude towards the world. It entrapped us all. It was a way of life from which few of us, including its beneficiaries, could escape.

Firstly, as a community it has to rediscover its natural sensibilities: a real and compassionate sense of justice, the capability to be angered, outraged and genuinely embarrassed once more by engineered and habitual mis-

46

demeanours perpetrated in your name that have caused and continue to cause suffering and despair.

Secondly, it must break decisively with Europe. The Australians acquired a new sense of freedom, a new identity that unleashed a great store of creativity when they made new friendships, redefined a sense of place and became one of the nations of the South Pacific. They broke with Britain and matured. What the white community will become when it has broken with Europe is the great adventure story of all South Africans.

Thirdly, it must ditch the National Party. I admit that this is a risky thing for me to say. It is too narrow a demand. I may sound as if I am campaigning for one party against another, that I am reducing important matters to the level of day-to-day political manoeuvring. Far from it. There is something more involved. Let me illustrate what I mean. It is now emerging why we had 2 February 1990, when the liberation movements were unbanned, political prisoners released including the announcement of Nelson Mandela's release, executions were suspended and many remaining apartheid laws were repealed. That date was not meant to bring in a new world. The promise of the future came by default. That day was designed to induce normalcy in politics so that the politics of the liberation movement could have its inspirational and visionary quality reduced to the mundane, so that it could be contained in such a way that there would be no difference between it and countless other demands that needed to be articulated through a regulated process. What was done forcibly in the past, that is, to break the back of opposition, was now achieved through an apparent concession. The point of this is that the government, in using the rhetoric of change, was doing no more than reinforce the past. When the white community thought it was moving forward, it was actually digging in. Is this what it really wanted?

To ditch the National Party, then, is not to engage in petty political manoeuvring; rather, it is to signal a decisive break with the past, and to accept the need for a truly liberating and human transformation. It is to signal the recognition that the struggle for liberation is not something that 'irritating' blacks claim to do, but that what is at stake is the community's own humanity, its own liberation. It is to have the humility to recognise that the struggle for liberation that has been raging for decades in our country represents one of the world's greatest statements on human freedom.

At stake, fellow citizens, is not the loss of power, its comforts and privileges of all kinds; it is not the preservation of official languages; it is not the loss of neighbourhoods; it is not the loss of a shallow and narrow intellectual culture, the result of banned books, films, and plays, separate schools and universities, a dismal political environment that prevented us from being enriched through the complexities and risks of intercultural contact. No.

What is at stake is the gaining of a new world that can free the white community from many debilitating illusions of the past. It is the gaining of a new world in which its creativity can draw full sustenance from its generous African environment, in which its humanity can be expressed more freely, more fully in the expanded human reality of its country, our country. We want nothing less than a new world with new people.

These are extremely difficult matters. But our history demands no less from us. What all this means for our universities and other institutions, both private and public, should be clear. We cannot come to terms with this situation through convenient adjustments. We have to effect principled changes commensurate with the magnitude of the challenge.

I hope that my fellow citizens will take up this call with resolve and determination.

Elections, Mountains and One Voter

on the morning of 27 April 1994

1994

Some two years ago, a few days after my arrival in the Western Cape to begin work at the University of the Western Cape, I remember driving home after work on a hot afternoon. I stopped at the traffic lights at an intersection along Modderdam Road. As I glanced this way and that as drivers are wont to do during that momentary boredom of waiting for the green light, my eyes rested on Table Mountain. At that moment I experienced an epiphany. I knew then one of the reasons that had me running away from Johannesburg after only a year. I was desperate to be surrounded once more, after years of exile in Lesotho, by mountains and their reassuring presence.

Those mountains have given me some inner strength and suggested to me the value of stability. In the many years of anxiety about whether I would ever see home again, the mountains of Lesotho offered solace and certitude. They seemed to offer the assurance that one day things would work out. So, during my stay in the Western Cape, I was to seek out Table Mountain by reflex each time I was outdoors. I was to see the mountain in all its moods: when it was uncovered or covered by mist and cloud and smoke, or when it braced itself against the winds and triumphed.

Part of the strength that mountains have given me is to show the value of stability in times of change. For instance, I have a peculiar personal trait. It is that I tend to be at my calmest and most deliberate when some remarkable event has made everybody else excited. I can receive the most stunning news with the utmost composure. I used to worry that I may be one of the most insensitive of people in the world. I have learned, though, over the years, that it is not so. I would simply be experiencing, at those moments,

---

SA 27 April 1994: An Author's Diary (ed. André Brink), Queillerie, Pretoria, 1994

that most incapacitating of feelings when one is torn asunder by the play of the clearest understanding accompanied by a momentary inability to turn insight into words. In that situation I have thought it best to resort to silence, for any utterance may not escape hints of insincerity precisely at a time when I felt most sincere.

All this is to account for the fact that when I opened my eyes on the morning of 27 April 1994, I sensed immediately the weight of the historic day, but although I felt awed, I registered no ebullient excitement. I was sure of one thing: I would, in my own time, wake up and find my way to a polling station to vote. I already knew that I would not vote at the polling station nearest to me, in Pinelands. I had been informed that voting would take place in the Dutch Reformed church. I reacted instinctively against that venue. But not wanting to yield to reflex emotion, I entertained an intense inner debate. Something told me that voting at that church would represent a special moral triumph. It would display starkly the symbolism of change and reconciliation.

It was not to be. My historical sensitivities were too powerful. I shied away from that moment of transcendence, not sure that I would be able to live with yielding to it in the days, weeks, months and years ahead. I shied away from a heroic public gesture in preference for a neutral venue where I would participate in the most personal of public events: the election. After all, had I not made some powerful emotional concessions at midnight in the centre of Cape Town during the ceremony to lower the old flag and hoist the new one? It was a most joyful moment. As I watched the new flag go up, I felt, for the first time in my life, that this country was really mine. All along, it had been an idea I longed for. Something I had hated and loved all at once. Now the ambivalence was gone.

During that intense moment, my eyes happened upon two white police-men whose faces registered pain, bewilderment and resignation. They were watching the end of all that had given the deepest meaning to their lives. They seemed lost. Yet, there they were, in the call of duty, ensuring the pro-tection of victorious celebrants. My heart went out to them. I confirmed something else at that very moment: how much I had been socialised into the values of the struggle. 'It is not the people but the policies', we had grown to learn. It had been hard to make that distinction. But I was influenced by it. That is why it is no miracle that during this moment of triumph, the mass survivors of oppression feel no special bitterness. So there were my two white policemen: I gave them my compassion, they protected me.

That is partly why, as I headed for the Civic Centre in Cape Town at about nine-thirty, I did not really feel bad about having decided not to cast my vote in the Dutch Reformed church. It was at the Civic Centre that I would cast my vote. That in itself carried its own special symbolism. I would vote at a place to which everyone had a civic right. In there we were made equal by right and legal precept.

But the reason for going to the Civic Centre was not entirely altruistic. I had received a report that the queues there were short and moving fast. As it turned out, I spent only an hour there.

As usual, on my way to the Civic Centre, I looked for Table Mountain. It was totally covered in low cloud. Why would the mountain hide from me on such a day? That was a distant thought but I registered it.

Inside the Civic Centre the atmosphere was quiet and dignified. I experienced what millions of other people in working democracies had learned to take for granted: queuing to cast a vote is a leveller of human beings. There we were – students, clerks, secretaries, teachers, chief executive officers, journalists, casual labourers, actors, the unemployed, all in a queue to do one thing. I talked to those close to me. Although we said very little about the election itself, we enjoyed the opportunity the election provided us to share some intimate experiences. We never exchanged names, but we will all remember that joyous hour in which we queued to make history.

When the voting moment came, it was fast and disarmingly simple, but profoundly intense. I trembled as I unfolded my ballot paper. It was really happening. I was aware of the terrible fear of making a mistake. I would not be able to live with a mistake. I began to look for my face of choice. This was my one and only face. Other faces were a blur as I looked for the one face that embodied all my hopes and, easing my trembling hand, I drew my X with the greatest care in the world. And it was done. When I proceeded to cast the provincial vote, I was already a seasoned voter.

As I left the Civic Centre to return home, I noticed that the queue was already all the way out of the building. So there were other voters who had taken their morning hours easy. Driving home, I looked at the mountain. It was still covered. When I went to a friend's house to celebrate the triumph of voting, the mountain was still covered.

I was never to see it that day. But, again as usual, I was confident it was there. Perhaps it was reaffirming its old lesson on faith, on Election Day. That the future is there for us: we need to have faith in it, and in ourselves. And so I ended my day unemotionally, but deeply affirmed.

The University of the North in the New Era

what the mosquito thinks

1994

When the state president and chancellor of the University of the North, Nelson Mandela, gave his address at the first opening of Parliament since our historic election of 27 April 1994, he began by quoting a poem by Ingrid Jonker. I want to follow in the steps of the president by beginning my address with a poem, albeit by a poet unknown to most of us. I came across it a few days ago and it made an immediate impression. Its impact must have something to do with its brevity and pointedness, which prompt an intensity of reflection that lasts much longer than its length. Written by Don Marquis, it is entitled 'Mosquito's Viewpoint':

> a man thinks
> he amounts to a lot
> but to a mosquito
> a man is
> merely
> something to eat

I found something radically sobering about these lines.

Why? Firstly, at the surface level of meaning, it says that there may be something humbling about being seen from another's point of view. Secondly, and perhaps more profoundly, this poem disturbed me because, like most South Africans, I have been agonising over our future. Our newly found freedom has filled us with a deserved sense of importance. Suddenly,

---

Public address as vice-chancellor, University of the North, 9 June 1994

each one of us counts. Each one of us is a valuable human being. We earned our pride through sweat and struggle; through countless agonies and ecstasies. We are here now, victorious. The meaning of our struggle and the manner in which it reached fruition have inspired people the world over.

But, at the same time, I sensed something that was later to be crystallised for me by Don Marquis' short poem. I sensed our vulnerability. I sensed that at our greatest moment of triumph, our weaknesses looked us directly in our eyes. I wondered whether, from the point of view of the future before us, we were going to be as a nation 'merely/something to eat'. Inevitably, I turned my reflective gaze towards our University of the North, and asked a similar question: are we going to be as a university, from the point of view of the future, 'merely/something to eat'? Or will we think we 'amount to a lot'?

If we are to survive as a successful nation in a highly competitive world, then we have to develop our economy as rapidly as possible. We will have to compete with nations that are far ahead of us in terms of the general quality of life measured by standards of education, high access to, and participation in, educational opportunities, levels of technology and technological skills, leisure time through arts and culture, and connectedness within the country and with the rest of the world. We think of North America, Europe, and Japan, on the one hand, and, on the other, China, Indonesia, Australia, Malaysia, South Korea, and India and other newly industrialised countries whose economies are increasingly competing successfully in the international arena. We have to join this latter group of nations.

But how can we, with our massive unemployment, massive housing shortage, illiteracy, poor schools and overcrowded universities, pervasive poverty, and diseases of all kinds? Are these things not actually working against us? Do they not make it very possible that we shall become 'merely/something to eat'? As we proclaim to the world our freedom, as we boast often times these days about the size of our economy in the African context, about our industrial infrastructure, about our roads, railways, airlines, minerals, and about our military might, we have to recognise at the same time the disturbing weakness at the centre of our national life. To the extent that we cannot deal with this weakness, we shall surely become 'merely/something to eat'. To the extent that we can overcome these weaknesses, we shall win the second revolution: the eradication of ignorance, poverty, illiteracy, ill-health, joblessness, and lack of housing. The second revolution is no less than the upliftment of the quality of life of every citizen. Then perhaps we can 'amount to a lot'.

The same can be said for our university. If we want to take any lesson from the way the mosquito looks at us, it is that we will have to be humble as a community in accepting what we are now if we genuinely want to be part of the struggle for the second revolution. What we are now is in many ways not pleasant. Like the country of which we are a part, we have to struggle to build for ourselves a new image. But that image is not something out there apart from ourselves. That image is part of each and every one of us; it is in our actions, in our activities. That is why one of the first things I decided to focus upon, when I arrived just under a year ago, was to rebuild the public affairs department. But it soon became clear that a public affairs department that told the world just how much we had changed as a university in the new South Africa would, in large measure, be lying. We have to project who we are, not who we claim to be. Spin doctoring and the academy do not go together.

How can we tell the world that we are doing well when we find it difficult to perform the simple professional act of acknowledging receipt of business letters; when it takes us ten months to fill a vacant post; when we make decisions that we do not implement; when our campus protection service sits back and watches millions of rands' worth of goods being stolen from us; when staff in the kitchen fight over carcasses of meat; when pay day is a holiday; when Friday afternoon is a holiday (not only did we add 'struggle holidays' such as 21 March and 16 June to our calendar, but we continued to observe even those old ones that symbolised our oppression – we did not add and subtract simultaneously, only added more days when we would not come to work); when a large number of teaching staff go home at midday; when some teaching staff refuse to mark examination scripts because they have a gripe with the university administration; when students insist on having a say in decisions regarding their academic evaluation; when some lecturers do not believe that students can be spoken to in a decent way; when some students think that to be radical is to be rude; when the failure rate is so high that some three thousand five hundred students have to sit supplementary examinations; when the research and publishing output is the lowest in the country; when some of us expect to earn higher salaries for low productivity.

We cannot build a positive image on a situation that resoundingly says: we are 'merely something to eat.'

On 31 March this year I addressed the Senate on my observations concerning problems that beset the university at the beginning of the academic year. The issues dealt with there remain alive and relevant:

> The 1994 academic year did not begin very smoothly. In fact, there was something approaching an anarchic state of affairs on campus. The causes of this situation are difficult to pin down, but if there is one thing these events indicate it is the urgent need for the university to create a new image of itself; to rediscover and to restore the value of internal institutional coherence, the restoration of a strong public opinion and loyalty based on productivity and service. There were illegal withdrawals of services or threats to that effect by the following: staff in the finance department; staff in academic administration; the 'concerned lecturers' group; part-time lecturers in the Xitsonga Department at the Giyani Teaching Centre; the professional library staff; administrative and technical staff. We also had problems in the Faculty of Health Sciences, partially resolved, which were quite debilitating.

The impact these actions had on the university during the critical period of registration was devastating. What we saw was simply another, ongoing, onslaught on the self-confidence of the campus body politic. These actions said to us: we can never do anything right. The common thread that runs through all these events was not so much the validity or otherwise of the issues raised but, rather, the debilitating manner in which they were highlighted, which resulted in grave institutional trauma. The work stoppages seem to suggest that, to the actors involved, the university, seemingly embodied in its administration, is still perceived to be an oppressive adversary that has to be brought to its knees. The university is still not seen by many of its members as something that belongs to them, something to be rebuilt and treasured.

Instead, these actions may consolidate certain negative images about our university. They help to define and typify that phenomenon called 'an historically black university.' They confirm the notion that an historically black university is an inferior institution, pleading for recognition at the same time as it does everything in its power to make such recognition impossible. They underscore institutional inferiority by bringing about such dysfunctionality as could confirm the racist notions of these universities as lost causes just because they are 'black institutions.' Nothing works there, is the message. Thus, at the same time that those who resort to such actions are calling for corrective measures, they are actually making sure that the institution is in fact incapable of ever effecting such measures. We thus reproduce institutional inferiority and ineffectiveness at the same time as we tell ourselves that we are working to improve the situation.

An intriguing psychology is displayed here. The more we engage in what has now become reflex protest action, the more dysfunctional the institution becomes; and the more dysfunctional the institution becomes, the more we engage in debilitating protest action, and the more we feel good that we are doing good. In effect, we are 'demonstrating' ourselves out of existence. We do not recognise that the context of activist action has fundamentally changed. If we continue this way, we can only cave in and self-destruct.

I do not recall these events to embarrass or blame departments mentioned. Far from it. I recall these events as an occasion for serious reflection. I present them as social facts without which we will not be addressing the real and fundamental issues that face us.

We often hear complaints about acts of corruption on campus. This happens when there is theft of money, apparent nepotism, and so on. This is a narrow view of corruption in our case. The situation I have described requires a broader definition of corruption. Corruption, in our case, is not just the theft of something, it is a pervasive social condition. It is a product of our history, showing how much we may have lost as we struggled to gain something else. If we do not accept this humbly, we are not going to succeed in developing a clear sense of where we want to go. We'll be busy making excuses for ourselves. For us, transformation and reconstruction mean committing ourselves to the eradication of a fundamentally corrupt institutional condition. It is a condition that has socialised us into doing less because we think everybody else is doing less. It is a condition that has made it almost impossible for us to appreciate one another. It has blinded us to the humanity of each and every one of us. It is a condition that has enabled us to say: why should I care? But we have to care! We will have to care.

We have to care because there are thirteen thousand five hundred students on campus, that is to say thirteen thousand five hundred individual talents whose contribution our country desperately needs. We have been given the honour as teachers to develop and nurture each talent for the benefit of our country. We have to care because we have some three hundred and fifty members of the teaching staff, that is to say three hundred and fifty highly trained personnel who took up this profession for the love of teaching, learning and research. We must create conditions that will enable them to strive towards excellence in the performance of their tasks.

The picture presented above is indicative of how much we have lost in the struggle to gain something. Despite that, we must perform our ethical duty, particularly during this period of reconciliation. We must take time to thank all those who have stayed on this campus throughout the years and continued to make their contribution under very difficult circumstances. Equally so, the humanistic vision of the struggle we fought forces us to remember even those who may have been perceived as enemies. Many were victims of the social engineering we have defeated. There are many who were perceived as victims and comrades. Many are in here. We must recognise them with gratitude, despite all the problems we are in. They have demonstrated their tenacity when everything was working against them. Now is the time to draw on that tenacity in order to build. Now, we must galvanise all our resources to make the contribution that is expected of us. In this connection, we must remember at all times, that we are not answerable only to ourselves, we are answerable to the public whose taxes sustain this institution.

It will take a lot for us to 'amount to a lot'. If we contrast the size of the mosquito with the enormous implications of its perception of us, we should surely rise from the ashes of our current state, changing ourselves fundamentally as we change our country.

Liberation and the Crisis of Culture

the ambiguities of change

1994

The South African stage is full of actors with many competing scripts. Before there had been only one legitimate actor with his one legitimate script: all other possible actors had been forcibly prevented from entering the stage. But after years of persistent pressure, the dominant actor has finally yielded some space on the stage, and we are witnessing the frantic entrance of new actors, all carrying their own scripts. We wait for the scripts to be opened, for some of them have been written many years back; and we wonder what possible exercises in rewriting and revising have been carried out. What is to be found in the scripts now? This is the foremost question of the times.

There is much to indicate that the once dominant actor still believes that his script is the best; that he wants to persuade everyone to participate in its enactment. But the rest are, understandably, sceptical, for they remember that ever since black people started competing successfully in South African athletics, new standards of performance have been reached in several events. Such a development ought to put into historical doubt all the records that were established before black people were allowed to compete. The limits of the once dominant actor's competence have never really been fairly and fully tested. No wonder that the emerging actors have no inherent confidence in the quality of the original script.

Assuming that they recognise the need to define a common destiny, how are all these actors going to work out a system that can accommodate their various artistic inclinations? Clearly, we have to know what individual inclinations are, which tendencies have enjoyed privilege and power and which

---

Altered State? Writing and South Africa (eds. Elleke Bohemer, Laura Chrisman, Parker),
Dangaroo Press, Sydney, 1994

have not, and why. Which tendencies, given the current state of events, are likely to gain ascendancy? What compromises are going to have to be made with the past? What resources will be required to train actors as well as to effect necessary structural adjustments to the theatre in order to accommodate new artistic demands? How are we going to define success and failure?

Our analogy is particularly useful in one important way: it concerns theatre. Yet the manner in which the actors are going to solve their problems will involve them in a political process. The social content of that process will consist of patterns of past behaviour that each of the contending parties bring to the collective search for new alternatives. As many of those cultural patterns as possible will need to be exposed to a scrutiny of the most comprehensive kind, for any emerging understanding has the potential of being a strong basis for a future political culture.

Where in the past so many have been silenced, we must now insist on as extensive an approach to social understanding as possible. All actors, speaking several languages, have an important role to play. These languages include the 'languages' of dance, painting, architecture, human movement, music, clothing, food, crafts, and forms of leadership. All these are languages that take time to be learned.

The challenge of culture in South Africa is one that results from the interaction of many languages yielding discordant meanings. In this situation we need to look for a creative point of convergence such as would inspire a universal confidence that our strivings towards a viable national culture are based on as inclusive an understanding as possible.

❑

South African television continues to throw up dramatically contrasting images of life. One moment there will be images of vast crowds demonstrating through the streets of Johannesburg, Cape Town, or some other city. The most unforgettable aspect of such demonstrations, whether on TV or in real life, is the dance: the call-and-response chant of the toyi-toyi. There are few things so remarkably symbolic of the purposeful coalescence of collective intention than the toyi-toyi dance. In the same newscast, however, will be a sports report in which white women in their immaculately white uniforms, in the deliberate composure of their surroundings, are seriously engaged in a game of bowls.

What separates these two forms of activity, is what constitutes the crisis of culture in the beloved country. Standing between these two is a chasm of engineered ignorance, misunderstanding, division, illusion, and hostility. It is a chasm that highlights the national tragedy of people who have long lived together but could do no better than acknowledge only their differences. They have done so with such passion as would suggest that perhaps they sensed something in common between them that neither side was prepared to acknowledge: the awesome responsibility entailed by such an acknowledgement may have been too daunting. After all, have there not been times in human history when the certainties of ongoing war and destruction were strangely preferable to the uncertainties of the peace that everyone passionately said they desired?

It is not possible that the women of the bowling club could be entirely unaware of the psychologically distant, yet brooding, presence of a world in ferment; one to which they owed, in large measure, their exclusive privilege. That world has typified for them every kind of social nightmare imaginable: overcrowded taxis, buses and trains; overcrowded schools; overcrowded stadiums. People everywhere, living in monotonously similar houses, killing without motive, screaming and hollering and laughing uncontrollably in the streets. Such people are not likely ever to make reasonable political demands. Most reassuringly, regular army patrols ensure that this nightmare never spreads to their white suburbs.

Writing about late nineteenth-century South African pastoral fiction in his book *White Writing*, J M Coetzee observes:

> The constraints of the genre ... make silence about the black man the easiest of an uneasy set of options. If the work of hands on a particular patch of earth, digging, ploughing, planting, building, is what inscribes it as the property of its occupiers by *right*, then the hands of black serfs doing the work had better not be seen. Blindness to the colour black is built into the South African pastoral.

Indeed, the South African pastoral was not just a way of writing; it crystallised a way of perception that was studiously cultivated into a way of life. Pastoral is the clinical tranquillity of the contemporary white South African suburb, with its security fences, parks, lakes, swimming pools, neighbourhood schools and bowling greens – all in a place that obliterates any suggestion that these are the products of human labour. Instead, Western civilisation has miraculously brought everything into being! Always hidden behind this legacy of imperial achievement has been the unacknowledged presence of black labour and the legitimacy of the political claims based upon that labour.

The advancing black struggle has brought about an understandably deep anxiety for our white compatriots. It is the anxiety of having to deal with what they had traditionally learned or preferred to ignore. Indeed, the new dawn must be, for them, something of T S Eliot's 'cruellest month', inevitably bringing forth the humanity of blacks as a factor to contend with, after a past of moral slumber. They had deprived themselves of the opportunity to develop social skills such as would enable them to deal with the complex issues of multi-cultural contact in South Africa, without the easy recourse to violent repression as a means of exerting social control. That is to say, the technical achievements of South African capitalism did not develop from an equally complex humanistic foundation.

It will need to be recognised, very quickly and right up to the highest levels of white political culture, that the history of black social experience has not been one long formless night. In spite of oppression, if not also in response to it, blacks have also engaged in the search for such social order as would make life predictable. They have developed forms of cultural experience that may have an impact on the reorganisation of national life in South Africa.

For example, the phenomenal success of the black taxi business is not unrelated to the long-established traditions of small money-making societies: burial societies, church groups, football clubs, the ballroom dancing club, drinking buddies, the networks of market women, home-boy and home-girl groups of various kinds and sizes, and the intricate network of extended family support groups. A predominant energising factor behind all these groupings is the sense that blacks are involved, no matter how informally, in a life of resistance. The ideology of resistance, the call for the uplifting of the black person, even if these are not immediately related to the material interests of a group being formed, are the ultimate justification for social effort. This political imperative has been a strong factor in all kinds of group formations in the townships. The success or failure of any political negotiations will be determined by the extent to which the black interest, defined by its strong and concrete social experience, is taken into consideration, for it defines perceptions of legitimacy and loyalty.

While blacks were busy forming an unofficial culture, as it were, black society at the formal level was, on the other hand, the object of white experimentation in social management: for example, group areas, urban Bantu councils, independent self-governing states and Bantu Education. Always underpinning such experimentation, even with the involvement of white universities, was the possible resort to institutionalised enforcement when the official intention did not tally with the black interest. That is why all the scenarios of the future, premised on the habitual experience of white hegemony, are likely to be seen as additional efforts at experimenting with black society. The opportunity to experiment has been the exclusive privilege of white society. Clearly, in the imagining of the future and the complex means for achieving it, blacks approach the promising dawn of freedom with a severe limitation. It is necessary for them to appreciate that situation fully.

❑

A few examples will suffice to show the inadequacy of white efforts to deal with this decisive moment in the black struggle. President de Klerk's lifting of the ban on the ANC, the PAC, the South African Communist Party and other political organisations on 2 February 1990 represents a momentous initiative. While the president then declared that his door was open, the follow-up has been predictably weak, if one can gauge from, for example, the debates in the media about the merits and demerits of privatisation or nationalisation, and from the crisis of black education or de Klerk's continued insistence on group rights.

The debate on nationalisation has largely been characterised by the paternalistic attitude that blacks really did not know much about economics. A typical example is a recent quote in the *Sunday Star* from Deryck Spence, managing director of Castrol:

> The vast majority of the followers of the ANC, UDF, MDM and other protest movements join them not for ideological reasons but because they look back on what, for many of them, is a lifetime of poorer housing, schooling, work opportunities and poorer quality

of life. Now they see a chance of all that falling away and that is where the big challenge to business leaders lies. We must not let them be confused by socialist slogans. And the only way we can do that is to put our money – and our hearts – where our mouths are. We have to create companies entirely free of discrimination and with genuine equal opportunities. If the opportunities are equal and the educational and training facilities are properly upgraded, then additional wealth will generate itself as naturally as a man breathes.

Recently, we witnessed a televised debate between the South African minister of education and two black educationists. In line with the president, the minister of education called upon the black community to come forward and meet him and his officials in the ministry to sort out together the problems of black education.

What is common to all these initiatives is the context of normalcy that they assume to emerge immediately after an appropriate declaration has been made. The rules of the marketplace will solve everything; the demand that black parents should knock on the minister's door with suggestions cannot but seem a self-serving exercise: to make accessible and available instruments of state without giving away power and control over them. Overnight, black parents are expected to behave like a normal electorate, visiting their minister as if there has never been a problem. The rules and regulations that determine white political and economic culture may actually have very little to do with the depth and extent of black disaffection. The government and the corporate world have simply resorted to an expedient and familiar system of state administration long set in place to administer to their needs.

❏

De Klerk's initiatives cannot be said to have left black people unaffected in very significant ways. Certainly, there has been some kind of confusion. The enemy of many decades seemed to disappear overnight, and the sudden withdrawal of prohibition may induce ambiguity. Is this real? Or is this another ruse? Should we cooperate, or should we continue to resist? Where politics is suddenly normalised, the most radical statement would not even be able to shake a molehill. Not only did the enemy seem to walk away from centre stage, he returned wearing the face of a permissive, even benevolent, liberator offering to be there to reassure whenever needed.

Such a situation cannot be experienced lightly. Attempts to understand the outcome of the recent elections in Nicaragua still continue where a party associated with radical politics over many years was overwhelmingly voted out of office. But the situation there suggests that the capacity of people to sustain a state of disadvantage willingly, while they appreciate the ultimate philosophical objectives of their resistance, should not be overestimated. In such a context, calls for the continuation of the armed struggle, whatever the tactical advantage as part of a strategy of negotiation, may result in no small measure of social anxiety. They can easily be seen as having the potential to jeopardise a perceived gain in the legitimate effort to lessen an historical burden. Their symbolic effectiveness may be compromised by a sense of the racist government's major departure from past actions. They may be seen as a restatement of an old position, where the appearance of resourcefulness in the form of a new approach may be required. The psychological need for change may compromise established positions irrespective of their validity.

A seemingly reflex resort to an established position may represent a kind of trap: the unintended trap of a self-evident moral advantage. It can blunt the capacity for initiative and resourcefulness. An appropriate response must be found that takes full advantage of the momentum of change underway. In that process, limitations and constraints from the past may continue to be exposed at the same time that new opportunities are accentuated.

❑

The crisis of culture referred to earlier is the crisis of transition, a process that should culminate in the emergence of something new. But seldom does the new in human history emerge so clearly as the sun at dawn. Rather, the new is experienced as a process of becoming. Recognition of this fact should underscore the heavy responsibilities of leaders in politics, labour, education, business, art and every other field of endeavour, to assist in bringing into being the self-actualisation of the oppressed in a way that will be in tune with their aspirations. In this regard, there is much that still has to be done.

Attempts have been made to create alternative structures to address the issues of education, health, manpower, and the crucial area of the redistribution of land. These efforts are the proper legacy of the history of resistance. They will have to be the basis on which a fundamentally new dispensation will be created. What this means in practice is that grassroots structures created to empower the oppressed must become the basis for a new national order.

The role of literature in this situation is not an easy matter. It throws up a problematic of its own within the broad cultural crisis I have been attempting to understand. Writers, rather than critics, are likely to provide the ultimate direction. Hopefully, critics will pose the kind of questions that will assist writers in their work.

Whither English in the 21st Century?

sharing a common language

1997

The *English Academy Review* of December 1995 proudly displays the English Academy's statement of mission. It reads:

> Recognising that South Africa (like its Southern African neighbours) is a multilingual, multicultural country, and that its population includes both first-language speakers of English and many for whom English is an additional language, the English Academy is committed to promoting access to English for all and English as a medium of communication, and to fostering the creative talents of all writers and speakers of English in Southern Africa.

So far, so good. The single paragraph continues:

> The Academy will continue to foster the linguistic and cultural interests of those for whom English is a first language, and will play an active role in investigating and promoting the interaction of languages and cultures in South Africa, which it sees as contributing creatively to the evolution of a unique and overarching South African culture.

This statement of mission is a product of its times. The linguistic signposts are there: 'multilingual', 'multicultural', 'promoting access to English for all', 'fostering the creative talents of all ...', 'promoting the interaction of languages and cultures of South Africa'. The spirit is impressively democratic.

Presented at AUETSA 1997, University of the North, 30 June 1997. Subsequently
published in *Current Writing* 10(1), 1998

But hidden in the verdure of 'democratic vistas', to borrow Whitman's expression, is an intriguing insertion: 'The Academy will continue to foster the linguistic and cultural interests of those for whom English is a first language'. The first effort in this regard is to deliver us from the American tendency towards canned descriptive expressions that bring attention to themselves, much like advertisements. Grammatical shortcuts are taken which result in sound bite linguistic expressions whose connection with their grammatical origins may eventually get lost. In this connection, there was something refreshing about being reminded that the expression 'mission statement' is actually 'statement of mission'. In this way, the academy brings attention to itself as an organisation with a mission to reclaim linguistic sanity.

However, the validity of this particular mission may be seen to oscillate between its profound relevance and its possible naïveté: an heroic gesture pitted against the indomitable tide of American English. Going with this tide, feeding it and being fed by it, is the march of globalisation and the concomitant tendency towards new forms of linguistic standardisation.

This trend has important implications for the dialectical relationship between the local and the global, a relationship that impacts on the possible range of uses to which language may be put. Thus, the academy, without saying so much, is issuing a warning (what the American State Department may call 'a travel advisory'): always ask questions whenever new linguistic trends emerge, assessing what impact they may have on your capacity to think creatively within your language community. For example, to what extent does the hiding of connections impede understanding? The hiding of connections will necessarily make it impossible for us to recognise process, making it easy for us to accept things as they are given. In this way a democratic society may espouse freedom and equality while actually making freedom and equality frustratingly difficult to achieve.

There is another reading of the academy's statement of mission I wish to offer. I confess to having felt a large measure of discomfort with an aspect of the statement of mission that made me so conscious of the fact that I was a member of the academy. I am referring, of course, to the insertion: 'The Academy will continue to foster the linguistic and cultural interests of those for whom English is a first language'. This commitment by the academy made me feel rather embarrassingly self-conscious that English was not my first language. There are many other members for whom this may be the case. Why was it being required of me to go out of my way 'to foster the linguistic and cultural interests' of a group I did not belong to?

It then seemed to me that perhaps I should not hasten to conclusions. Is it not true that first-language speakers of English are not people only of English descent? Of course! The demographic composition of this group includes not only South Africans of English descent, some Afrikaners, a large number of South Africans of Indian descent, Jews, a large number of coloured people, third or fourth generation Greeks, Portuguese, etc, but also an increasing number of black Africans. Is it this diverse group that the academy is thinking of? If so, although these people may constitute a first-language linguistic interest group, do they constitute a single cultural interest group? Probably not, my instinct tells me.

Of course, this situation is not new. The English and the Americans may share the same language, but, as someone has observed, they are also divided by it. I am then forced to conclude that the academy is really thinking of the interests of a small, discrete group of South African English speakers of English descent. Why should the special linguistic and cultural interests of this group enjoy the privileged support of a culturally diverse academy membership? Why shouldn't the academy also support my very strong Zulu and Sotho cultural interests? It seems untenable, then, that an academy with a multicultural membership brought together by a common interest in the English language should identify one linguistic and cultural group for special attention. While I respect the culture of this group, I may not necessarily want to be involved in fostering it.

What this tells me is that the drafters of the statement of mission were unable to shake off understandable group anxieties over the future of their language and their ability to have a major say in determining that future. So the English-speaking South African of English descent should understand the anxieties of Afrikaners over the future status of their language. The difference is that although other linguistic and cultural communities were made to find it difficult to develop real affection for Afrikaans, people tended to gravitate towards English for many different reasons. Despite that universal gravitation, it would seem that our South African English speakers of English descent have yet to accept that, although they may belong to a linguistic and cultural group that gave the world a language, this language no longer belongs to them. They may continue to contribute to its growth and development, in exactly the same way as others, but not from an exclusive domain.

This point has of course been made before. In particular, it was a central feature of my address to the Jubilee Conference of the English Academy of South Africa thirteen years ago (and collected in my book *Rediscovery of the Ordinary*). But it seems necessary to restate this point in the context of my reading of the academy's statement of mission.

I do not in fact wish to discuss right now the role of the academy in the development of English in South Africa. Rather, I use my comments on the academy's statement of mission as a point of entry into the central subject of my thoughts: the place of English within a diverse community of languages in post-apartheid South Africa. Approached from this perspective, the most immediate issue is not languages as such, but appropriate strategies for national reconstruction and development in post-apartheid South Africa. My aim is not to offer definitive answers to the questions around the future of English in South Africa; rather, it is to characterise a situation in which English and other languages are likely to develop, to explore the implications of certain questions rather than provide answers to them. We still need to understand where we are and the impact of our ongoing transition on the way we think about it.

Some time last year I was requested by the new Academy of Science of South Africa to prepare a discussion regarding the role of the new academy in our national life. Although the discussion document was prepared, the project remains uncompleted: a victim of my having too many pots on the stove, including the biggest pot: the University of the North (now the University of Limpopo). Some comments made in that unpublished document are relevant to my current project. I set out to be provocative, posing rather than answering questions, to be exploratory rather than definitive. I did that not just to sound clever, but because I deeply believed in that kind of intellectual process. I believed in the relevance of that process to the reinvention of South African society through the intellect.

South African intellectual activity, I began my argument, reveals, like many other aspects of national life, key features of the society in which it flourishes. The apartheid era was characterised by a structure of hierarchies and the legislated parallel development of its various communities.

Horizontal interaction between racial and ethnic groupings was discouraged. It can be said that this situation engendered and consolidated an analytical epistemology with its tendency to break up and divide phenomena into constituent parts. Such an epistemology was wont to emphasise differences rather than similarities; isolation rather than interaction; description and definition rather than interpretation. Accordingly, knowledge was rigorously structured into discrete disciplines with stringent regulatory mechanisms to control the crossing of boundaries. Witness how difficult it is in general for students in our universities to register in more than one faculty, or to move from one university to another.

In the last three years, our society has moved away from parallel development towards horizontal relationships; from the security and certitudes of isolation towards the creative risks of interaction; from repression towards expression; from secrecy towards revelation and exposure; from analytical towards integrative modes of thinking. All this strongly suggests a major shift from an analytical towards an integrated epistemology that gropes towards relational coherence.

An integrative epistemology would enable us, as the constitution of the Academy of Sciences of South Africa puts it, to 'remove barriers between knowledge disciplines and obstacles to the full development of intellectual activity'. It promises to extend our intellectual horizons, in the South African context, in ways not previously possible.

❑

Anyone familiar with the so-called science of complexity and related theories of chaos will be able to appreciate all at once the strengths of our historic transformation towards democracy, as well as our distressing vulnerability. Our emergent democracy, viewed as a complex adaptive system, has released enormous human energies. How to permit those energies full expression, while ensuring at the same time that they are harnessed for sustainable creativity, is not only a political objective, it is also an intensely intellectual one. The central questions are: in what ways is our complex society attempting to reinvent itself? How does our society get to know itself in a constantly transforming environment? How do we characterise its complexity, and grope towards ways of explaining how it is able to establish order at the same time that it is being seriously threatened by all forms of

71

disorder? Thus, our society becomes an enormous laboratory of world historic significance. Seen in this light, the task facing South Africa's intellectuals is an incredibly immense one.

Our university system is currently plagued by historic divisions and, within particular institutions, debilitating internecine strife of varying degrees. The system as it currently exists is incapable of developing a coherent intellectual agenda. By 'coherent intellectual agenda' I do not mean systems of thought linked by common dogma. I am referring to creative intellectual activity energised by and informed by a unique historicity. The results of the current process of reconfiguring the higher education system, in the first instance, seem to be driven more by the political imperatives of structural transformation. Sustained intellectual projects arising out of the new configuration will follow later, but not too soon. Until that happens, much of ongoing intellectual work will remain 'locked' into passing paradigms.

I suggested at the time, that the new science academy could play a major role in enabling our intellectual culture to develop a unique character in the transitional phase. The academy was, to my knowledge, the only formal multi-disciplinary body organised at national level. That situation presented the academy with immense possibilities. What kinds of questions could be posed, from different disciplinary perspectives, about the transition? Was there a link between interdisciplinarity and our ability to comprehend social complexity? Seen in this way, interdisciplinarity was a central principle of intellectual revival, suited to the transition, rather than a mere strategy of inquiry.

With this perspective informing our approach, we can confront a major national context of the language issue: the new constitution of the Republic of South Africa. The last of the six founding provisions of the constitution deals with the languages of the republic. Subsection 6 of Chapter One in its entirety reads as follows:

(1) The official languages of the Republic are Sepedi, Sesotho, Setswana, siSwati, Tshivenda, Xitsonga, Afrikaans, English, isiNdebele, isiXhosa and isiZulu.

(2) Recognising the historically diminished use and status of the indigenous languages of our people, the State must take practical

and positive measures to elevate the status and advance the use of these languages.

(3)　(a) The national government and provincial governments may use any particular official languages for the purposes of government, taking into account usage, practicality, expense, regional circumstances and the balance of the needs and preferences of the population as a whole or in the province concerned; but the national government and each provincial government must use at least two official languages.

　　　(b) Municipalities must take into account the language usage and preference of their residents.

(4)　The national and provincial governments, by legislative and other measures, must regulate and monitor their use of official languages. Without detracting from the provisions of subsection (2) all official languages must enjoy parity of esteem and must be treated equitably.

(5)　A Pan South African Language Board established by national legislation must

　　　(a) promote and create conditions for the development and use of
　　　　　(i)　 all official languages;
　　　　　(ii)　 the Khoi, Nama, and San languages; and
　　　　　(iii) sign language; and

　　　(b) promote and ensure respect for
　　　　　(i)　 all languages commonly used by communities in South Africa, including German, Greek, Gujarati, Hindi, Portuguese, Tamil, Telegu and Urdu; and
　　　　　(ii)　 Arabic, Hebrew, Sanskrit and other languages used for religious purposes in South Africa.

The linguistic environment being addressed by the constitution is an inherently complex one. It is characterised by the affirmation of political principle within the national value system embodied in the constitution. At the same time a field of negotiation is provided in respect of the implementation of principle. The use of official languages within the context of 'taking into account usage, practicality, expense, regional circumstances and the balance of the needs and preferences of the population as a whole or in the province concerned' opens for us a vast field of negotiation and interpretation. It makes things possible and impossible all at once. It prescribes rights while underscoring the fact that, for those rights to be enjoyed, certain things need to be put in place.

What are those things? How long will it take to put them in place? How long will it take before desired outcomes occur? These are difficult questions of process, political will, and dogged monitoring of activity stretched over a possibly vast period. But, for the moment, one of the spin offs of negotiation and interpretation promises to be the laying of a firm foundation in the short to medium term of the transitional period, but with benefits that might stretch far into the future – the development of an intellectual frame of mind that seeks not definitive answers as yet but, rather, deliberately sets out to observe, describe, and then to pose as many questions as possible. The more difficult the questions posed, the more rigorous the methods to find answers, and the more complex the process of interpretation.

I have not had the opportunity to explore the implications of this approach in relation to a specific language issue. One possible starting point is that the constitution places enormous responsibilities on both the national and provincial governments in decisions regarding the use of 'any particular official language for the purposes of government'. It seems to me that the responsibilities placed on provincial governments are particularly onerous. It is at the provincial level that language issues may be at their sharpest, and where the capacity to deliver on ultimate constitutional rights may be at its weakest. In this situation, the politicisation of language rights may generate more heat than light. Demands asserted even though their validity is accepted may be impossible to meet. 'What if?' scenarios, backed by research, and which, although informed by political considerations are not ultimately determined by them, which may result in more studied interventions.

One such scenario starts from the premise, articulated by Albie Sacks in the *English Academy Review* of 1994, that it was the height of constitutional wisdom that the English language was not declared 'to be the working language of government and the functional medium of public discourse, reserving to other languages a protected but subordinate status'. Such a

situation would be politically unacceptable. In this regard, Sacks goes on
to speculate:

> It might well be that, one day, English will emerge as the working
> language of most of government and business in South Africa.
> Perhaps it will come to be the language that everyone wants to learn
> because of its utility. That, however, would be evolution through
> choice. Nothing could be more inimical to the widespread accept-
> ance of English than to make it the common language by command.

Yet, where all of us are both constitutionally and conceptually not free to
possess English for our own ethnic interests, ignoring the de facto position of
English as a working language would have devastating consequences for all of
us. Communication would be greatly affected in education, commerce and
industry, in the judiciary, and in many other areas of national life. Thus the
place of English, in the immediate instance, as a tool for economic development cannot be underestimated. This recognition suggests that our agenda
right now is to doggedly affirm the equality of all languages while ensuring
that a language that enables all of us to participate fully in the economic life of
our country, at this juncture, is made more accessible. Nor should such accessibility imply the lessening of access to other languages. This current informal
situation does not negate formal linguistic group interest. In this connection,
English may be the only language that many of us may approach, possibly
through choice, without an attachment to it that defines our identity.

Once more, Albie Sachs comments in a most illuminating way on
this issue:

> The basic concept of the new South African nation is that we come
> into it as we are, bringing our languages, beliefs and world-views in
> with us. Citizenship is culturally and linguistically unqualified. To be
> a South African, you do not need to prove to anyone's satisfaction
> that you are civilised, assimilated, exempted or honorary. We share a
> common humanity, occupy a common territory, and fall under the
> protection of a common constitution. We do not have to share a
> common language. Equality does not mean identity, but denotes
> equal rights to participate, as we are, in a common citizenship.

The importance of the informal, rather than prescriptive, choice of English means that those languages, including English for first-language speakers, that define us culturally and otherwise, need to receive simultaneous attention to promote their development. In the long term, the possibility is that their successful development may be linked to the availability of greater resources. An assumption can be made that economic growth promises a more realisable, more viable, linguistic democracy.

What I have tried to suggest, in a deliberately speculative sort of way, is that our language situation necessarily predisposes itself to a complex approach. I pose this approach in the light of politically correct tendencies to call for instant solutions. These tendencies may be understandable in the short term, post-election period when it is necessary to flex the muscles of rights, but they should quickly give way to persistent ingenuity.

Moral Anchor

an interview with the Arch

1998

Although I had an intuition about it, I was not to know the difficult reality of interviewing Archbishop Desmond Tutu as chairperson of the Truth and Reconciliation Commission until I arrived at his office in the TRC's Cape Town headquarters late one afternoon. Perhaps both of us registered the faint awkwardness of the situation when he remarked that I had found him at that time of day when, he said, 'I am not at my most scintillating.'

Responding to that human moment, when people meeting for some formal purpose are wont to adjust to one another before settling down to business, I said, 'Well, what you have just said, you said in a scintillating manner.'

We laughed, the familiar glint of jocular mischievousness struggling to ignite in the Arch's eyes. But it failed to erode the effects of another long and busy day. For me, there was the added delicate strain of the many intervening years between this rather formal interview and my previous intimate encounter with him in 1971, when, as a student, I had approached him with a spiritual crisis. The tension between having seen this man personally years before and approaching him now professionally wreaked havoc with my ability to carry out my mandate: getting an insight into Tutu the person within the context of the TRC and its activities.

'I could maybe to some extent pride myself on being not too bad as a chairperson,' Tutu observed about himself much later in the interview. But I mention it now, unexpectedly, hoping it will have a shock effect in the same way that, before the interview began, the archbishop motioned me to a table and said, 'Let us pray.' A few minutes later, as we said 'Amen', I noticed that

---

this unexpected prayer had done much to make the office atmosphere more tolerable.

In his comments on his ability as a chairperson, Tutu was referring to his capacity to pull a meeting through agonisingly difficult moments. One example is how the commission survived a traumatic credibility test when one of its key officials, investigation unit head Dumisa Ntsebeza, faced potentially damaging allegations of complicity in political murders. Ntsebeza's accuser subsequently confessed that he had been coached to discredit him.

The meetings on this crisis, attested the archbishop, were agonising. 'We hardly had a meeting of the commission where, when you finished, you felt happy.' It seems Tutu pulled the commission out of its agonies by resorting to means beyond the limitations of discursive logic. I wondered to what extent his management style resided in his ability to recognise those precise moments at which a resort to spirituality provides a unifying transcendence that allows him to assume, and remain in, authority.

It is clear that one of the archbishop's primary objectives at the start of the commission's life was to build a team linked not only by professional expertise, but also by human skills: 'Our first meetings as a commission were some of the most difficult. We came from all sorts of backgrounds. It was important that we started off with a [spiritual] retreat and more or less ended with a retreat.'

It was important that professional skills were shored up by developing loyalties, such that when the integrity of Ntsebeza was vindicated it could be said that the integrity of the commission was also affirmed. Loyalties to the commission, a body that is the enactment of a crucial principle in nation building, were consolidated.

'Now I think that if the Ntsebeza thing had happened earlier in the life of the commission, it would have torn us apart. It split maybe not the commissioners as such, but the staff. There were many who believed the gardener [Ntsebeza's accuser],' Tutu said. 'Some formidable human weaknesses had to be overcome. How many colleagues in the commission chided themselves for having entertained doubts, wishing they had believed in a colleague without the help of a confession from his accuser?'

In this regard, he observed, the commission 'in many ways became a microcosm of South African society', with many untested attitudes, prejudices and agonies of conscience to overcome. It is difficult not to conclude that with such powerful human intangibles at play, the archbishop was a crucial source of stability.

The hearings on the 1992 Bisho massacre in which twenty-nine demonstrators were mown down by Ciskeian soldiers provided one telling example of human magnanimity about which Tutu remarked, 'Oh God, people are wonderful! I was myself upset by the testimony of the first witness who had been the head of the Ciskeian Defence Force. The next set of witnesses was four officers, three black and a white who was their spokesperson. He said to this packed hall where the tension was so thick you could cut it, "Yes, we gave the orders for the soldiers to open fire." And in the hall were people who had been injured in that incident; others had lost loved ones. Then he turned to the audience and said, "Please forgive us, please accept back my colleagues into the community." An incredible moment! The same angry audience broke out into deafening applause. And when they finished, I said, "I think we need to keep quiet because we are in the presence of something very special and very holy." And so, those are my abiding experiences.'

Tutu had asked for a minute's silence to let the profound significance of the moment sink in, leaving a lasting impression on everyone in the hall. Few could fail to be affected by such an experience. It seemed to me that, once again, he had recognised the correct moment to validate the event with theological authority.

The TRC was a massive human effort. It must have drawn heavily on the physical, mental, intellectual and spiritual resources of the archbishop. 'How would you describe yourself as having been the manager, in this situation?' I asked.

'It gives me great joy to pay tribute to an incredible team, really. It's not just being conventional,' said Tutu. 'We were enormously fortunate to have Alex Boraine as the deputy chairperson. I can't imagine how we would have been able to start as quickly as we did. I keep saying, I would not want to wish on my worst enemy the job of being asked to take up [the commission]. It's the worst possible ordeal to start up an operation as complex as this one de novo. We were singularly blessed. Boraine very quickly helped to put in place the staff.'

Incorrigibly self-effacing! While it may be true that Boraine complemented Tutu by being there to handle many of the daily public relations and hard-grind management issues, the archbishop lent overwhelming moral

authority to the entire process. His self-effacement in the interests of recognising and paying tribute to a collective effort itself derives from that
authority. Such self-effacement is far more than a display of modesty. It is a
key feature of ecclesiastical authority successfully tested in the long and bitter
struggle against apartheid. It is authority derived from active intervention in
many difficult moments during the struggle: the activist man of God who
would fearlessly hold both the oppressor and the oppressed to account.

In this context, whatever political or philosophical limitations can be
pointed out about the commission and its chairperson, they come up
against an almost unassailable moral authority. Each criticism of the archbishop and the commission can induce in the one who makes it a mixture
of inadequacy, ingratitude, and even a hint of meanness. Surely this man has
earned the right to his words! Your experience compared to his, no matter
how much intellectual argument you have to deploy against him, appears
minuscule.

In other words, resistance to the theological authority of the archbishop
succeeds only in making it stronger. His effectiveness as manager of this
historic process lies precisely there.

And criticisms there are. One is that the commission's interpretation
of its mandate reduced apartheid to its worst perpetrators; that it allowed
apartheid's beneficiaries, whites, to distance themselves from it because
these perpetrators would then become its most compelling examples. It did
not succeed, on the other hand, in putting across the banal reality of apartheid
in the life of every black South African: the pass laws, the forced removals,
the inferior education, separate amenities and so on. How does Tutu react to
this view?

He stresses that there is a context to the commission. 'People, I hope, will
be aware that there were statutory constraints on the commission. We had
to give as complete a picture as possible of gross human rights violations
that happened as a result of the conflicts of the past within a thirty-four-
year period – 1960 to 1994.

'The definition of gross human rights violations was also restricted to
four categories: killing, abduction, torture and severe ill-treatment. But it
is not true that all the commission concentrated on was perpetrators. We
had a hearing on the health sector. We had a hearing on the business sector.
We've had hearings on youth, women and the faith community.'

People must read the commission's final report, says Tutu, to judge whether it was 'the naïve commission that some people think we might have been. Many of us were involved in some of the things, forced removals, for example. We didn't just experience them as observers. We were victims of forced removals, many of us.'

I was intrigued that he thought some might dismiss the commission as naïve. Indeed, when one sees television pictures of victims embracing perpetrators in an almost ritualistic display of forgiveness, it is difficult not to register the delicate play between magnanimity and naïve sentimentality, the feeling that people have been manoeuvred into righteousness.

Either way, the politics of negotiation and compromise have led us to this situation, forcing us to skate on the thin ice separating reconciliation and justice, a continuum that makes African Studies Professor Mahmood Mamdani wonder exactly 'when justice turns into revenge (Rwanda), and when reconciliation turns into an embrace of evil (South Africa)'. One is compelled to ponder: we are either tragically naïve, or profoundly wise.

There is a story, I tell the archbishop, of some Afrikaners who believe that black South Africans, oppressed for so long yet willing to reconcile instead of avenge, confirm in doing so that they are not quite human. A real human being hits back. What is at stake here? I ask the archbishop. Is it the very concept of a human being?

'I must say I'm very deeply saddened,' he says, 'if this person's idea of the normal human being is one who must lust for revenge. There always has been the idea that only the weak forgive. In fact, it's the strong who are able to forgive. It's the strong, ultimately, who can ask for forgiveness. The weak person is the one who never wants to acknowledge that they can be wrong.

'I'm sad, because, if the person who says this claims to be a Christian, then he is saying something quite subversive about Jesus Christ. What he is saying is that Jesus Christ was really not human.

'He is really saying that Madiba is not really human, when the rest of the world is saying "What an incredible man who, after twenty-seven years, instead of looking to hit back at his tormentors, invites their wives to tea!" Is this guy saying, "Madiba, you really are sub-human"? There must be something wrong with his assessment of people. I would weep for him.'

It is probably why such people, Tutu thinks, deserve visionary white leadership. Former presidents F W de Klerk and P W Botha failed to provide this kind of leadership for the white community. De Klerk 'got very close. But you remember this wonderful description somebody once made of theological statements: that they purport to be assertions and then they die the death of a thousand qualifications. De Klerk made a very handsome apology, and then somehow he didn't just go that extra bit where he would have said "we take responsibility". In this connection, de Klerk displayed weak leadership at a crucial moment. In his defiance, on the other hand, P W Botha continued to live in a world without moral complications.'

The archbishop seems to imply that there is a dire need for white leaders of stature who can redefine and reposition the moral and ethical world of white South Africa so that that community can regain a sense of balance in a new order.

Of a 1998 survey on public attitudes toward the commission's hearings, Tutu says, 'What has shattered me and also exhilarated me is that eighty per cent of the victims of apartheid say they believe reconciliation is possible. Now those are the people who should be saying we want revenge, but they're saying "we feel it [reconciliation] is possible".

'What is shattering is that the beneficiaries of apartheid – whites, coloureds, Indians – are the ones who are dubious about whether the thing [reconciliation] can work. It seems to confirm whites basically shunning, spurning the offers of reconciliation.'

But for Tutu reconciliation surely means believing that all South Africans are capable of appreciating the need to reconcile. There is no doubt that the Arch's considerable moral authority has left an indelible mark on the national character of South Africa. This is partly because he has achieved the kind of spiritual clarity that can only come to one who has engaged the agonies and the ecstasies of leading people over many years of travail. Only those who have travelled on that road can understand the extent of human complexity embedded in that single word: reconciliation. Not an alternative to justice, or vengeance, but a means to enrich human conduct.

But it is precisely this concern with human conduct in the midst of all the pressing social and economic problems that lays open reconciliation to the charge of political naïvety. The pressing problems of the economy, power politics and social inequities always tend to render vulnerable the best value systems. Nevertheless, the commission places human conduct at the centre of our national consciousness. In this context, it is our national capacity to affirm our value system against great odds that will be a major test of our resolve to succeed in creating a new society.

Perhaps for the archbishop, the commission hearings, beyond revealing to us the facts of engineered iniquity, were also an opportunity for us to acknowledge them formally. But that acknowledgement comes with enormous responsibilities, and sometimes people may have to be pushed to recognise and accept those responsibilities. This seems to be the only meaningful way for one to understand why Tutu pushed Winnie Madikizela-Mandela into a public expression of contrition. 'Did you really believe her,' I asked, 'after you relentlessly squeezed out a confession from her?'

Her contrition, says the Arch, is a 'flickering flame' we should not extinguish. 'Let's say, well, we've got the flame. It's there. Can we imagine what it would have been like if she had said "Nonsense!" How would we have felt?' This commission had also accorded P W Botha the same opportunity 'just to say to the people "I am sorry!" He spurned it. He just wasn't ready to go that way. She, at least, you could say, opened a small door. And that is what we were trying to coach out of her.'

Clearly, in Tutu's view, it was not so much whether Madikizela-Mandela could be believed, but whether she had been made to do the right thing. Perhaps being pushed to yield to the imperatives of a moral position may later enable one to accept and live with the implications of that morality.

In the end, the archbishop's moral authority also became his biggest tool of management. Given the objectives of the commission and that it was intended to be an important factor in stabilising the process of change, he was its ideal leader. He had paid his dues. Fortified in spirituality, strong in action, dauntless, persecuted yet resilient, he could be trusted to approach the task before him with principled equanimity. He leaves behind a legacy that will be interpreted for many years to come: the TRC as political agency, driven by a legal instrument, and, in the hands of Tutu, often assuming the contours of religious ritual.

Our parting pleasantries after the interview are interrupted by the telephone. As I leave the office, I glance back at the Arch. He is already on the phone, paying full attention to the needs of someone else at the other end of the line.

The Triumph of Narrative

telling the stories of the TRC

1998

When it was announced that a group of former police generals of the old South African Police were going to apply for amnesty, I thought that a new chapter had opened in the work of the Truth and Reconciliation Commission (TRC). No sooner had I registered this thought than I was struck by the irony contained in it. The stories of the generals would be more than simply the next event in the activities of the TRC. They would, indeed, be a new chapter in the narratives being told at the hearings of the TRC throughout the country.

I remembered that at the end of the historic first round of the TRC hearings which took place in East London, Archbishop Desmond Tutu, TRC chairperson, was quoted as having said, 'The country has taken the right course in the process of healing to hear these stories. Very few of us can be the same today as we were on Monday [the day the testimonies began].' This was one of the first pronouncements I remember in which the TRC testimonies were referred to as stories.

Is it not so that we often think of stories as imaginary events, which we may call tales, fiction, fables, or legends: stories as narratives of one kind or another? Yet the testimonies we continue to hear at the TRC hearings are the recall of memory. What is being remembered actually happened. If today they sound like imaginary events it is because, as we shall recall, the horror of day-to-day life under apartheid often outdid the efforts of the imagination to reduce it to metaphor.

But time seems to have rescued the imagination. Time has given the recall of memory the power of reflection associated with narrative. Isn't it

---

Negotiating the Past: The Making of Memory in South Africa (ed. Sarah Nuttall & Carli Coetzee), Oxford University Press, Oxford, 1998

that there is something inherently reflective about memory, as there is about narrative? If so, narratives of memory, in which real events are recalled, stand to guarantee us occasions for some serious moments of reflection. Hopefully, it is this reflective capacity, experienced as a shared social consciousness, that will be the lasting legacy of the stories of the TRC. Possibly, this is what the archbishop implies about the capacity of these stories to change us.

What seems to have happened is that the passage of time which brought forth our freedom has given legitimacy and authority to previously silenced voices. It has lifted the veil of secrecy and State-induced blindness. Where the State sought to hide what it did, it compelled those who were able to see what was happening not to admit the testimony of their own eyes. In this connection, the stories of the TRC represent a ritualistic lifting of the veil and the validation of what was actually seen. They are an additional confirmation of the movement of our society from repression to expression. Where in the past the State attempted to compel the oppressed to deny the testimony of their own experience, today the experience is one of the essential conditions for the emergence of a new national consciousness. These stories may very well be some of the first steps in the rewriting of South African history on the basis of validated mass experience.

And so it is that we are privileged to experience social change as the incremental exposure of an elaborately constructed intrigue of immense size and complexity. The narrative of apartheid, which can now be told, has reached that part of the plot where vital facts leading to the emergence of understanding are in the process of being revealed. While some key elements of the intrigue are emerging, I believe we have yet to find meaning. In fact, it is going to be the search for meanings that may trigger off more narratives.

If and when that happens, the imagination, having been rescued by time, will be the chief beneficiary. The resulting narratives may have less and less to do with facts themselves and with their recall than with the revelation of meaning through the imaginative combination of those facts. At that point, facts will be the building blocks of metaphor.

This point is worth emphasising. One of my favourite quotations is from T T Moyana's essay in *Aspects of South African Literature*, where he speculates on why it was often so difficult for artists and writers to extract metaphor from the day-to-day horror of apartheid:

An additional difficulty for the creative artist in South Africa, especially the black writer, is that life itself is too fantastic to be out-stripped by the creative imagination. [Lewis] Nkosi calls the theme of the absurd a theme of daily living in South Africa. Indeed, many writers of the absurd school would find their plots too realistic to startle anybody into serious questioning of their deeper meaning. How would the quarrel over a bench in Edward Albee's *Zoo Story* startle anybody in a country where thousands of people have been daily quarrelling over who should sit on a particular park bench, and the country's Parliament has had to legislate on the matter? That's much more startling than Albee's little quarrel between two men. And Kafka himself could not have bettered the case told by Lewis Nkosi. He was arrested by a policeman who then phoned his superior to ask, 'What shall I charge him with?' Or the incident of a white man and a coloured woman who were tried for being caught kissing. The court got bogged down over the question of whether the kiss was 'platonic or passionate'. One reporter who covered the case for a local newspaper wrote: 'Lawyers and laymen are certain that the Minister of Justice will now have to consider an amend-ment to the law which will define the various degrees of kissing from the platonic to the passionate.'

It was not only difficult to see logic behind this sort of thing, it was also impossible to detect coherent philosophical justification for it. And this is the nub of it. At its best, the achievements of apartheid society took place in the context of a moral and intellectual desert.

The extent of this moral desert has only now been confirmed. The stories of the TRC expose not only previously silenced voices, but also methods employed in silencing them. That is why the revelation of these methods has received so much attention. The silencing of voices through various forms of brutality, torture and humiliation induced anger and bit-terness. In the end, particularly for the writer, the ugly reality of oppression became impossible to articulate. This is because it became itself the only story, but one which, once enacted, had to be denied. The story of apartheid became adept at self-denial.

And so, what can no longer be denied has come out. We now learn how people's hands were cut off and put in bottles; how a woman was forced to watch her husband being tortured. The police were later to boast to her how, in order to remove evidence of his death, they roasted his body to ashes, observing how it hissed like ordinary meat on a braai pan. It is even said that as they roasted a human body they drank beer and had meat roasting on a braai a few metres away.

We now confirm what we have suspected all along: the different methods of torture. We can confirm the details of the terrible deaths of the Mxenges. We can confirm how a man's head was reduced to blood and brains by a booby-trapped walkman, and how that instrument of death was first tested on the heads of pigs. We have heard about people being falsely accused of being informers and dying horrible deaths at the hands of fellow members of the oppressed. We could go on and on and on. But there is no need to do this. What it all represents is the acknowledgement of such pain and suffering that only now is it meaningful to ask: why? It also enables us to wait for that moment when the perpetrators acknowledge their deeds. We see pictures of alleged perpetrators dressed in business suits which make them so ordinary, like the person next door, and we begin to wonder about colleagues next to whom we may sit in a lecture hall, in a meeting; about business colleagues across the negotiation table; about fellow passengers on a plane. Could any of these have been a compulsive killer on duty? At this point we begin the search for meaning.

What kind of explanation are we going to find? I have argued before (see the essay, 'The Brilliant Trick') that the creative aspects of apartheid society, from the point of view of its proponents, ended when that society became inordinately preoccupied with methods of domination, which became the basis on which privilege could be maintained. Any transcendent values that may have initially informed apartheid's value system gave way to the psychology of maintenance. This was the psychology of habit which made prejudice a standard mode of perception. This mode of perception flourished in its crude aspects among members of the white, mainly Afrikaner, working class, for whom jobs were reserved in the police force, the army, railways and harbours, the civil service, and small-scale farming. The ruling elites in both the political and industrial sectors, satisfied that they had bought the compliance of the white electorate, gave a blank cheque to the military and law-enforcement establishments. Where, in these establishments, the enforcement of apartheid degenerated into a science of torture and death, in the general society it informed social habit. It occurs to me that in this situation, black people were not hated as such; in time they simply became objects at the receiving end of elaborate institutionalised processes of maintaining domination. For those dispensing oppression, their jobs became an official vehicle for their received prejudices. Social conditioning and the work process became two sides of the same coin.

That is why the National Party is unable to apologise for the moral desert they took time to create. Their project did not succeed in anything beyond an elaborate political programme. The political programme became everything. The resulting depravity in the polity became generalised. It is not only to be found among personnel in the security services. It is also the measure of the general moral condition among the ruling elites who are now no longer in power. Power and wealth became the dominant determinants of behaviour: two key ingredients in the recipe of socially embedded corruption.

That is why many intelligent Afrikaners still clamour for a volkstaat or for language rights that they already have, as if nothing significant has happened in our country in the last few years. They are unable to link the failures of the past to the need for a new moral vision that includes others. They have yet to accept such a vision as a basis on which to reassess the past more fundamentally. Their demands, however valid they may be, represent a tragic failure of social conscience. In this connection, the future of Afrikaner culture may lie in its rediscovery of social morality.

Fortunately, this process has begun. In fact, there may be an informal truth and reconciliation process underway among the Afrikaners. Its contours are taking shape in the form of such novels as Mark Behr's *The Smell of Apples*. Karel Schoeman's *Promised Land* anticipated it some years back. Jeanne Goosen's *Not All of Us* gave it further impetus. I am certain that there are more such narratives which have not yet been translated. Their distinguishing feature is their focus on ordinary social details which pile up into major, disturbing statements. The ordinary Afrikaner family, lost in the illusion of the historic heroism of the group, has to find its moral identity within a national community in which it is freed from the burden of being special. Afrikaner culture and its language will triumph from the resultant honesty of self-revelation, the resonances of which will appeal to many others whose humanity has been newly revealed by a liberated present.

Somewhere, the story of the agony of the contemporary Afrikaner family will converge with the stories of millions of the recently oppressed. That convergence may very well be the point where ordinary Afrikaners recognise, through confronting their own histories, the enormity of the horror that was done on their behalf, and which, as willing agents, they helped bring about.

As we negotiate the difficult task of normalising freedom, it will be important for us to realise that a political accommodation such as we have achieved does not imply that all the moral, intellectual and philosophical questions have been solved. To stop at that point is to risk repeating the apartheid mistake of making politics everything.

Early this year, my wife and I were flying back home from Mauritius when the pilot announced that Bafana Bafana, the national soccer team, was ahead of Cameroon in the first game of the African Nations Cup. My wife and I and a few other passengers cheered merrily. A wealthy corporate South African turned towards us to ask, 'This team that we are playing, is it a good team?' After noting the self-consciousness around the use of 'we', I vaguely remembered the tone behind this sort of question that evokes my resentment in a Pavlovian sort of way. Not only did the man know nothing about the sporting preferences of his fellow South Africans, but the glory of the Cameroon team, the pride of Africa, had passed him by.

The tragedy of this situation is that that man felt superior in his ignorance. And while he ritualistically sought information that was of no use to him (as the important thing for him was to demonstrate lack of racism in himself by seeking information from a black person, without realising in the process that he was being his own usual inordinately condescending, racist self), we were being reduced by him to explaining 'our people'.

As I have observed, he was not asking for information; he was demonstrating his lack of prejudice. Little did he realise what he was actually saying to us. Here is what he was saying: 'I do not know you to be good enough to beat a good European team. This other team, whatever it is, can't be that good. So you are beating a useless team. Therefore you can't be that good either. But am I not wonderful that I am asking you?' It is highly unlikely that he would have asked the same kind of question had we had a South African cricket or rugby team, both almost exclusively made up of white players, competing in an international tournament.

I am presenting, of course, the archetypal image of the bleeding-heart, English-speaking liberal South African, who has no understanding of why he is hated so much when he sacrificed so much for the oppressed. In this connection, our fellow passenger would, of course, readily donate jerseys to a black team as long as he was convinced these jerseys 'were going to be properly used'.

Fellow South Africans of this kind are blissfully unaware that they should appear before the TRC. They are convinced that it is only the Afrikaner who should do so. 'It is often said,' Mandela has recently been quoted as saying, 'that an invisible wound is more painful than the visible one.' These are the wounds these South Africans have generally been good at inflicting. With their condescending platitudes, they have massacred hundreds of thousands of souls. I have never been to jail, but I have, at various times in my life, been in the prison of these platitudes.

Yes, they have a story to tell. Its setting is in the interstice between power and indifferent or supportive agency. In that interstice, the English-speaking South African has conducted the business of his life. Now he was indignant and guilty; now he was thriving. This no-man's land ensured a fundamental lack of character. With a foreign passport in the back pocket of the trousers, now they belong – now they do not. When will they tell this story?

In factoring in the bleeding-heart English-speaking liberal, I am proposing one of the greatest dangers to the TRC hearings. From the point of view of one very large sector of the South African population, the TRC hearings may confirm the image of blacks as helpless victims, suffering complaints before whites who claim to understand their plight and declare themselves to be willing to help. In this way blacks will always be the numerical majority weighed down by the psychology of suffering minorities. They will be the eagle that grew among the chickens and is no longer able to fly. English-speaking South Africans have yet to acknowledge their willing compliance, by developing their own particular version of oppression, in the oppression of black people.

At the risk of setting up simplistic binary oppositions, one should state that, on balance, the guilt of English-speaking South Africans is as extensive as that of Afrikaners. The latter were the primary agents. They had the power. They accumulated new wealth. They ruled with a firm hand. Their resulting self-confidence rendered them collectively insensitive. On the other hand, the guilt of the English-speaking South African was prone to greater moral agony, to more wrenching agonies of conscience. Those who had no power remained with their consciences, while those who had it died from within.

We cannot afford to condone any aspect of racism at a time when racism should be permanently buried. Let all the stories be told. The gift of our freedom partly lies in our ability to ensure that where oppression is no longer a major defining characteristic of the social environment, the different features of our society will now emerge as aspects of a more complex definition of that environment.

And so it is that the stories of the TRC seem poised to result in one major spin-off, among others: the restoration of narrative. In few countries in the contemporary world do we have a living example of people reinventing themselves through narrative. Only now has South Africa succeeded in becoming metaphor, in becoming a true subject of philosophy. That is why the real challenge is not in maintaining competitive levels of capability in science and technology. That is a relatively easy task. The real challenge is in grounding science and technology in lived life, in the capacity for our society to stimulate the imaginations of its peoples through voices that can go beyond the giving of testimony, towards creating new thoughts and new worlds. Only then does our experience resonate with moral import.

Innocence Lost, Opportunity Gained

a path towards renaissance

1998

The story of our four years of democracy is really the story of how it has affected millions of personal lives. For that reason it is an infinitely complex story and is bound to get even more complex the older our democracy becomes.

The agonies and ecstasies that result from our diverse efforts to try to understand this story are perhaps some of the greatest gifts of our freedom. Much more interesting than the story of how much we expected the new government to deliver on promises is the story of our capacity to push personal initiatives, taking advantage of openings suddenly available. All this strongly suggests that government be the great facilitator, carrying visionary and moral authority, and making it possible for enormous personal energies to be released.

Yet, while the release of so much energy can be an expression of optimism, it introduces into national life a profound element of uncertainty and risk. The challenge for the State is how to cope with potentially massive dissonance at the same time that we are pursuing the declared national objective of finding the best ways of giving meaning to our freedom. Released energies may flow in different directions, prompting reactions that are equally divergent, and which may result in a chain reaction of activity whose efficacy is difficult to assess or predict at any particular moment. This situation makes the art of governance an extremely demanding enterprise. It is a situation that will often test the limits of democracy to the full.

A few days ago the SABC showed a documentary, *Apartheid Did Not Die*, by the legendary John Pilger. It would appear from media reports that the

---

Cape Times, 27 April 1998

SABC agonised somewhat over the wisdom of showing the documentary. I could not understand why they should have worried. Coming at a time when we customarily ask how we have been doing since the first democratic election, the documentary was a useful piece around which to reflect.

It showed a reality that we know so well: the progressively narrowing wage gap between blacks and whites; the widening wage gap between the black elite and the rest of the black population; the erosion of memory by sudden wealth; the arid rationalisations of corporate white South Africa; the colonial origins of apartheid dramatised in the obscene contrast between Alexandra and Sandton; the faded memories of Dimbaza, and the indestructible self-help schemes of the women of South Africa. Far from being denunciatory, the documentary was a dramatisation of concern, never mind a title suggesting betrayal.

Nevertheless, I thought the overall effect, encapsulated in the very title, was an oxymoron: a powerful revelation of the known. Surely, the death of apartheid is a social process not an event! Apartheid had continued to die in one way or another every day since the dying process was speeded up by the election of 27 April four years ago. The real flaw in John Pilger's documentary is that he took us on a journey he was unable to complete.

Recently, we have witnessed several related events which, looked at from the conventional perspective of John Pilger's film, may soon be seen to confirm the belief in some quarters that perhaps we should not have had a negotiated settlement. Let us recall them.

An Afrikaner farmer allegedly shoots a black boy to death after the farmer's son, who was playing with the black boy, came home complaining of an injury sustained during play.

Another farmer runs over a little black girl with his bakkie. She dies. The farmer declares it an accident and says he is not responsible for the girl's death. As if he has not inflicted enough pain, he chases the dead girl's family away from the farm.

In another incident, the very latest one, a farmer allegedly shoots a six-month-old black baby girl to death, and reportedly threatens the baby's grieving family with death should they dare report the killing.

Some white farmers, responding to the outrage these events have roused, remind the public of the spate of killings of white farmers, as if implying that there has now been some form of justice.

The stories of brutality emerging from our farms indicate there are many South Africans for whom the doors of perception and opportunity are yet to open. They are still trapped in small feudal fiefdoms that resonate with the terrible, brutal emptiness of the past. Nothing illustrates such emptiness more than the tragic-comic figure of P W Botha, a figure once feared, yet totally without capacity to strike fear, wagging his finger, hoping it still has the same effect.

Fortunately, he is no longer the head of the armed forces. Unfortunately, many like him, his erstwhile followers, still have their guns in their farmsteads. Socialised by what P W Botha represented and defended, they go on shooting in an illusory world in which the make-believe of their specialness entitles then to the habitual expectation of impunity. It would appear that the farmer who allegedly shot the six-month-old baby and the local police who apprehended him, were old cronies. They would take care of him. Unfortunately for them, they were to be hit, only now, by the gale of the new reality.

Something tells me that it is out of such psycho-social dramas that the character of our new society is taking shape. The contours of new relationships have yet to take shape. This terrain of struggle, though, is a particularly intense, but perhaps sobering, meeting point. It is this that John Pilger may have intended but did not arrive at. It is that all of us have lost our heroic specialness. The specialness that derived from fighting oppression, or from administering it, is gone. Suddenly, for the newly liberated, the mistakes we may make in our different stations of responsibility have become the subject of embarrassing exposures, revealing glaring weaknesses of experience, testing the purity of our motives, revealing temptations around which to navigate, subjecting us to the pains of not being understood, telling us that the mere expression of commitment to a vision is no longer enough.

Where the intention to do good may have assumed the status of law, there is now the necessity to subject intention to the rigours of procedure: a requirement of commitment to accountable processes. And so it is that we have painfully seen people we have admired, and continue to admire, burning in the fires of new demands on our understanding and behaviour. Many continue to fall by the wayside, hopefully to be remembered for having shown us what to avoid in future.

In this respect, democracy can be unsparing. Unfortunately, that is what seems to be normal about it. Perhaps the next election will see the emergence of a professional state (is there such a thing?), driven by processes intended to make things work. The broad sweep of vision and charisma could only take us up to a point.

This does not make vision redundant; it suggests, rather, the requirement that vision also becomes practical. That is to say, the new policies and laws must work. Land restitution must work; the criminal justice system must work; the school system must work; the health system must work; the informal sector must flourish; houses must be built; economic investment must succeed; and the landscape of apartheid be redesigned.

Yet, we do have strong and terrible memories. We catch ourselves wondering why we should submit to 'normality' when terrible things happened to us. When we shied away from the path of vengeance, we chose to live with our memories, to live with the consequences of remembering without vengeance or, worse still, to forget. The latter would represent a serious threat to our future.

Were we fooling ourselves? What do we make of the sentimentality of programmed forgetfulness of the kind that lingers uncomfortably long after the spectacle has passed: such as when Archbishop Tutu pleaded with Winnie Madikizela-Mandela to say 'sorry'?

She finally said so, under the compelling public pressure of impeccable moral authority. I didn't believe her. Her declaration was not consistent with the combativeness of her testimony in the giving of which she succeeded in winning some admiration. She had accepted no wrong-doing; so what could she be sorry for? But, in the end, she had played the game. And so we move on, hoping we are right.

Yes, we are an ordinary society now, perhaps still reeling under the expectation that destiny owes us something. But when we became free, we lost our innocence. Yet we have to realise, too, that our new status does carry enormous opportunities. These opportunities suggest that a new kind of greatness will begin to be forged once we get down to mastering the new values and rules by which we have chosen to govern ourselves; to embrace the future boldly with a flexible, if somewhat pained, creative intelligence. That could be one of the many paths towards renaissance.

African Renaissance

a new kid on the block

1998

We have had them before: slogans of optimism. Through powerful evocations of authenticity, they inspired and boosted self-confidence. Through intellectual speculation, they offered explanatory possibilities and fired imaginations. They promised self-deliverance in a world whose interest in Africa seemed to be only to exploit its resources, to humiliate its peoples and to cultivate its underdevelopment.

These slogans have come and gone: Negritude, the African Personality, African Socialism, African Philosophy, African Humanism, and Authenticity. A new kid on the block has arrived: African Renaissance.

Some common threads run through them. They have been reactive calls of self-assertion where there was a perceived universal, if not racist, denial of the human worth of Africans. They have attempted to prove that, if other continents or powerful civilisations think they have some distinctive characteristics, then they are in for a disappointment: Africans have them too.

If there is socialism in Europe, we have our own in Africa. If there is Christianity in Europe, we have our own version in Africa. Look at our communal life of sharing! And it all happens naturally without doctrine or dogma!

We are then led to a second feature of the slogans: they suggest notions of African essentialism. Not only do we have our own brand of socialism, but that very socialism is a special feature of being African. It is a unique possession which no other humans in the universe could ever have.

At best, the essentialist argument can make one feel good. At worst, it is a divisive instrument. In a complex world in which none of us can fit easily

Siyaya, issue 2, winter, 1998

into neat holes, those with sophisticated proclivities towards doctrine may soon declare an essentialist norm of enforced solidarities.

Some may be included and envied while others are excluded and shunned. This situation can engender a shallow politics driven by a shallow objective: the search for the authentic African. These days, the essentialist, authentic African is often is said to possess ubuntu.

In the end, the early slogans of optimism were severely undercut by an infinitely more complex reality. This inescapable reality is that there are many kinds of Africans, but that the conditions of African underdevelopment, while not reducible to a simple formulation, reveal some common, recognisable patterns of socio-historical behaviour.

At this point enters the African renaissance, the only one of the slogans of optimism that gives the impression of being grounded in the realities of history and the dynamics of social progress.

In a recent document, 'African Renaissance: Reality or Hope', William D Carmichael refers to Deputy President Thabo Mbeki's proclamation of the beginnings of an African renaissance by citing 'four highly encouraging developments':

- the successful transition to majority rule in South Africa;
- the cessation of lengthy and debilitating conflicts in various parts of the (African) region;
- a significant upturn in the region's economic performance; and
- a growing reliance on elections and democratic governance.

'These claims of renaissance seem based on some tangibles,' says Carmichael. 'In place of the quest for some elusive authenticity is the quest for successful social arrangement. This approach offers the real possibility that the immense human potential of Africa can actually be unleashed.'

That is why the historian Jacob Burkhardt, writing about the European renaissance, introduced the notion of 'the state as a work of art'. He saw the Renaissance as representing the crystallisation in social awareness of recognisable patterns of social development and the purposefulness of organised effort in helping them along.

That is why the African renaissance is not reducible to some notion of ubuntu, nor is it a formula to be applied, or a tap of progress to be opened or closed. Nor is it coincident with African authenticity. Rather, it is a life to be lived in which emergent forms of successful social practice are recognised and helped along through innovative, purposeful and relevant means that are political, economic, scientific, artistic and professional.

The African renaissance declares multi-dimensional creativity and transformation as an open-minded social quest. It says that the quest for authenticity, while not entirely irrelevant, is subsidiary to the quest for a society that yields some desired deliverables, and actually changes peoples' lived lives.

Game Lodges and Leisure Colonialists

caught in the process of becoming

1999

I n July of 1997, while holidaying on the north coast of KwaZulu-Natal, I struck up a friendship with a family of American tourists. As we exchanged experiences of life in a game lodge, one of my new friends commented, 'Now I understand what it meant to be a colonialist.' I was intrigued by this comment because it seemed to ring true of my own experience of game-lodge living. Does the game lodge not represent the ultimate 'leisuring' of colonial history? Honed to a commercial fine art even more dramatically in post-apartheid South Africa, the game lodge resonates with an aspect of our history that has remained relatively untouched in the discourse of freedom. In essence, the game lodge impedes the emergence of an image of Africa and its diverse cultures as transforming historical phenomena.

But how did it feel to be a colonialist? There I was, having secured my own space through an advance booking in a game lodge that promised relief from the accumulated stresses of professional life. It promised isolation, unobtrusive personalised care, campfire camaraderie and pre-dinner drinks with a small number of fellow guests in the evenings, a dinner presided over by the managers, and late-night or early-morning game drives. Much of the lodge was built on stilts so that it would be environmentally friendly. This, I thought, was a slight departure from the usual style where you felt that you were entering a precious cleared space in the middle of a frightening, threatening forest. To make up for the loss of that sensation, this particular lodge, raised up on its wooden posts, allowed you to enjoy the illusion of being lifted protectively above all the 'creeping things' of the earth. But wouldn't

---

Architecture, Apartheid and After (eds. Hilton Judin & Ivan Vladislavić),
NAi Publishers,

those things still come creeping up the stilts? Soon I learned to put this niggling anxiety aside and got down to enjoying myself.

There are some interesting features common to game lodges. There is
the clearing in the middle of the bush, signifying civilisation. This clearing
will have neat green lawns, which contrast with the dense, chaotic bush just
beyond their trimmed edges. That clean-cut edge is crucial. It indicates the
perimeter of civilisation. In the precious clearing you 'unexpectedly' yet
gratefully find all the modern conveniences. Although they were promised
in the promotional brochure, it is most reassuring to confirm the presence
of comfortable, elegantly decorated bedrooms, each with its own bathroom
containing toilet, shower and bathtub, hot and cold water. The towels and
toilet paper, the rugs, the bedside reading lamps never fail to convey a sense
of hospitality warmly offered, 'far from home'. Thank God there is no television set! Its pervasive absence enhances the general silence. This occurs
especially at night when you finally lock the door and turn off the light to
sleep, vaguely grateful that there is a key.

The pleasure of the game lodge lies in its ability to provide personal conveniences and luxuries far from home. These conveniences are an essential
link to the home base. Signifying the success of conquest, they are the concrete manifestation of the movement of the dominant culture across time
and space, and its ability to replicate itself far away. Of course, in the case
of the contemporary game lodge, the violent and bitter history of conquest
is long over. So you visit the lodge, the secured space in the bush, not to
administer the threatening wilderness that presses in on all sides, but
to participate in the continuing enjoyment of the fruits of conquest. There
is nothing 'out there' to subdue and control. Whatever it is out there, it is
guaranteed to stay at bay.

The contemporary tour of duty in a game lodge is of a special kind. It is
to reaffirm and celebrate a particular kind of cultural power: the enjoyment
of colonial leisure. For is it not true that relaxation comes from the uncontested simulation of hardship in the bush, enduring the chill and the bumpy
tracks on night drives, sweating through walking trails, living by the light
of the campfire rather than the television screen? The sense of stimulation
is enhanced by the ease with which escape is possible. In case of trouble,
or in a bout of weakness, the telephone at the bedside is within arm's
reach. Keeping the hand away from the phone is the measure of the leisure

colonialist's discipline and determination to be isolated successfully. After all, you could simply drive away. Moreover, finding in the morning that your car had been miraculously cleaned, and every trace of the bush removed, you could drive away feeling overwhelmed by the greatness of small gestures, thinking: how thoughtful they can be! So, whether you succeed or fail in your simulated enterprise, you will be rewarded with care. Colonial leisure is the pleasure of risk without danger, or risk with the guarantee of safety.

Guaranteed safety? Not quite. If there is any guaranteed safety it is safety from the past. But if the past is gone, there can be no safety from the future. The thought occurs to me that the game lodge has become a leisure sanctuary where moneyed white South Africans can take refuge from the stresses of living in a black-run country. Once, the game lodge was an extension of their power; now it is a place where those who have lost power go to regain a sense of its possession. Everything there is still in place: the measured conveniences, of course, but also the faceless black workers, behaving rather meekly, who clean the rooms, wash the dishes, make the fire, baby-sit the children, and make sure that in the morning the leisure refugees find their cars clean. Living somewhere 'out there', beyond the neatly clipped frontier, the black workers come into the clearing to serve. And then they disappear again. In their comings and goings, they are as inscrutable as the dense bush from which they emerge and to which they return. The servants, in their coming and going, trigger off among the leisure refugees a low-intensity anxiety. Who knows what the potential of these 'servants' is for turning into the unknowable nightmare, so frequently reported in newspapers, in which a white farmer and his family are brutally murdered by killers, most probably black, who appear out of nowhere and vanish back into it again? After all, they have political power on their side these days, they can join trade unions and come and go as they please.

Into this situation enters the black tourist. Until very recently, one of the distinguishing features of the game lodge was the marked absence of black tourists, but now they are beginning to show up in steadily increasing numbers. Being there, they experience the most damning ambiguities. They see the faceless black workers and instinctively see a reflection of themselves. They may be wealthy or politically powerful, but at that moment they are made aware of their special kind of powerlessness: they lack the backing of cultural power. They experience cultural domination in a most intimate way. This is apparent especially when it comes to the viewing of game. It is difficult not to feel that, in the total scheme of things, perhaps they should be out there with the animals, being viewed. Caught in a conversation with their white fellow refugees, brought together with them by an increasingly similar, stressful lifestyle, they can engage in discussions that bring out both the artificiality and the reality of their similarity.

The black tourist is conditioned to find the political sociology of the game lodge ontologically disturbing. It can be so offensive as to be obscene. He is a leisure colonialist torn up by excruciating ambiguities. He pays to be the viewer who has to be viewed. He is expected to engage in conversations around the campfire, about bush stories and lion kills, and hunting jokes that hold no interest for him. He is expected to be knowledgeable about 'white things' at the same time as he is transformed into an informant about 'black things', which are then analysed and interpreted by his campfire companions. Whenever he is asked his opinion about these interpretations, he is irritated by a tone of questioning that suggests that he ought to confirm their correctness. The more generous ones treat him with studious respect, wondering if they are not in the presence of a member of the new black elite, someone who may have useful connections. Desperately wanting to forget momentarily where he comes from, he is held up for display in the structure and content of the pleasure laid on for him as a paying customer. He finds no peace here. He can only experience himself as a caricature of a tourist. Seeking peace, and sensing that he may succeed only in adding colour to the white leisure colonialists' pleasant memories of the game lodge, he pays for being pushed into a stressful state of simmering revolt. The entire world of contemporary tourism carries no intuitive familiarity for him.

But his travail does not end there. The relationship between the black leisure colonialist and the black worker at the game lodge is full of pitfalls. For a moment, the black worker is not sure how he should respond to the black leisure colonialist who is caught up in the structure of 'white things'. Should he enter into a conspiracy of familiarity? Or should he play the game in which one of his kind is to be treated as if he were in fact 'the other'? If he chooses this last course, he puts the black leisure colonialist in a terribly invidious position. For the black leisure colonialist it is difficult to distinguish between being treated like a pampered guest or like a black guest who is doing 'white things'. The comfortable status of the privileged guest is possible only where there is a shared culture of leisure between the worker and the tourist, a culture that flourishes and finds legitimacy within a hegemonic political, social and economic dispensation.

On the other hand, if the black worker enters into a 'conspiracy of familiarity' with the black leisure colonialist, familiarity may breed contempt. Given that the black worker may regard the black leisure colonialist as his admired 'representative' in the white world, if the conversation between them becomes an exchange of gossip about 'white things', as it well might, the black leisure colonialist is in danger of losing his dignity. How can he, from his position of 'power', complain with the powerless about the powerful? This ludicrous position clearly confirms him as a caricature. Surely this conspiracy is impotent! After that, the professionalism that the black leisure colonialist, as a paying customer in search of peace and relaxation, expects from the black worker is compromised. Having been exposed as lacking an integral identity, the guest is left with a terrible choice: either to treat the workers with masterful aloofness or to engage them in harmless pleasantries. Either way, he gets to keep his dignity, but he keeps it at the cost of avoidance and self-deception. Both the structure and the content of leisure offer no escape.

But there is a possible escape route. It is to engage the white leisure colonialist and the owners of the game lodge in a cultural contest, in which the cultural history of the game lodge is deconstructed and a new structure and content of leisure are brought into being as expressions of a new society. The liberation of leisure is an essential aspect of the new experience of freedom. To begin that liberation we need to pose some questions: How can the game lodge evolve forms of leisure that are rooted in contemporary South African experience, catering for a new leisure clientele and guaranteeing profitability? How can the game lodge participate in the general liberation of leisure? How can the game lodge become more than an antiquated colonial outpost routinely (yet probably unintentionally) tolerated by black governments? A new black government will surely be concerned about being seen to guarantee the survival of negative, outmoded anthropologies by allowing culturally entrenched forms of white privilege to continue to exist unchallenged!

This leads me to what is perhaps the most frightening aspect of culture in post-apartheid South Africa, something that speaks to the nature of evolving forms of national consciousness. Is it possible that South Africa is one big game lodge where all its black citizens are struggling to make sense of their lives, like people who awake in an enormous vacation house which is now supposed to be theirs but which they do not quite recognise? Do they strive to be just like their fellow citizens who have mastered the economics of the game lodge, and who may seek to consolidate a cultural condition in keeping with their strategies of survival by marketing an image of South Africa as a haven of safety and success in a dark, violent and threatening continent? Does it not pay to belong to South Africa, to be free from the 'chaos of the north', to keep the north at bay at all costs? Does it not pay to be the onlooker, gazing out at 'the rest of the continent' from the window of a vacation house that offers comfort and security? What does it take to keep things this way?

Are we evolving a split personality which may generate its own forms of creativity? What does it mean to use the vacation house as a vantage point from which to look down on others when we have yet to prove that the house belongs to us and that we are its rightful owners, when we still live in an environment in which we are the ones being viewed? As I write, the land-scape of apartheid is reproducing itself with a vengeance. Townships are bursting with informal settlements, reinforcing old dichotomies in the land-scape. The psychology of apartheid, the culture of the game lodge, would teach us to regard informal settlements as a potential threat to civilisation, menacing the Europe in our midst. While defending this European residue may allow us to keep the vacation house intact, it may also prevent the emergence of the recognition that what is going on in the townships carries the defining characteristics of our new society. The informal settlements and all the problems they present – are they not a vital context in which we can define, plan and build for ourselves, not merely maintaining the vaca-tion house but constructing a new home? Could the game lodge itself be transformed in the service of rural development?

The ambiguities and choices are difficult, even painful. Now we want to throw off the psychological burden of our painful past; now we want to hold on to it. We know that death may be a very real consequence of throwing off the burden altogether in one big heave. Surely who we are and who we finally become is bound up with all these questions and contradictions!

Surely we are an inseparable part of Africa, our home! Yet our history intricately binds us to the rest of the world, and such ties cannot be broken without a serious threat to our survival. And again: we are very much ourselves, we have many demons to exorcise, and yet much has been achieved that we can build on. We remain complex and we have a responsibility to confront that fact. Our survival will depend on our ability to develop successful skills in carving coherent and sustainable meanings out of this definitive field of complexity.

And so, as we leave the game lodge, we notice the electrified fence that surrounds the whole reserve (we remember the electrified fences on our northern borders). The fence reminds us that the game lodge, that inner core of cleared space, is not carved out of an unbroken wilderness but out of another contained space, sealed off from the country at large. It is a world of make-believe whose charm depends on the brief enjoyment it gives us to be a colonialist. On the edge of the real world we stop the car, as the black gatekeeper opens the gate with an expectant smile. If we are white leisure colonialists, we will wave with a smile or give a generous tip. Either gesture will be appreciated. If we are black, we wonder if we should tip at all. How will it be interpreted? If it is too little, the gatekeeper will think we are insulting him. If we don't give anything, we will fit the stereotype of the stingy rich blacks. If we give too much, perhaps he will think we are ostentatiously displaying our wealth. In the end, we rationalise. We give what we think is generous under the guise of 'spreading wealth'. It seems to be appreciated. Then we drive away, a bundle of mixed emotions and troubled thoughts. How is it that a simple quest for peace and restoration turned into an unexpectedly painful journey into the self? We think: there is no peace for those caught in the process of becoming.

The Lion and the Rabbit

freeing the oppressor

1999

Y ou will all remember that famous tale in which Lion caught Rabbit in the act of stealing in a cave. Rabbit was helping himself to a meal he had found in a trap that Lion had laid. Lion was enraged and pounced on the thief. As Rabbit was about to be devoured, he screamed that the cave was collapsing and that both of them would be saved if Lion, who was stronger, could prop up the ceiling with his powerful limbs while he, Rabbit, rushed to get help.

Lion, caught in the suddenness of a dangerous moment, and instantly grateful that he had not recklessly eaten a source of vital and prompt wisdom, sprang up on his hind legs, propping up the roof of the cave with his front paws. Rabbit sprinted away, and of course never returned. Lion remained there in the cave, a living rafter, holding his dear life in his own paws and realising with dread that he was getting tired. Doom hung over him as he pondered why lions were also made to be vulnerable to fatigue. He prepared to be buried alive as he finally let go of the roof. Nothing happened. His relief at being alive was momentary as it dawned on him that he had been fooled.

No doubt many of us will admire this small animal, Rabbit, for getting out of a tight spot by means of superior intelligence. Our popular trickster has done it again, reducing the brawny king of the jungle to a piteous fool. The narrative frame of the tale easily paints a story of escape in which the weak enjoy a moment of triumph over the powerful, and live to tell the story. The dramatic sequence of entrapment and escape easily attracts and captures our attention, enabling us to settle quickly to the most apparent

Delivered at the After the TRC: Reconciliation in the New Millennium conference, University of Cape Town, August, 1999; published in *Pretexts: Literary and Cultural Studies*, Vol 8, No 2, 1999

point of the tale: some entertainment at the expense of the powerful. By the same token, we are made to appreciate the value of intelligence.

In the imbalance of forces at play, Rabbit is in danger of losing his life. In order to safeguard it, he deftly manipulates Lion into a position of trust. The instant violation of that very trust restores the balance as Rabbit escapes with his life and both of them continue to live. The moral considerations involved in breaking trust become secondary to the higher goal of escaping with one's life.

We think further that in the final analysis no harm befell Lion. No cave fell in. He suffered only a slight loss of dignity from being fooled. Even more, he remained behind to eat his catch.

But that would not necessarily be the end of our dialogue with this tale. Some would strive to argue that Rabbit is not such a wonderful fellow after all; and that Lion does have redeeming qualities. When faced with the prospect of saving both his and Rabbit's lives, Lion was willing to suspend the act of meting out punishment, and chose rather to cooperate with Rabbit for the safety of both. What if, indeed, the cave was collapsing? Rabbit's capacity to discover danger matches Lion's willingness and capacity to keep the danger at bay. There is thus a real basis for mutual trust, no matter how temporary.

All is well until we remember that Rabbit is, in fact, a petty thief. No matter how brilliant he is, anyone who dares enter into a pact with him in future is warned: there is a good chance you may be betrayed. The very ease with which Rabbit gets out of a tight situation should tell you to watch him closely in the future. While you may admire his escape, he also leaves you with niggling anxieties. Surely there is something volatile and incendiary about his intelligence? The energy and brilliance of his inventiveness may not always wait for moments of self-defence to act themselves out. Rabbit may take advantage of anyone and strike in unprovoked malice, wreaking havoc and chaos. Certainly, not only will Rabbit live to tell the story of his escape, he will live to steal again.

The tale presents us with at least two frames of interpretation. There is the larger frame, dependent on the most observable features of the drama: entrapment and escape. It yields an unproblematic hero against an obvious, powerful victim who deserved what he got. Lion, whose catch was being stolen, receives less sympathy in the light of his intention to punish, perhaps with death, a small but clever fellow. The second frame emerges from within the larger frame and subverts it. It is the frame of detail, which emerges as we ask further questions about the tale. It yields us a somewhat complex, vulnerable victim, and a brilliant hero with serious flaws. We discover, to our surprise, that we might sympathise with Lion and have serious reservations about Rabbit.

There are many in this country who think that South Africa has been a cave facing inevitable collapse, and that its black citizens have been left holding up the roof while the whites have escaped to get on with their lives. But if the majority black population is the Lion, it should be remembered that this Lion was no longer king of the jungle, the colonial wars of conquest having taken his title away. And Rabbit has been stealing all along, albeit within an enabling code of legitimacy imposed by himself. But the power of the black majority was rising steadily, leading to the negotiations that finally led to the elections of 1994. The contours of a lion were emerging once more, and Rabbit, uneasy that he might be pounced upon, can see the value of the story of a collapsing cave.

Many of the black majority may have the definite impression that Rabbit is getting on happily with his life. Isn't this impression confirmed by a casual inspection of the divided landscape of our country? Who is it who still has to rush into trains, buses and taxis, paying heavily to travel long distances to work and back? Whose children still attempt to get an education in overcrowded classrooms? Who is it who still dominate as bosses at the workplace, and are still privileged to think and plan and issue instructions, albeit with decreasing confidence? Who is it who continue to live in better houses and suburbs, and play cricket and rugby, while others live in deprived townships and play soccer? Certainly, in this view, the negotiations leading to the elections of 1994, and such instruments as the Truth and Reconciliation Commission (TRC), look like one big trick to keep Lion holding up the roof.

But the situation can get a little fuzzy, if not downright complicated. Let us consider this. According to the South African folklore of tribal politics, which, like all people, we indulge in from time to time, the Xhosas have become Rabbit, now running this country, while all the other tribes, black and white, are holding up the roof. As if that were not all, have you noticed all the new popular words which are used to get people to do something: 'Masakhane', 'Bambanani', 'Zama Zama'? No doubt, there is a Rabbit language taking over while the rest of the African languages are holding up the roof. Of course, if the Xhosas are running this country and the Zulu language is running amok, it must be that the conspiring Ngunis are walking away, while everybody else is holding up the roof.

Look at the Afrikaners, the big Lions that dominated the army and the police, and probably still do, and who ruled with an iron fist for close to half a century. Look at them. They are holding up the roof while the English walk away with their second passports! This world is truly unjust. The 'coloureds' in the Western Cape – are they not holding up the roof while the alliance of the Democratic Party and the New National Party walks away?

And what can be said about the workers of this country? Are they not holding up the roof while the exploiting, manipulative capitalist Rabbits continue to prosper? Recently, new capitalists have arrived. They are as black as the workers. They may be Rabbits themselves, but may feel that they are holding up the roof while the rest of their Rabbit capitalists, who do not have to worry about being accused of greed and corruption, get on with their lives. At some point the ANC must have felt that it was being made to hold up the roof while the Communist Party walked away with the Reconstruction and Development Programme. Or, have black men left black women holding up the roof? It's all very confusing.

Who, really, is the Lion? And who is the Rabbit? Identities seem to shift constantly, depending on the classification of participants involved in any particular situation. They can fall into any of the categories of race, ethnicity, class, political affiliation, geographical location, gender, generation, and numerous others. Depending on the function or location of a category in a particular drama, someone may be Lion today and Rabbit tomorrow. There is a constant ebb and flow of shifting identities in South African history that subverts any tendency towards simplification.

In fact, the greatest simplification, apartheid itself, constantly worked against the complicating forces of history, enforcing a tendency towards denial among its beneficiaries, often through willed ignorance. On the other hand, the victims of apartheid tended to expose and affirm the hidden realities of interacting identities as they converged daily in the drama of economics, but they lacked the capacity, until recently, to turn that tendency into a strategic advantage. And this is what seems to be happening now: the real possibilities of South Africa may lie in our ability to face the full implications of the tendency towards interaction, away from the past of artificial separation.

Perhaps our tale, and the different forms it takes as its characters wear different masks, enables us to take stock of the extent of social anxiety in South Africa. For example, there is the fear that magnanimity has not only been misunderstood as weakness, but that it has, in fact, become weakness. There is the fear that the perception of a loss of face may restore old feelings of inferiority, or rage, in proportion to the increasing levels of confidence among those who lost very little else besides political power. There is the fear that right and constitutionality, which were fought for, so long and so hard, by the magnanimous are being used to frustrate redress, to insult and denigrate. There is the fear that the demands of a modern state, itself subject to powerful global forces, might overwhelm the project of emancipation.

On the other hand, all rabbits who have left the cave to the lion realise they have to return to the cave. At what cost? Exactly what do they stand to lose or gain? They are not sure what Lion really thinks, but they know that he is in power. They feel guilty about what they have done to Lion in the past, but pride will not allow them to acknowledge the feeling. They may have to resort to the constitution and the bill of rights to assert themselves, but many among them may feel that doing so does not really enable them to push anxieties away. What to do?

Allister Sparks in *Tomorrow is Another Country* tells of how, in the run-up to the historic elections of 27 April 1994, a solution had to be found to the increasing conflict between the ANC and the white right, which could be mobilised effectively into an army of resistance. We are told that a series of meetings took place between the ANC and the generals of the white right. The first meeting, it is reported, turned out to be one of the defining moments of the road towards freedom and reconciliation. 'If you want to go to war,' Mandela told the generals, simply,

> I must be honest and admit that we cannot stand up to you on the battlefield. We don't have the resources. It will be a long and bitter struggle, many people will die and the country may be reduced to ashes. But you must remember two things. You cannot win because of our numbers: you cannot kill us all. And you cannot win because of the international community. They will rally to our support and

they will stand with us.' General Viljoen was forced to agree. The two men looked at each other … [and] faced the truth of their mutual dependency.

The new dependency is based on the recognition of an emergent balance that hinges on a common awareness that the survival of South Africa is a common responsibility, and suggests a major shift in the flow of power and influence. A dependency once based on, and sustained by, the organising of oppression was reluctantly recognised as a condition of stability from which a new order could emerge. In order to make a new society possible, an apocalyptic disintegration of South Africa was perceived not to be in any-one's immediate or long-term interest. The preconditions of reconciliation laid in recognition of Africans, to establish relationships across inherited boundaries, are a real feature of our national experience today. If there is any one thing the hearings of the Truth and Reconciliation Commission have done, it is to reveal the range of content at the centre of our interactive public space. The common interest is to preserve an imperfect zone of sta-bility in which the imbalance of morality is nevertheless recognised to be tipped in favour of an emergent order.

There is another way in which the new binary relationship distinguishes itself from the old one. It is infinitely more interactive. Its character can be exemplified in the following questions which reflect many of the unresolved anxieties already mentioned. How can South Africans reconcile what Allister Sparks has phrased as 'the black demand for majority rule [with] white concerns stemming from this demand'? How can the redistribution of resources and opportunities occur without the destruction of the economy? How can South Africa protect the rights of its white citizens without entrenching the privileges of old? How can the cultural rights of groups be reconciled with a broader national project? How is equity possible in the face of continuing historical disparities in housing, education, income, media control, in the broad cultural and linguistic dominance of a demo-graphic minority? How is justice possible when perpetrators of terrible crimes and human rights abuses can walk away through amnesty?

These questions present us with formidable dilemmas, whose horns demand to be addressed simultaneously. In doing so, we may need some working principles to guide our conduct. One of them is that in this space of high interactivity it is important to accept that answers to problems may not be easy to arrive at. Indeed, the difficulties faced in arriving at answers represent an investment towards the value of possible answers. This applies even when the solutions arrived at are later found not to work. The energies invested are of inestimable value in allowing parties greater opportunity to fully establish their good faith. It is in the interactive struggle for the solutions that new relationships are forged between individuals, within and between groups. The overriding challenge of governance is to provide and maintain public space so that the resolution of difficult dilemmas can take place in a controlled, legitimate environment.

There is yet another principle. Our ability to shift into several identities in a multicultural society allows us the potential to locate ourselves within questions posed by others. In a fascinating article called 'Dominance Concealed Through Diversity: Implications of Inadequate Perspectives on Cultural Pluralism' published in the *Harvard Educational Review*, Dwight Boyd states that:

[A]nyone with an effective sense of democratic reciprocity will recognise that, as exactly the same claim can be made from the perspective of any of the differing cultures in question, any democratic collective answer to the question (of conflicting values, for example) must locate the speaker within the problem and must be affirmable from positions different from one's own.

The interactivity of our new binary relationship is a humanising space of immense complexity. It is space brimming with risk-taking, trust and suspicion, intrigue, transparency and obfuscation, real and imaginary boundaries, negotiation and imposition, honesty and dishonesty, concealment and discovery, alignments and realignments, shifting identities, the pains and horrors of lapses, loyalties and betrayals, idealism, greed, courage, doubts and certitudes, redeeming truths and insights leading to optimism and progress, and the excitement of infinite possibility. The interactivity generated releases energies that have the potential not only to make the inherited binary relationship a transient one but also threaten its explosion into a multiplicity of relationships. The potential for an individual South African to establish relationships across inherited boundaries is a real

112

feature of our national experience today. If there is any one thing the hearings of the Truth and Reconciliation Commission have done, it is to reveal the range of content at the centre of our interactive public space.

I will recall elements of this content very briefly. It ranges from the personal, through the experience of local communities, to matters that involve government and governance. In this way the TRC attempted to take us through a wide spectrum of contemporary South African history in the period it was mandated to cover. It made a valiant attempt at an impossible task, but its reach, given the short life of the commission, has been extensive.

The report brings together the real extent of what the victims of apartheid have known all along: pervasive, State-organised violence which permeated the entire fabric of South African Society. It documents the pains and traumas of individuals. It shows us random invasions of homes, arrests of family members, often followed by their inexplicable disappearance. Some families would later witness exhumations of disappeared family members, now painfully accounted for. We are shown how communities of the oppressed, torn apart by fear, suspicion and mistrust, and desperate to build and preserve unity, were often led to hunt down people thought to be informers and collaborators, who met gruesome fates at the hands of groups convinced that they were working in the interests of the community.

Documented also is the history of 'bannings and banishment', a spate of judicial executions, 'the use of force on crowds and gatherings', 'torture and death in custody', infiltration, abductions, interrogations, and gory assassinations. We see how much law enforcement agencies had become corrupted by a culture of impunity as a result of laws that granted them sweeping powers. The TRC was able to capture vividly the history of perpetrator brutality. In some memorable incidents, former torturers demonstrated their methods of torture.

The 'homelands' were another theatre of gross violations of human rights. The 'homelands' of KwaZulu, the Ciskei and KwaNdebele, in particular, come in for a closer focus. Concerning the latter, the commission reports on 'cyclical attacks and counter-attacks' in which 'the line between victims and perpetrators blurred, as comrades and vigilantes assumed both roles. The youth, relentlessly pursued by Imbokodo vigilantes for months, initiated their own campaign against suspected vigilantes, frequently resulting in the most brutal of murders'. In the townships we witnessed 'necklace killings', burnings of houses of suspected spies, and the reign of terror of groups acting in the name of liberation.

We are shown the war machinery of the apartheid state and how it wreaked havoc on neighbouring countries, violating their sovereignty, in pursuit of South African citizens. It intimidated and harassed civilians of those countries; bombed targets at will, turning the whole of Southern Africa into a zone of insecurity.

We are also shown the agonies and ecstasies of waging a war of liberation. While the liberation movement was engaged in a just war and there were many successful strikes against the apartheid state, there were also failures of judgement, particularly under the threat of infiltration by the enemy. Fear and insecurity resulting from the sense of being invaded from within led to some gross violations of human rights in which comrades became enemies to be arrested, tortured, and purged. Lapses in chains of command led to some 'unplanned military operations' with outcomes impossible to anticipate. The call for the country to be rendered ungovernable may have been a genuine strategy to incapacitate the State, but it also led to unintended consequences.

The picture presented is broad but incomplete, yet such incompleteness was to be expected. It was unavoidable in view of the limitations around the life and activities of the TRC. Nevertheless, we do have sufficient material to enable South Africans not only to acknowledge the terrible aspects of their immediate past but also to ponder the meaning of that past for their future. The TRC, its hearings and its report on their own cannot bring about reconciliation. They began a process that should continue.

❑

I want to make some observations, according to the account so far: the anticipated disintegration of South Africa in a conflagration of violence did not take place. Many South Africans just prior to the elections of 1994 saw threatening clouds of apocalyptic disintegration gathering in the sky. That the collapse did not occur has led to the peaceful transfer of power being called a miracle. I believe we do need to look for explanations. We may find, for example, that South Africans were more predisposed to cooperate than fight to the bitter end. If we take the farms of South Africa as a case study, following the remarkable scholarship of Charles van Onselen in his book

The Seed is Mine, we may find there are more significant binding factors at play. These may explain more fully why the fear of disintegration may be less significant than a greater awareness of what van Onselen called the 'nooks and crannies' of social life during the days of apartheid. In these nooks and crannies, the daily intricate intimacies of cooperation between master and servant may have created reluctant bonds, particularly in the farming and sharecropping communities.

Coagulated by years of paternalism, authority flowed one way, resulting in various kinds of mutual accommodations, adjustments and readjustments. Such relationships may have played themselves out also with greater conflict and rebellion over time. Indeed, the bonding that took place among the major political negotiators seems to me too remarkable not to have had an historical or social basis. The South Africans who sat together at the negotiating table were not total strangers to one another.

What has now happened is that power relations have changed radically, and relationships that were mediated by paternalism, largely unarticulated, have emerged into the open and tensions generated are being fully articulated. The verbalisation of pain and suffering through an official medium recognised as a result of change that was fought for, and the enforced revelation of the deeds of perpetrators, complicate relationships that were based on internalised assumptions. Their articulation raises the social temperature, which at the same time needs to be lowered. It is the lowering mechanism that demands our attention, for bringing down the temperature should translate neither into platitudes nor buying time. Rather, it should yield visible measures for improving the lives of the victims of the past who, even while they are still in a state of severe disadvantage, ought no longer to experience themselves as victims. The temperature-lowering mechanism is a direct matter of social policy.

There are two other related factors that may also have contributed to the lessening of any push towards disintegration. Firstly, the geographical boundaries that delineate South Africa as an entity enjoy a near-universal acceptance in the country, I believe, although there are some low-intensity threats to this position. For example, the Afrikaner far-right wing entertains hopes for a mythical country of Afrikaners only. This demand is based on an elastic constitutional interpretation of the rights of cultural communities. The attitude of Mandela's government, faced with the impossibility of meeting this demand, seems to have been to try to find a way of living with this issue rather than rejecting it out of hand, like a recessive gene that will from time to time rear its head and then disappear again, temporarily.

Secondly, an increasingly familiar commercial and industrial landscape has progressively drawn the population into a unifying pattern of economic activities. A replicated landscape of major commercial chains throughout the country has, over the decades, become a feature of how the land is imagined. Spatial familiarity of this sort renders the land familiar, less strange and more accommodating wherever you may be in the country. This kind of familiarity may have a binding effect which cuts across the particularising tendencies of geographic and ethnic location. Linking the country is a complex network of a communications system which promised the accessibility of every part of the country to every citizen. This sense of universal accessibility was sensed as an achievement even before the Congress for a Democratic South Africa (Codesa) was under way. Later on, land restitution and economic empowerment emerged as attempts to translate optimism and potential into tangible gains.

These observations may lead us to ponder the possibilities for democracy and reconciliation in an environment charged with both expectation and the counter-pressure of limitations we are called upon to accommodate. Reflecting on its activities in Duduza, the TRC observes in its report that:

> Reconciliation involves various stages of development and change. One essential step is dialogue between adversaries. The victim-oriented and perpetrator-oriented aspects of the commission's work are broken into separate functions. Victims tell their stories in one forum and perpetrators in another. The interaction is thus often mediated purely by the media coverage of these events. While this may have been useful in providing safe space to engage them, or to maximise information gathering, the subsequent step of facilitating more direct dialogue still needs to be addressed.

This view of reconciliation enables us to go well beyond the moral and religious connotations around it which have thus far dominated discourse. It pushes us towards the notion of reconciliation as a human project grounded in social process. The affective connotations of reconciliation as forgiveness often gain centre stage owing to a tendency for us to focus on its intended results rather than on the difficult process of working towards them. Instead, reconciliation is something to be earned by South Africans. They will achieve it through facing the uncertainties and contradictions inherent in our transformation. To navigate through a great deal of human turbulence, the constitution and the bill of rights provide a democratic framework within which the process of reconciliation can act itself out.

The commission's report is very clear on this point. Responding to 'erroneous notions of what reconciliation is about', the chairperson of the commission in his foreword – on its own a remarkable document – asserts that reconciliation 'is not about being cosy; it is not about pretending that things were other than what they were. Reconciliation based on falsehood, on not facing up to reality, is not true reconciliation and will not last'. Later in the report the point is made again: 'reconciliation without cost and pain is cheap, shallow and must be spurned'.

In fact, the more I read the commission's report, the more I became convinced that the predominance of religious connotation in the public discourse on reconciliation resulted from a tendency for many of us to focus on the chairperson of the TRC as a man of God. The linking of reconciliation directly with forgiveness closed off many other angles of discussion. If reconciliation was a matter of confession and forgiveness, if things change while they remain the same, then it should not be surprising that there could be room for cynicism, disillusionment, and the feeling in many of having been fooled: of holding up the roof. How do we avert this kind of feeling?

To return to the tale. Rabbit has walked away. Maybe he wants to come back and talk. But he is too clever to put himself at risk. He fails to appreciate the extent to which his cleverness may create intractable problems for him. That happens when his anxieties get hidden behind his cleverness; when his instincts lead him to create and maintain the illusion of continual control. The best among the rabbits recognise the illusion for what it is. But to face it squarely, they will require Lion to reassure them constantly that Rabbit will not be grabbed and eaten; that Rabbit has a role in the social ecology. But Rabbit may find it difficult to make the move. Making the move is the primary responsibility of Lion.

After all, he embarked on a liberation struggle. And in the process, he told everyone that he learned from Paolo Freire's book *Pedagogy of the Oppressed*, thirty years ago, that:

> [I]t is only the oppressed who, by freeing themselves, can free their oppressors. The latter, as an oppressive class, can free neither others nor themselves. It is therefore essential that the oppressed wage the struggle to resolve the contradiction in which they are caught: and the contradiction will be resolved by the appearance of the new man: neither oppressor nor oppressed, but man in the process of liberation. If the goal of the oppressed is to become fully human, they will not achieve their goal by merely reversing the terms of the contradictions, by simply changing roles.

Indeed, who is complaining today that the future is bleak? The results were released a few months ago of a survey that sought to find out how optimistic or pessimistic South Africans were about the future since the advent of democracy five years ago. It was found that those South Africans who lost very little in material wealth and general standard of living, whose rights were never really violated, were significantly pessimistic about the future, and were at their unhappiest with the current changes. Many were disgruntled and either wanted to leave, or were nostalgic about the past. Freire wrote perceptively about them:

> But even when the contradiction is resolved authentically by a new situation established by the liberated, the former oppressors do not feel liberated. On the contrary, they genuinely consider themselves to be oppressed. Conditioned by the experience of oppressing others, any situation other than their former seems to them like oppression. Formerly, they could eat, dress, wear shoes, be educated, travel, and hear Beethoven; while millions did not eat, had no clothes or shoes, neither studied nor travelled, much less listened to Beethoven. Any restriction on this way of life, in the name of the rights of the community appears to the former oppressors as a profound violation of their individual rights – although they had no respect for the millions who suffered and died of hunger, pain, sorrow,

and despair. For the oppressors, 'human beings' refers only to themselves; other people are 'things'. For the oppressors, there exists only one fight: their right to live in peace, over against the fight, not always even recognised, but simply conceded, of the oppressed to survival. And they make this concession only because the existence of the oppressed is necessary to their own existence.

On the other hand, those whose human rights were violated consistently by a racist state were hopeful about the future. They perceived that they had gained something from the changes. They had far more access to water, electricity, telephones, houses, than before. They experienced a great deal more official responsiveness.

Lion is the maker of the future, he has the responsibility to take the initiative. It is not enough for him to read the commission's report where it says about Duduza that: 'The commission hearings were not attended by local whites' and leave it at that. Even more worrisome, he may see in this a sign of racism. 'They are racists!' he may shout, not telling us anything new. Of course whites did not attend, and they are unlikely to attend unless they are engaged in the matter. They are highly unlikely to come out and say they need help. And if Lion does not come forward and exercise responsibility, he will see a recurring situation in which there is more and more racism to condemn, and then Lion will be in real danger of reducing the enormous power of his position and transforming it into a hole from which he voices endless complaints about racism. What a let-down it would be!

In the total scheme of things, the main reason millions of Africans in South Africa have a poor education is our history of institutional racism. But a question arises whether racism as causal explanation can provide us with all the tools necessary to find appropriate solutions. For example, we may find that certain aspects of the legitimate struggle for liberation may have compounded the problems of education. Looking for racists to blame will not improve the situation.

This question may suggest that, in the new democracy in which the black majority is centred, white racism as a central category of analysis may lead to a distortion of the real project of post-apartheid society. It may condition us to focus on what we were denied, in a time past which cannot be returned, rather than on what we need to create for a future to be made. To clarify this matter further, a question may be asked: is there a difference between the resort to race as a received category of social and political analysis on which decisively to ground public policy and the resort to race as merely a corrective tool to measure the progress of a policy of achieving equity, particularly in opportunity? In the former case, race carries the entire burden of explanation. In the latter, race is subsumed under a strategy of change.

One of the fundamental challenges of emancipation in South Africa is for the emancipated to avoid the conceptual trap of ascribing to the past of white racism centrality of explanation. The real challenge is how, through appropriate strategies of development, a country ruled by an African majority can come into being, where that majority no longer feels the social and political pressures in which there are serious consequences to being characterised as black. And where such characterisation is ultimately rendered irrelevant by the actualisation of emancipatory goals. This is not to ignore the fact that some continuing inequities are a result of a racist past. But the point is made to illustrate how a subtle change in the point of departure can lead to significantly new possibilities.

For many South Africans, the last five years have been a time of euphoria. Many horizons have been pushed open as people have assumed new roles and new responsibilities. There have been many remarkable successes, but there have also been many fingers cruelly burnt. In the enthusiasm to serve, some corners were unwittingly cut, resulting in painful reminders that public service was subject to systems and rules of accountability. More painful was the realisation that, although some of the systems and rules were an inheritance from a painful past, their legal force could not simply be pushed aside. There are, of course, others whose euphoria enabled them to see calculated opportunities for quick enrichment.

Whatever the case might be, many actions, whatever they were, were seen and experienced as the enactment of freedom. The new laws passed in Parliament in the last five years, for example, have been more significant as definitive acts of freedom than as instruments of regulation. The regulatory impact of these laws will become more pronounced as they are increasingly tested against the capacity of the new State, the people and their government, to deal with all the problems unravelled by the TRC. The disengagement between law-making as an act of freedom and law-making as regulation is only now beginning to happen. The question is, at what point will we feel that the lingering effects of the former are sufficiently rooted in the national consciousness to be assumed to inform regulation and the maintenance of the State? When does social practice change from creativity to maintenance? In many areas of national life, that transition is still a long way off. But as we move along we may wish to set up indicators to measure and trace the continuum of transition.

The real point to be made is that as the new laws that embody the emancipatory vision of the new democracy are tested against the harsh realities of unsolved problems, such as those that will arise from the challenge of reconciliation, they result in frustrations. It is such frustrations that may mistakenly be thought to indicate the failure of the larger project, but they really indicate setbacks that may require a redoubling of effort. And that is the point of danger: when Lion really thinks that he has been duped.

The TRC was one mechanism to resolve difficult dilemmas, but by no stretch of the imagination did it offer a permanent solution. Rather, it allowed the country to cross a particular river of time and circumstance. Seen in this light, the negotiated settlement appears to have delivered, unexpectedly, the disposition to live with unresolved tensions by seeking to ensure that the sore points do not fester into incendiary wounds; to enter instead into controlled engagements in which fixed positions are progressively abandoned until a comfortable, if imperfect, solution is accepted as a *working position*. These working positions are crucial to ensure that compromise is not seen as a manipulative gesture, but as an option that offers something substantial to the negotiating parties.

The TRC has yielded us a potentially destabilising complex of dilemmas. The resulting tensions require that they be handled with a high level of social skill, a rigorous intellectual disposition, and an inventive social imagination.

In the third frame of interpretation, Lion has much bigger things to do. He cannot afford to be distracted by the antics of a clever little fellow like Rabbit. Indeed, his task is to prop up the roof. So far, the roof has not collapsed, and there is a meal to share in the cave. Hopefully, Rabbit has learnt to make a humble request not only to share what is in the trap but to bring along a contribution.

The Race Card

playing a fair hand

2000

Early in December, the *Mail & Guardian* became involved in a strident exchange with the office of President Thabo Mbeki. It began with an editorial on 10 December accusing the president of running a 'backroom government' and 'threatening to make nonsense' of South Africa's fledgling democracy. These charges prompted an outraged response from Parks Mankahlana, the president's spokesman.

Mankahlana's reaction came in the wake of persistent complaints from many sectors of the public that, since the end of apartheid, the *Mail & Guardian* has shown disdain for the black-dominated government through biased reporting, slander by innuendo, unsubstantiated allegations of corruption and incompetence, unprofessional annual ratings of government ministers and attacks on the reputations of black public figures. A pattern had emerged which convinced many that the *Mail & Guardian* had become a vehicle for the expression of racist anxieties about the future of white South Africans under a black government.

The *Mail & Guardian* denied these charges, claiming they were a veiled attack on press freedom. But the persistence of racist reporting finally prompted the South African Human Rights Commission (SAHRC), a body established under the terms of the constitution, to undertake a survey of racism in the media. The interim report was released to outrage from the editors of several newspapers, including the *Mail & Guardian, Star, Cape Argus, Cape Times* and *Sunday Times*. These editors have since been subpoenaed to appear before the SAHRC to answer allegations of 'subliminal racism'.

One thing is certain: for a newspaper that enjoyed solid anti-apartheid

---

Index on Censorship 2, 2000. Initially submitted to the *Mail & Guardian*, which declined publication.

credentials, the *Mail & Guardian* has changed into a right-of-centre voice for disgruntled white liberals. This should come as no surprise. The arrival of democracy has fractured the easy solidarities of the anti-apartheid struggle; South Africans are now free to be who they really are, or want to be. In this respect, the *Mail & Guardian* no longer represents a progressive vision of the present or future for many South Africans, regardless of colour. Press freedom is not currently under threat in South Africa. What is under attack is the kind of racism that comes through the columns of the *Mail & Guardian*. And the exchange between Parks Mankahlana and the newspaper revealed some of the mechanisms by which that racism is articulated.

Mankahlana's response to the *Mail & Guardian*'s editorial on 10 December did not fit editor Philip van Niekerk's riposte in his follow-up editorial on 17 December. It was neither 'hysterical' nor 'tawdry'; it did not 'resort to emotional racial invective'; nor was it a descent 'into paranoid nonsense about natives and basket cases'. Rather than being a 'dangerous display of defensive arrogance', it was a pained attempt to get the *Mail & Guardian* seriously to consider becoming a credible source of information and intelligent commentary.

Mankahlana began with a point-by-point refutation of the *Mail & Guardian*'s allegations about Mbeki's political conduct. His point was that a responsible newspaper could not claim that the government was 'threatening to make nonsense out of our democracy' without deploying a good deal of verifiable evidence and persuasive analysis. Van Niekerk conceded that Mankahlana had made 'some good points which we accept in the spirit of debate', without indicating which these were, as opposed to those that remained in contention.

When the editor of a serious paper proclaims the 'right to be wrong' as the *Mail & Guardian* did in its 17 December editorial, it does nothing for reader confidence. Such a right, if it exists, has to be earned and to earn it a newspaper has to demonstrate a consistent record of integrity in its reporting, commentaries and analyses. Without that record, the 'right to be wrong' becomes the right to misinform, defame, scandalise and exploit through damaging innuendo, all in the same name of the 'free flow of criticism and debate' – and, of course, selling newspapers.

There have been other cries of agony recently from individuals and institutions that felt unfairly treated by the *Mail & Guardian*. Barney Cohen, chief executive of Urban Brew Studios, complained on 10 December about what appeared to him to be a 'campaign of slander' by the *Mail & Guardian* 'achieved by using unsubstantiated information from a vindictive inside informant'. After revealing further inaccuracies, Cohen appealed: 'It's about time we put an end to highly damaging speculation and innuendo.'

In an article on 10 December headlined 'Principal raises his pay', the paper reported that Attie Buitendacht, vice-chancellor of Technikon SA, 'gave himself a 35% salary increase' and, in doing so, 'neglected to seek the governing council's approval', an act that allegedly forced the chair of council to resign. In its response, the technikon revealed that the increase was approved and the chair had, in fact, not resigned. The *Mail & Guardian* has still failed to correct the error. The headline's implication that Buitendacht had engaged in corrupt conduct has been left in place to wreak havoc with his reputation. The newspaper does not care. 'The right to be wrong' is out of control.

The second part of Mankahlana's response sought to understand why a supposedly reputable publication consistently gets its facts wrong; routinely fails to verify and investigate the authenticity of its sources; displays a persistent inability to 'balance' the evidence; and routinely fails to publish the defence of those it targets for exposure and damns by innuendo.

Van Niekerk should have answered some of Mankahlana's questions. Was it true that the *Mail & Guardian* had 'virulently opposed the Pan Africanist Congress and Azapo [Azanian People's Organisation] accepting the offer to participate' in Nelson Mandela's government? Was it true that the *Mail & Guardian* later suggested that the Democratic Party's (DP) participation would be 'in the national interest'? If so, then surely van Niekerk was obliged to explain the basis on which his newspaper had preferred the participation of one group against that of another?

If the *Mail & Guardian*'s Howard Barrell writes in his column that the DP 'may *also* be led by a bunch of venal, ambitious, self-serving bastards', is it not the legitimate right of any reader to ask who the other 'bastards' might be? If Mankahlana was wrong to suggest who, in his opinion, these 'bastards' really were, then van Niekerk should have demonstrated why this was so.

Given our history of racism, is it unreasonable to suspect racism behind an inconsistency in which the option for a white party, in place of black ones, remains unexplained? In the same way, it is not unreasonable for a reader to fill in the missing term in the syllogism involving Howard Barrell's 'bastards'? Van Niekerk's heated response strongly suggests that Mankahlana had touched a nerve.

I concede that many white South Africans find themselves in an invidious position when they sense that the race card is being raised to silence them. There are many black South Africans who will be tempted to use that card with effect. White South Africans must learn to recognise when the card is being exploited, and deal with it appropriately. Otherwise, they will be charged with crying 'racism' whenever it suits them. The resort to evasion rather than argument results in ridiculous postures intended to demonstrate that there is at least one white man who cannot be intimidated.

Van Niekerk has a penchant for shifting the terms of discussion in an attempt to undermine a respondent's arguments on grounds other than their substance. This he invariably does under the heading 'The Editor Replies'. He disingenuously invites readers to take his side when he poses a heavily loaded question: 'Is the criticism of the presidency the same as an attack on the country's new democracy? What do you think?' Firstly, this question strongly suggests that the issue it raises is, in fact, a position held by Mankahlana. This is false. Secondly, it pretends to initiate a serious inquiry when it already contains its own answer: a resounding 'No!' As a tactic, this represents the ultimate disrespect for the public intellect.

Van Niekerk is unable to distinguish between the act of criticism, which is not under attack, and the content of criticism, which Mankahlana legitimately challenges. Failure to recognise this distinction apparently leads him to accuse Mankahlana of what he himself does routinely. The *Mail & Guardian* consistently equates criticism of itself with an attack on press freedom. Van Niekerk deploys this argument in his assault on the Human Rights Commission's decision to call for a study on racism and the media. Surely he should accept the logic of his own argument: that if the press should be beyond criticism in defence of press freedom, then so should the presidency in defence of democracy. Strangely, he votes for the immunity of the press, but not of the presidency. We are faced with another baffling inconsistency.

But what do we make of habitual inconsistency; of mundane reliance on rumour and leaked documents as sources of information; of headlines that have no bearing on the substance of an article? I suggest that what we are facing here is something serious. We are witnessing not only the decline of professionalism but a profound failure of intellect.

This prompts some important questions:

- What is the process by which a newspaper determines its editorial stance? Who is involved in the process of determining it?
- What understanding of social transformation informs its formulation?
- How does it influence strategies of presentation?
- How are the resulting representations of society contested and negotiated with the reading public that responds to them?
- More crucially, does the newspaper have sufficient and diverse intellectual resources to answer these questions?
- Can it transcend methods of representation trapped in outmoded yet subliminally powerful intellectual paradigms?
- Does it have the capacity to interrogate itself?

One thing is clear: we need to move forward. The mandate of journalism in today's South Africa urgently needs revision. Public confidence needs to be restored in a sector that has a responsibility to project more complex images of our society. We need a press that is trustworthy; that deepens public knowledge, enriches insight, nurtures a vigorous and courageous atmosphere of public discussion and, above all, respects its public.

Iph'indlela?

finding a way through confusion

2000

There is a small story to the origins of my title. A formidable frustration for most writers is what to do with a blank page. It stares at you with silent, intimidating power. To deal with this situation, I decided to put down words at random. Here they are: peasants, foreign policy, the environment, HIV/AIDS, higher education, the media, Zama-Zama, racism, globalisation, Tito Mboweni, culture, the Truth and Reconciliation Commission, black intellectuals, poverty, two nations, xenophobia, Brenda Fassie, penguins, street children, *Thath' amachance, thath' amamillion,* Trevor Manuel, abortion, market forces, crime, size and shape, game parks, identity, African bourgeoisie, witches, taxi wars, the African renaissance, cities, tribalism, Cosatu, farm murders, Human Rights Commission, Northern Province, primary schools, TV, Tim Modise.

After this brief burst of automatic writing, I leaned back to see if I could spot any emergent trends that would suggest a possible title. I stared at the words and found no sustainable connections to hook onto immediately. But, just as I was about to decide that my random collection of words had not helped, I sat forward as a question formed itself without any effort on my part. I wrote 'Iph'indlela?' I did, indeed, feel lost. I could find no immediate path through this forest of words.

The only thing that was certain was the realisation that the act of writing was a supreme effort at finding your way through immense confusion. It is the act of 'finding your way' through a turbulent sea of words. The only thing that sustains you is a daring act of faith. You'll get somewhere. Somehow, I did. Hence, I arrived at this title.

This experience hit me as a fitting metaphor for what our country is

Steve Biko Memorial Lecture, 12 September 2000; published in *Social Dynamics* 26 (1). 2000

going through. It struck me that, through some daring act of faith, we are 'finding our way' through a turbulent sea of events. These events are the words that we write down almost randomly on the pages of our future. We work our way forward through a continuous play of random events. At each point along the way, we have to respond to events both anticipated and unanticipated. We remember, for example, how the elections of 27 April 1994, on which we put so much hope, threatened to explode each time a series of unanticipated obstacles loomed in the way, making us sway precariously between deliverance and desolation!

But by the time we got to the elections, we had done some surviving. We survived the hope that flew on the wings of the release of Mandela and crashed with the assassination of Chris Hani, threatening never to rise again from the harrowing commuter train killings and Boipatong. At the same time, kwaito flourished. Later, after the elections, art and politics did a delicate dance over AIDS. Mandela had tea with Betsy Verwoerd. P W Botha, facing a black magistrate, wagged his notorious finger more out of habit than conviction in a tired effort to relive some of the past.

In the Northern Province [now Limpopo], many old women were chased away from their homes or burnt to death on the grounds of being witches. Elsewhere, initiates began to die in increasing numbers from circumcisions that went horribly wrong. The Mandelas divorced. Members of the new black elite took up membership of the wealth-making class, driven by compelling visions of instant wealth. Some crashes and disappointments occurred as empowerment dreams faded. We were so excited as we formulated new policies to cover every aspect of national life. But we also saw student activism falter and waver, losing its visionary vitality as it strangely began to look like P W Botha's wagging finger. The hearings of the Truth and Reconciliation Commission came, often tearing us apart, and then left, leaving us emotionally drained but still holding on to our faith.

I refer to these events almost randomly in order to convey the very real sense of finding our way through randomness. But I also want to suggest that this is our own kind of peculiar randomness. It prompts a set of responses that incrementally define us. It is impossible to approach randomness from a singular perspective. We look for trends and shifts and react, sometimes in control, sometimes drifting until we find a foothold that enables us to regain control. It seems to suggest that the process of looking for the way is not to focus on specific issues but to let emerging tendencies provide an explanation which, even while not totally clear, opens up more room for new, innovative solutions. I locate this search in the realm of consciousness: something that Steve Bantu Biko struggled with intensely in his brief but dramatic life.

❑

On this day, 12 September 1977, Steve Biko died in detention. It is twenty-three years ago. Two days later, the then minister of justice, Jimmy Kruger, is said to have 'provoke[d] laughter among delegates to the Transvaal Congress of the governing National Party with remarks about the death: 'I am not glad and I am not sorry about Mr Biko ... He leaves me cold. The minister also agree[d] with a delegate who applaud[ed] him for allowing the black leader his "democratic right" to "starve himself to death". Commenting to the press on his verdict after the inquest into Biko's death, the presiding magistrate, Prins, followed his political leader and declared some three months later, 'To me it was just another death. It was a job like any other.'

Of course, the cause of death was not starvation. It was 'head injuries' which led to 'extensive brain injury'. This leads us to the memory of what must be one of the most imagined events in South African history – imagined, because only four men witnessed it. Yet, the rest of us, who were deeply affected by the horror of the situation, the outrage it evoked, and the bonds of solidarity and empathy that it strengthened, can still see it vividly in our minds, almost as if we were there in that journey through the night.

I am reminding you of the naked, manacled, and lonely body of Steve Biko lying in a Land Rover being driven through the night from Port Elizabeth to a prison hospital in Pretoria by Captain Siebert. It was a distance of more than seven hundred miles, which ended in Biko's death. According to S W Kentridge, counsel to the Biko family, Steve 'died a miserable and lonely death on a mat on a stone floor in a prison cell', as Millard Arnold poignantly tells it in his book *Steve Biko: Black Consciousness in South Africa*.

There is a continuum of indescribable insensitivity and callousness that begins as soon as Steve Biko and Peter Jones are arrested at a roadblock near Grahamstown on 18 August 1977. It starts with lowly police officers who make the arrest in the relative secrecy of a remote setting, and ends with a remarkably public flourish, when a minister of government declares that

Biko's death leaves him cold. This situation lets us go deep into the ethical and moral condition of Afrikanerdom, which not only shaped apartheid but was itself deeply shaped by it.

It strikes us now just how terribly unreflective Afrikanerdom became once apartheid had wormed its way into the centre of its moral fibre. When apartheid culture became both a private and public condition, defining a cultural sensibility, Afrikanerdom significantly lost much of its sense of irony. In this situation, the combination of political, economic and military power, validated by religious precept, yielded a universal sense of entitlement. Afrikanerdom was entitled to land, air, water, beast, and each and every black body.

At this point, the treatment of black people ceases to be a moral concern. Speaking harshly to a black person; stamping with both feet on the head or chest of a black body; roasting a black body over flames to obliterate evidence of murder (not because murder was wrong, but because it was an irritating embarrassment); dismembering the black body by tying wire round its ankles and dragging it behind a bakkie; whipping black school-children; handing to, in the words of Biko himself, 'an illiterate [black] mother presenting her ailing infant for treatment … a death certificate in order that the [white] doctor should not be disturbed in the night' *when* the infant died … These are things one who is white, in South Africa, can do from time to time to black bodies, in the total scheme of things.

No wonder the death of Steve Biko left the minister cold, and that Magistrate Prins could admit to having witnessed another ordinary death, just as he would have had another glass of water. In all this, there is a chilling suggestion of gloating that borders dangerously close to depravity. Suddenly, 'the heart of darkness' is no longer the exclusive preserve of 'blackness'; it seems to have become the very condition of 'whiteness' at the southern corner of the African continent. Its expression will take on various degrees of manifestation, from the crude to the sophisticated.

That is why such instances of the desecration of the black body have yet to evoke significant expressions of outrage from the education, religious, cultural, and business leadership of this country, caught in the culture of 'whiteness' which they built. Certainly not to the extent of anything that signals an historic movement towards a new social and moral order. Indeed, the quest for a new white humanity will begin to emerge from a voluntary engagement by those caught in the culture of whiteness of their own making, with the ethical and moral implications of being situated at the interface between inherited, problematic privilege, on the one hand and, on the other, the blinding sterility at the centre of the 'heart of whiteness'.

❏

I confess to being one of those who have had an ambivalent attitude towards the recent national conference on racism. On the one hand, I welcomed the attention paid to this national problem of racism. On the other, I remain deeply worried about the terms on which the problem was highlighted and engaged. I am bothered by the phenomenon of a black majority in power, seeming to reduce itself to the status of complainants as if they had a limited capacity to do anything more significant about the situation at hand than drawing attention to it. It is not that the complaints have no foundation; on the contrary, the foundations are deeply embedded in our history. But I cannot shake off the feeling that the galvanising of concern around racism reflects a vulnerability, which could dangerously resuscitate a familiar psychology of inferiority precisely at that moment when the black majority ought to provide confident leadership through the government they have elected.

I worry that the complaining may look confusingly like a psychological submission to 'whiteness' in the sense of handing over to 'whiteness' the power to provide relief. 'Please, stop this thing!' seems to be the appeal. 'Respect us.' I submit that we moved away from this position decisively on 27 April 1994. We cannot go back to it. It should not be so easy to give up a psychological advantage.

I am bothered by the tendency that, when a black body is dragged down the road behind a bakkie, we see first proof of racism rather than depravity and murder. When we give to racism in Africa this kind of centrality of explanation, we confirm the status of the black body as a mere item of data to be deployed in a grammar of political argument, rather than affirm it as violated humanity. The inherent worth of a black body does not need to be affirmed by the mere proof of white racism against it. The black body is much more than the cruelty to which it is subjected. If we succeed in positioning ourselves as a people above this kind of cruelty, we deny it equality of status. We can then deal with it as one among many other problems in our society that needs our attention.

I think this is what Steve Biko meant when he cautioned against 'the major danger' he saw 'facing the black community … to be so conditioned by the system as to make even our most well-considered resistance to it fit within the system both in terms of the means and of the goals'. I quote from his book *I Write What I Like.* It is possible we are not entirely out of this danger.

Is the foregrounding of race and racism a veiled admission that perhaps there is as yet no material basis for the black majority to contain this scourge through the imposition of its own versions of the future? Does this speak to the black majority's perception that perhaps they are not yet agents of history?

I ask these questions in the knowledge that white racism in South Africa no longer exists as a formalised structure. We conjure in our minds the continued existence of such a structure to our perceptual peril. There is no evidence of a Ku Klux Klan that is regrouping somewhere in the far-flung corners of the country. On the contrary, with the disintegration of apartheid as a formal structure, white racism has reacted in a number of ways.

In some cases it has simply died.

In other cases, particularly where strong pockets of white power remain, such as in commerce, industry, and in higher education, it has either mutated and assumed the colour of change while retaining a core of self-interest, or has genuinely struggled with the agonies of embracing necessary change.

In other cases, racism also continues to exist as individualised pathology, frequently exploding into acts of suicide or desperate acts of brutality against any black bodies in sight. In almost every case, we witness a crisis of identity with various degrees of intensity. But what these various forms of reaction do show is the danger inherent in a singular approach.

That is why the black majority carries the historic responsibility to provide, in this situation, decisive and visionary leadership. Either it embraces this responsibility with conviction or it gives up its leadership through a throwback psychological dependence on racism which has the potential to severely compromise the authority conferred on it by history.

❏

In an essay, 'Martyr for Hope' in *I Write What I Like,* Father Aelred Stubbs writes:

Given the circumstances he faced of a strongly entrenched, power-fully armed minority, on the one hand, and a divided, defeated majority on the other, perhaps the political genius of Steve [Biko] lay in concentrating on the creation and diffusion of a new *consciousness* rather than in the formation of a rigid *organisation*.

The relationship between emergent social process and organisational forms created to define and assist such social process is a complex one. A way of life is not reducible to institutional forms designed to support it. Indeed, when the Black People's Convention was established in 1971, there were arguments to the effect that Black Consciousness was a quality of being rather than an organisational project that could be subjected to harassment and banning. In our own day, the African renaissance as an emergent historic phenomenon is often used interchangeably with the notion of the African renaissance as an institution-driven project seemingly designed to midwife the African future. In my view, the latter cannot meaningfully come before the former, although it can anticipate it.

The problem is not so much the establishment of organisational forms as the threat of a constricting rigidity in organisational interpretations of social processes. Potential rigidity and ownership of definition can pose a number of threats. I think that, despite the wars, the famine, outlaw governments, and HIV/AIDS, some reawakening is underway. Some economies are growing. There is a creeping spread of democracy. The Southern African Development Community and other regional economic formations are making a committed effort to contain decay and help on positive trends. Like all social processes, the African re-awakening is a messy yet creative development, far from being subject to a body of predictive rules and regulations, nor is it reducible to a political programme. It has yet to be satisfactorily characterised as an irreversible process.

It goes without saying that my approach is to put more stress on emergent phenomena than on evoked realities. I will now explore briefly what I mean.

David Philip Publishers published a remarkable little book earlier this year. It is entitled *Marketing through Mud and Dust* by Muzi Kuzwayo. I was fascinated by the central idea behind this book. It is this: 'The economic future of this country lies with blacks.' This remains a singularly simple but profound statement. What it states cannot be otherwise in a country with our kind of demographic profile, and the place where the currents of history have taken it at this point. From this perspective, this book fundamentally re-writes the textbook of South African marketing.

Kuzwayo tells the story of a township taverner's contact with the 'rep' of a certain company. 'Most reps,' says the taverner, 'do a sterling job, but man I don't know where they get some of them from. You can see that the guy is well educated but is not street smart at all. The problem is that reps are interviewed in an office environment and the human resources people want to see how they fit into the office as opposed to the streets where he'll be marketing the product.' What this suggests is that the pressures of life in the township will significantly exert influence on the strategic choices to be made in company boardrooms and in academic departments and faculties of universities. Such institutions will be responding to the pressures of increasingly dominant social forces which will, over time, exercise a decisive hegemonic effect. A situation such as this cannot be led by policy. Policy can only be developed from it in order to support it.

Commercial and industrial enterprises and institutions of higher learning that fail to recognise this fundamental shift in the orientation of the economy will not survive in the medium to long term. To survive in the future, they will have to rethink and innovate around the needs of the emerging black market. This market, of course, has always been there. But it was rendered officially invisible because the State was primarily constructed around meeting the needs of its white citizens. Clearly the white market is not big enough to shoulder the burden of economic growth. It can accommodate only so much growth before it begins to run aground and stagnate.

Similarly, there will be an optimum capacity in both economic and cultural terms beyond which white residential areas can become a home to black people to any significant degree of rootedness, in the short to medium term. By the same token, white-based commercial and industrial concerns with a large base of white shareholders can absorb only a certain number of black experts before their number peaks. In a paper delivered at the inauguration of the Institute for Justice and Reconciliation I argued that there are some advantages to this situation. I noted:

It should not be expected that the levelling off of black participation, and the subsequent limitation in black influence in such institutions, should lead to their destruction. On the contrary, the service they provide remains essential to the survival of the entire country. The perceived limitation in total black control results in the maintenance of essential productive capability and some measure of predictable stability. By the time a critical mass of blacks is in place, there will be an institutional tradition of company practices into which new members are socialised. This situation may not be desirable from the perspective of a short-term radical project. But such an understanding may be crucial for a long-range perspective.

This long-term transitional process may have some particular benefits for a white society that has lost political power. It retains for them a certain measure of cultural familiarity, which assures them some basis for working levels of self-confidence. But to the extent that this familiarity may become an expectation that is not shared by the new order it may run aground and self-destruct in decay. To prevent such an outcome, it will have to ensure a large measure of buy-in by a critical mass of participant black members.

All this suggests that traditionally black localities around the country will become new zones of economic growth and evolve complex economies built around meeting the needs of embedded black communities. The success of this historic trend will largely depend on an extensive distribution of inventive capacity in the scientific and entrepreneurial fields throughout the entire population, freeing us from the current dependence on limited white expertise.

Although this development may emerge on its own, it will require a great deal of stimulation and steering in the form of complex public policy interventions. This may involve developing an active capacity to build thirty- to fifty-year planning scenarios involving, at their centre, high-quality social planning that stresses the creation of functional and productive living environments throughout the country. From such a perspective, a great deal of current policy perspectives take on a fresh significance: urban and rural planning; a high-quality schooling system; lifelong learning; adult basic education and training; strong provincial and consolidated local governments. The aim would be to maintain reasonable levels of service to privileged communities while considerably improving service provision in traditionally black localities.

❑

What is the connection between the project of development so essential to our finding the future and this critique of 'whiteness' and what our response to it has been? Of course this question has to be considered alongside the hegemonic growth of a black consciousness (not in the sense of a philosophy or movement associated with Steve Biko, although it may not exclude it, but, rather, in the more fundamental sense of the inevitability of a particular kind of social process).

It will be obvious that the flow of social influence is not going in one direction from the black to the white community. There is a two-way process setting itself up as a critical stabilising factor as we negotiate change. Because the process will not always be smooth, it will require a number of negotiated positions. On balance, though, white South Africa will be called upon to make greater adjustments to black needs than the other way round. This is an essential condition for a shift in white identity in which 'whiteness' can undergo an experiential transformation by absorbing new cultural experience as an essential condition for achieving a new sense of cultural rootedness. That is why every white South African should be proud to speak, read, and write at least one African language, and be ashamed if they are not able to.

This matter of rootedness is important. For example, from a black perspective, whatever the economic merits of the case, it is difficult not to see the transfer of capital to big Western stock exchanges as 'whiteness' de-linking itself from the mire of its South African history to explore opportunities of disengagement, where the home base is transformed into a satellite market revolving around powerful Western economies, to become a market to be exploited rather than a home to be served.

This kind of 'flight of white capital' may represent white abandonment of responsibility towards the only history that can promise salvation to 'whiteness'. 'Whiteness' has a responsibility to demonstrate its bona fides in this regard. Where is the primary locus of responsibility for white capital, built over centuries with black labour and unjust laws? A failure to come to terms with the morality of this question ensures the continuation of the culture of insensitivity and debilitating guilt.

In the past, 'whiteness' proclaimed its civilising mission in Africa. In reality, any advantages for black people, where they occurred, were an unintended result rather than an intended objective. An historic opportunity has arisen now for white South Africa to participate in a humanistic revival of our country through a readiness to participate in the process of redress and reconciliation. This is on the understanding that the 'heart of whiteness' will be hard put to reclaim its humanity without the restoration of dignity to the black body.

We are all familiar with the global sanctity of the white body. Wherever the white body is violated in the world, severe retribution follows somehow for the perpetrators if they are non-white, regardless of the social status of the white body. The white body is inviolable, and that inviolability is in direct proportion to the global vulnerability of the black body. This leads me to think that if South African whiteness is a beneficiary of the protectiveness assured by international whiteness, it has an opportunity to write a new chapter in world history. It will have to come out from under the umbrella and repudiate it. Putting itself at risk, it will have to declare that it is home now, sharing in the vulnerability of other compatriot bodies. South African whiteness will declare that its dignity is inseparable from the dignity of black bodies.

The collapse of 'white leadership' that would spearhead this process has been lamented. On second thoughts, perhaps this situation represents a singular opportunity. The collapse of 'white leadership' ought to lead to the collapse of the notion of 'black leadership'. Where there is no 'white leadership' to contest 'black leadership', where these descriptions of leadership were a function of the outmoded politics of a racist state, we are left only with leaders to govern this country. There can be no more compelling argument than this to urge for care and caution in addressing the issue of racism at the southern tip of the African continent. The historic disintegration of 'white leadership' imposes immense responsibilities on how we frame notions of leadership in the resultant political space we are now inheriting.

This way, the South African State is placed in a unique position to declare its obligations to all citizens. It should jealously and vigorously protect all bodies within its borders and beyond.

❑

When I began to write this talk, I had no idea where it would take me. Faced with a daunting randomness, I settled on the themes of race, consciousness, and social process around which to explore any possible ways into the future. I am humbled by the knowledge there can never be one, single, definitive way. There are many other possible paths.

Muzi Kuzwayo, in the conclusion to his fine book, tells the story of how, a year before the 1999 elections, a 'white guy' who discovered that Muzi was in advertising came to him with a bizarre proposal. He sought advice on how to market a coffin-manufacturing company, which would flourish from the violence being anticipated at the time, and from all the HIV/AIDS deaths. As Muzi relates:

> I refused to help him because I have faith in this country and its people. And every day my faith is reaffirmed by the millions who get on buses, trains and taxis to go to work. Lately, increasing crime, disease and interest rates are causing justified desperation. But I still have faith. And faith doesn't have to be justified. My future depends on South Africans spending their hard-earned money on bread, books, alcohol, savings or investment accounts or anything else that keeps our economy going. If you are in marketing, advertising or any other industry, you must have faith. Irrational as it may be. Sometimes it will waiver and when that happens remember those people who stock-piled tons of food, water and petrol before our first democratic election. They were all wrong.

It is my act of faith in the act of writing that has got me where I am now with a few ideas.

138

Reaching out to the World

new identities on the horizon?

2000

The workings of history are remarkably unpredictable. But when events come to pass, they seem the result of a great plan. Certainly, I am the first vice chancellor of this great university to be installed by Mrs Graça Machel since she became its chancellor in December last year. Seven years earlier, in September 1993, I was the last vice chancellor of the University of the North [now the University of Limpopo] to be installed by a very close relative of hers, who was then chancellor of the University of the North, Mr Nelson Mandela. Today, of all days, I cannot be denied the right to say, truly, I am a member of the family.

Could I, in only one sentence, highlight the meaning of this family whose membership I have just claimed. It represents the convergence of personal and public histories journeying across vast distances in time and space. It is the quintessential experience of millions of southern Africans. A small number of us have traversed these great distances of history and have come to this one spot, to engage in a brief moment of celebration and reflection. I have travelled my own journey for twenty-nine years of a fifty-two-year life, with my lifelong friend, lover, partner, and mother of our children, Mpho. I can think of few other blessings greater than this.

There have been other blessings, such as having been the child of my mother and father, Makhosazana and Nimrod, both ancestors now, who taught me compassion, the love of learning and the life of the imagination. It has been a blessing to have been the pupil of numerous dedicated teachers who inspired me to persevere. My journey with them began from the crèches of Western Native Township and Charterston Location, through the lower and higher primary schools of Charterston to St Christopher's

---

Inaugural address, University of Cape Town, 21 September 2000

Anglican High School in Swaziland, where I and many of my peers began a long life of exile.

Other blessings were a triumph over adversity. They include many years living in Lesotho, an island of freedom in the dark days of the total onslaught, a country that gave many of us the unforgettable experience of being students at the University of Botswana, Lesotho, and Swaziland, where lecturers and professors from all over the world taught freely an equally international student body. Above all, Lesotho was a place to call a home from home, and a base from which to see the rest of the world. It was from there that I became a citizen of the world.

I am at this moment also aware of another vast distance of time and space, one heavy with meaning and responsibility. It is the distance between me, the eighth vice chancellor of the University of Cape Town, and the first. I am conscious of having been asked to play a role that others in between, all remarkable and distinguished individuals, have played in the history of this university. I am awed by the continuum of immense significance, which links the present to the past in ways that South Africans are only beginning to learn to accept and appreciate as something inseparable from the definition of who we are. President Mbeki captured this complex definition in his famous 'I am an African' speech to the Constitutional Assembly on 8 May 1996.

Indeed, as we meet one another across vast distances of time and space, we cannot but come to realise that each one of us brings a high store of value, up until now unknown in the public domain, because we have come from a past that did not allow us to share our value. Now, after some hesitance, flickers of recognition are occurring. That is why those moments and places where we can meet, in our schools, in our universities, in our churches, are so important as sites of mutual discovery.

This mutual discovery I am talking about is not a sentimental process. Rather, it is an historic phenomenon that comes in the wake of the initial assertiveness of South Africa's black, newly enfranchised citizens, and the anxious withdrawal from centre stage of its white citizens. But the assertiveness and confidence was later to be tempered by an increasing sense of vulnerability in the face of the enormous task of having to confront not only national and regional challenges, but global ones as well.

Concomitantly, the anxiety and loss of power among white fellow citizens is compensated for by an increasing confidence that may come from the sense of being needed. These subtle shifts in interdependency can often be misinterpreted as powerlessness, on the one hand, and racist arrogance, on the other. They actually represent a process of mutual discovery that presents us with a unique opportunity to explore an interdependency that has immense cultural implications.

We are pushed towards diversity, no longer by a political imperative but by felt social necessity. Demographic diversity in the workplace, in our schools and on university campuses becomes a principle of survival rather than a mere political objective. It ought to be a central, energising feature of the factory floor, the corporate boardroom, church service, and of schools and universities, shaping their curricula.

❑

The recent 'shape and size' report of the Council for Higher Education recognises the need for a fundamental attitudinal change in the manner in which South Africans look at the higher education sector. It makes a very significant statement:

> The 36 public higher education institutions inherited from the past are all South African institutions. They must be embraced as such, must be transformed where necessary and must be put to work for and on behalf of all South Africans.

This statement recognises that a new South African identity expresses itself through an inclusive possessiveness of the human and physical landscapes we have inherited. It addresses a major concern I have had over many years, that the higher education sector has been one of the most conservative institutional sectors in our new democracy. Embracing the racial and cultural divide even more vociferously after 1994, it has been difficult to change. For this reason, this sector is crying out to be freed from the psychic prison of inherited divisions, vigorously defended, among other things, through the discourse of redress and institutional autonomy.

It is all tied up, of course, with the politics of race. While the concept of institutional autonomy has been counterbalanced with that of 'accountability', that of 'redress' remains locked in with 'entitlement'. I have always argued, even from the perspectives of the disadvantages I have experienced, that institutions should not receive special attention because of their positions within a system of colour coding, but because they have been identified to play defined functional roles within the broader perspective of national development. The abandonment of colour coding ought to promise greater, unexplored freedom. But enjoying this freedom comes at the price of embracing vulnerability and demanding hard work.

It is increasingly problematic that institutions compete on the basis that one institution has more black students than another. The potential abuse of 'blackness' through high-enrolment and programmes of inferior quality that yet generate subsidy income may become a dangerous trend. Having black students should also mean providing the programmes of the highest possible quality. Diversity should become a quality-assurance issue at a fundamental level rather than a posture signifying deracialisation. Deracialisation is about more than numbers; it is about bringing to bear new influences on inherited institutional cultures.

It needs to be stated that black students who qualify should have the freedom to walk into any institution of higher learning in this country and feel at home. We cannot limit the field of possibility for any student. But, by the same token, the responsibility on all institutions to offer quality learning environments is one that should be shouldered in partnership with government and the funding agencies willing to assist. What is unacceptable is for black South Africans to limit their options through a reflex resort to an outmoded system of colour coding, by turning their backs on any of the thirty-six institutions of higher learning they have inherited. To do so would amount to no less than a surrender of historic rights achieved through sacrifice.

All South African institutions of higher learning have a responsibility to build on some inherited strengths. But as they do so, they should strive to remain true to the values of democracy, equality, nonracialism, and academic freedom. These inherited strengths should be supported by policy positions that are able to recognise inherited value even while subjecting that value to a necessary critique of its origins. Such a critique is an essential condition for holding any particular institution accountable to the broad democratic and humanistic goals of our country. This perspective should go a long way towards rendering our institutions of higher learning refreshingly normal. Then we can focus on the pressing issues.

All our institutions of higher learning face similar problems: declining enrolments; global competition from private higher education providers; an economy that is not growing fast enough; a government subsidy that will not significantly grow in the short to medium term; the unfolding impact, as yet not fully grasped, of the HIV/AIDS pandemic; the phenomenal growth of knowledge economies; the formation and increasing power of regional economic communities; high levels of poverty and illiteracy; and the demand for high-level skills in management, science and technology, arts and humanities, media and communications.

In this situation, every institution is called upon to assess its possibilities. This means any number of things: focusing closely on the core functions and roles of higher education institutions; accurately identifying competitive strengths and channelling scarce resources towards strategic choices; forming complementary institutional relationships through regional partnerships; urgently setting in place and implementing quality assurance systems; enhancing institutional ability to expand resource bases; and achieving high levels of relevance.

In the context of this picture, I look at my new university, my home for the next few years, and feel excited. I am excited by the fact that our students, members of the next generation of South Africans, have an opportunity to extend the wings of their minds and characters in an intellectually stimulating and culturally diverse environment. They learn in an environment with students from more than seventy different countries. It is wonderful that they do not have to travel far and wide in order for them to acquire membership of the new network, which will effectively replace the old white schoolboy networks that have run this country for so long. The networks of the future will be culturally diverse and global.

I am excited by the prospect that the University of Cape Town, located in a city decidedly multicultural and increasingly identified as an international city, the destination of many around the world, is well positioned to be our country's international university. Already locked into world-class research in several fields, we have an obligation to consolidate our position in this regard. It is a competitive advantage we have a responsibility to maintain.

With our strong research base, we are positioned to build new sustainable partnerships providing high-level expertise to local, provincial, and national governments. We do also have the capacity to be world players through similar partnerships with international and global institutions in Africa and beyond. We are committed to establishing strong partnerships with the private sector through innovative joint ventures with the potential to yield considerable mutual benefit. This trend is not only desirable, it is mandatory.

It is important for us to remember, though, that universality always arises out of local experience. Our strong research base would be even more valuable if it did not forget the community within which the university is located.

The concentration of highly talented people, highly dedicated to the university, although the pool of talent is not yet sufficiently diverse, has to be maintained and broadened, motivated to stay, urged and rewarded to innovate. But we do have to make strategic choices about where we want to be most effective in the short to medium term. For example, we have to be more adventurous and less complacent about being a traditional, medium-sized, residential university.

If it is correct that education in the Western Cape is the second revenue earner after tourism, then further investment in our solid regional education infrastructure is guaranteed to yield immense, long-term benefit. The Western Cape as South Africa's and Africa's knowledge centre is not only a possibility, it is an emergent reality.

The opportunities for regional partnerships among educational institutions in the Western Cape are enormous. For example, institutions of higher learning in the Western Cape will have failed the people of this region and the country if they do not, in partnership with the national and regional governments, rescue our ailing provincial health sector from the clash of institutional missions. Inventive collaborations must be the new norm. But such collaborations will not yield their full benefit without a partnering of strong individual institutions.

I have become intensely aware of the consistent support that the University of Cape Town has received from its diverse alumni in this country and all over the world. Equally so, there are donors and foundations who, in their various ways, have believed in the future of this university and the special role it can play. We invite them to continue to take the journey with us. It is of tremendous significance that in the massive fundraising exercise that resulted in our new and magnificent library and other upper campus developments, the bulk of our funding came from South African sources.

This immense asset, as it reaches out to the world, will be put to the service of the people of this country and our continent. It is a special privilege, for which I am eternally grateful, to have been given the opportunity to take the University of Cape Town towards higher levels of commitment and engagement with its diverse communities. This is a project that has to succeed.

An Encounter with My Roots

vexing questions of language, identity and culture

2000

Just over a year ago, as part of my research towards a fiction work-in-progress, I visited a village outside Durban to spend the day with nine *izangoma*. As my research assistant and I approached the village, I grew increasingly apprehensive. Would I be able to communicate effectively with these healers, who had graciously agreed to let me observe and even participate in some of the rituals by which they communicate with ancestors? I felt I was about to be exposed.

After twenty years of exile in Lesotho, I had gradually adopted Sesotho as my preferred African language of communication, leaving my own mother tongue, Zulu, in some kind of limbo. Clearly, I could not communicate in Sesotho in a Zulu village, more so as I was on a mission so intimately connected with language. Supplications to ancestors should be in a language they understand. Nor could I resort to English without the risk of feeling and looking ridiculous, if not insulting. But how was I going to communicate in a language I had not used with any degree of consistency for twenty years? How was I going to overcome the feeling of helplessness arising from the conviction that I had forgotten my language? My assistant's reassurance in the car could not really shake off my anxieties. He had assured me, on his word of honour, that I spoke excellent Zulu. No one could tell that I had not spoken it for so long, he said.

The moment of truth came after my assistant had introduced me to the *izangoma* and requested me to explain my mission in my own words. We sat on the floor in the right half of the divination hut. The nine venerable women sat to the right of me in a line that curved away from me along the wall of the round hut. It will be a long time before I forget the twenty seconds or

---

Connect: Art, Politics, Theory, Practice, Fall 2000

so of silence in which my mind attempted to converge to a single point the urgent immediacy of a speech moment and almost the entire history of my life. It was a chasm of silence between disaster and deliverance.

I began: *'Ngcolosi!'* saluting Mrs Alvina Bhengu by her clan name. That is who she told me she was later when I asked for her postal address. In her *umyeko*, an impressive headgear of green, white, pink, purple, black, and blue beads which streamed down her neck and shoulders, she radiated leadership and authority. Here and there within the tapestry of beads hung dry sacks of goat bile, testimony to the number of goats slaughtered in her honour. There could be no other fitting way of signalling my acknowledgement of so many things about her life than through her clan name.

'*Mina,*' I continued, poking at my chest with pointing fingers even after I had already been introduced, '*ngingu Njabulo Simakahle Ndebele, ozalwa ngu Nimrod Njabulo Ndebele, ozalwa ...*' The outline of my brief family history and the story of its origins and movements across the land, ending with my sojourn in New York at the Ford Foundation, poured out with decreasing hesitancy. By the time I explained what my visit was all about, I had been miraculously reborn as a Zulu.

After an invocation to the ancestors, after the passing of the *ukhamba* for all of us to drink from in unity, after the sacrificing of the goat I had been asked to bring along, after the systematic distribution of its meat according to ritual, after the communal meal that followed, and the visit to the herbarium where I was given the Zulu names of the various plants and what they were used for, I felt an overpowering sense of belonging to a people such as I had never experienced before. Up to that point South Africa had been, for me, a broad political community with a generalised political identity. But, I had often asked myself, what was there beyond the politics? What I experienced that Saturday in May 1999 seemed to be an answer. It seemed as if the specificity of my feelings and the immediacy of their source yielded a more concrete, more vital, sense of discovering belonging.

And who were these Zulus? They were a people who had existed in my mind as an evocative notion through language association and a fascination with aspects of their momentous history in southern Africa. Suddenly, on that Saturday, they became real to me as they had never been before. I had not really known them until then. I had not really bothered to know them more, except when assailed, from time to time, by insecurities around my identity. Otherwise, I was a confident, if complacent, product of South Africa's townships, one who considered himself completely detribalised.

Like many of my fellow detribalised, I have often had moments when I looked at any manifestation of tribal behaviour with amused contempt and a sense of political, but never cultural, superiority. Never, until that Saturday, would I have thought myself capable of experiencing the strong stirrings of tribal feeling in the most affirming sense of belonging and identification. How did I come to sense so vitally the cardinal points of an, up to then, elusive identity? This is an identity that I had not actively sought but was simply given at birth. So this was it? Was this how it was for many people the world over, not to have to explain and justify their existence? One simply became, through the existential feeling of being slotted into place.

❑

But my day in rural KwaZulu-Natal was not going to be without its problems. They began when, at some point while I was basking in the warmth of a newly rediscovered identity, I looked at the green rolling hills around me. I noted how still they were. They were serene. Voices of people shouting across hills, the sound of truck engines struggling up a hill, or dogs barking, intensified the sense of stillness and gave birth to interfering images stirred up by unsettling memories. At first I felt uneasy. Then I got frightened. And I became horrified.

Had not these same hills also been a theatre for the spilling of so much political blood in the last twenty years? Were these same hills not the sites of ancient feuds and vendettas which in recent times became mixed with conflicting political and social visions, often the result of evocations of tribal solidarities? Was this how, drunk with belonging, I could be a willing instrument of death? Could this have anything to do with the unrelenting ugliness of tribal hostilities in Kosovo? Could this be how Hutus and Tutsis in Rwanda and Burundi sought intimate justification?

These intriguing extremes of feeling I experienced within a day. Partly they represented the displacement of a certain kind of benign naïveté that comes from a strand of political thought among some of South Africa's detribalised elites. It is characterised by a superior contempt for 'tribal things', which are then wished out of existence. Aspects of it are understandable. Black South Africans countered the atomising tendencies of apartheid by counterpoising an uncomplicated trans-tribal solidarity.

This kind of political unity was not only wished into existence as a strategic goal, it was also aided, for more than a hundred years, by the growth of South African capitalism. For more than a century, South African capitalism built multi-tribal entities across the economic landscape, which worked profoundly against apartheid's atomising tendencies. What this meant for most black South Africans was that their identity as part of a national political community intersected with their ethnic identity. But the nature of this intersection has not been fully understood. It is this intersection that, in the specific context of South Africa, may form a theoretical basis for experimentation with multilingual narrative forms.

My personal linguistic experience is located in the intersection of three major language communities: English, Sesotho, and isiZulu. My experiences with each of these languages represent significant moments in my life. English, for example, has been a major vehicle for my education and creative writing. Sesotho, on the other hand, carries special memories for me. In almost two decades of exile in Lesotho, I experienced the integrity of a self-referential African world with its language, customs and traditions, and its social and political systems functioning as a contemporary society and not as a relic of colonial anthropology. I fell in love with the beautiful language of Thomas Mofolo in his novels, and with the music of J P Mohapeloa. I spoke Sesotho with relish despite an accent that constantly betrayed me. My life in Lesotho was a most enriching experience of being home from home. Sesotho resonates for me with an experience of social complexity, the quality of which I never had with isiZulu. I saw in Lesotho the immense possibilities of an historically rooted African society which survived colonialism largely intact, retaining a strong sense of identity. Being an orderly society, Lesotho had internal mechanisms for mediating between creative and destructive tendencies within it.

I described earlier my re-encounter with my mother tongue, isiZulu. The impact of its sudden and dramatic return into my life heavily suggests that the intervening years have been a profound interruption, as if my relationship with the language was frozen in time, only to be triggered back into life through an unexpected, tribal experience. It was an instant reconnection that opened up new possibilities for my relationship with it.

A real question emerges: which of these three languages is my language? In South Africa, a country engaged in building democracy, the question is more academic. An answer hinges on clarity in any number of possible strategic objectives. For example, Section 6 of the constitution identifies all eleven major languages as official languages. These include English, Sesotho and isiZulu. Subsection 6(2) further states: 'Recognising the historically diminished use and status of the indigenous languages of our people, the State must take practical and positive measures to elevate the status and advance the use of these languages.' Not only has the political equality of all South Africa's languages been secured; so has the State's responsibility towards the advancement of those languages that were previously disempowered by colonialism and apartheid. Sesotho, within South Africa, has been as disempowered as isiZulu. A strategic commitment to the cultural development of these languages is a vital element in the strengthening of democracy.

Such a dramatic arrangement makes it possible for me to claim all three languages, and precisely because of that claim I can assert my responsibility for the enhancement of the role and status of Sesotho and isiZulu. What nature this responsibility can assume may be a collective social matter involving, for example, the eradication of illiteracy, and the aggressive monitoring of the implementation of constitutional language provisions; or a personal one involving artistic choices. In this latter connection, I now experience the choice to write either in English or in an African language as primarily a cultural rather than a political question. The legitimising force of the constitution has significantly reduced the urgency of political choices, so overwhelming during the struggle for liberation.

Thus far I have attempted to lay the groundwork for a speculative exercise on the possibility of a multilingual work of fiction, with particular reference to how, in my case, the situation might play itself out. For a year I have been thinking deeply about my literary project and the directions it might take. What kind of novel would I write after my encounter in KwaZulu-Natal? How would I deal with situations inspired by this visit? Would English measure up to the challenge?

If there is any lasting significance in my experience with the *izangoma*, it is that my fictional work-in-progress cannot be carried entirely by English. Whichever way I am going to use elements of my visit to KwaZulu-Natal, for example, an expressive logic dictates that these elements need to be grounded in a fitting linguistic and artistic medium. There are aspects of my experience that I cannot imagine in English. This leads me to the conclusion that if my linguistic experience as a South African has grown in, and been influenced by, the intersection of three communities whose respective languages I speak, read, and write (with different levels of capability), I am forced to confront the task of exploring artistic possibilities resident in that intersection.

First is the possibility of fiction woven together in at least three languages. In this regard I must begin with the acknowledgement that my history of using English as a medium for artistic expression is incomparably much longer than my use of Sesotho and isiZulu for that purpose. A further use of the latter languages would require extensive experimentation during a period of self-imposed apprenticeship. A critical artistic challenge is how to ensure intelligibility for readers who are outside my three-language intersection. The same consideration would apply for other multi-language intersections. The more intersecting languages there are, the greater the artistic difficulty.

Secondly, the experimentation with multilingual fiction is far from being an artificial exercise in multilingual tinkering. It arises out of the fact that the eleven official languages are likely to coexist in close proximity well beyond the foreseeable future. This situation suggests that English, a dominant language with vast global reach, is no longer a foreign language to be abandoned. It has become one possible artistic medium among others available to a South African. This understanding opens up vast possibilities for a resourceful South African writer by delimiting the exercise of language choice and conferring legitimacy on any choice made.

Thirdly, who are the likely readers in such an experiment? The average South African speaks any combination of at least two languages. The average black South African speaks any combination of at least three languages. In the Johannesburg area, the average rises to four or five languages. On balance, the average black South African speaks more languages than does his or her white compatriot. This means that a multilingual fiction has a potentially large multilingual black readership, on condition that a speech community located at a multilingual intersection actually amounts to a reading community. Such a development cannot happen on its own. Readers of multilingual fiction have to transform speech habits into a reading discipline, making possible the growth of a dialogue between writers and readers.

As the economy gradually shifts its attention away from focusing on the needs of the increasingly shrinking white market that it currently serves, towards a growing and vigorous black market as a fundamental basis of its growth, so will there be greater opportunities for a progressive increase in the public use of African languages – provided, of course, that the provisions of the constitution are relentlessly pursued. In the same way, I see myself experimenting with multilingual fiction in which, in the first instance, English is highly likely to carry the burden of maintaining the intelligibility structure of the novel as the primary narrative language. In time, English may be displaced from within as the other languages increase their narrative space.

However, the constitution envisages that the task of achieving such displacement will not be easy:

6 (3) (a) The national government and the provincial governments may use any particular official languages for the purposes of government, taking into account usage, practicality, expense, regional circumstances and the balance of needs and preferences of the population as a whole or in the province concerned, but the national government and each provincial government must use at least two official languages.

(b) Municipalities must take into account the language usage and preferences of their residents.

The number of variables to be taken into account in the formulation of national, provincial, and local government language policies strongly points to a process of language development that takes place over time. Planned interventions in this regard will be essential. But a planned approach does not preclude unanticipated social upheavals that speed up the process.

I have attempted to suggest a correlation between social possibility and artistic experimentation through the medium of language, in which the visionary possibilities of South African democracy can be extended and realised. It is a speculative and intuitive venture, in its initial stages, intended to open up other avenues to vexing questions of language, identity and culture.

The Ties that Bind

a search for common values

2001

J ust under a year ago I returned home after living overseas for eighteen months. I recall many times thinking about what it meant to be a South African. There were a number of things about New York that forced me to think these thoughts: most strikingly, the many nationalities from all over the world that have established a physical, cultural and economic presence in that world city. Koreans, Indians, Dominicans, Jamaicans, Irish, French, Pakistanis, Chinese, Italians, West Africans, Arabs, Persians. The list goes on. They each appear to have brought with them to New York a social or cultural distinctiveness that provides them with a zone of collective comfort in a highly competitive, and sometimes hostile, environment. Soon, however, they fit into a matrix of multicultural activity that enables them to contribute to the vitality of the city. It is not long before their cultural or physical strangeness is compensated for by their economic usefulness. Their niche in the economic ecology of New York accords them a position within the quilt of multiculturalism, one of the defining features of a world city.

I would then pose the question: if fifty thousand South Africans of various races, classes, ethnic groups, and religions were airlifted into New York right now, what is it, once they have settled, that would make them gravitate towards one another? What is it that would distinguish them from other nationalities in such a way that their distinctiveness becomes a basis on which they might become economically or culturally useful to New York? Would the answer to this question matter if they were airlifted in one major operation, or if they were carefully brought to New York through a simulation of a migratory process over time? Would they be bringing something

---

Keynote address, conference on Values, Education and Democracy in the 21st Century,
22–24 February 2001, Cape Town

with them, or would they evolve new forms of social practice, remembering mainly their geographic origins instead of compelling memories of the texture of organised social life?

And so it is that, in the calendar of cultural and economic events in New York, many nationalities gather once a year in festivals or carnivals of all sorts to display some essential features of their cultural history. They make statements about themselves through their clothes, their music and dances, their food, their languages, and various other aspects of their culture displayed on floats slowly weaving their way through the streets and attracting crowds of spectators. What would South Africans display about themselves annually through the streets of a world city?

I want to speculate further about our fifty thousand compatriots of various backgrounds finding themselves in New York at this moment. What is it that they would bring to this new environment? Finding themselves in a strange land, it is highly likely that they would rearrange themselves into social groups that offer ready comfort to individuals who immediately recognise themselves as having much in common. Without a doubt, they would rearrange themselves, if only psychologically, into two major subgroups: one white, the other black. Whatever interaction occurs between the two groups by individuals will not be socially significant. It would be no more than the interaction of friends or like-minded people. It does not matter that our immigrants are relocating to a new environment six years after the first democratic elections of 1994. This is how they are likely to start out.

Our compatriots would certainly bring along with them their many languages. It is highly unlikely though, that those whose mother tongue was not English, whose languages do not exercise a strong presence in the South African public discourse on national policy around education, science and technology, commerce and industry, and the law, would exert cultural demands on the public school system. Nor would they embark on a heroic effort to maintain their languages and struggle for their survival through purposeful language transmission to their children. They would not struggle very much to ensure that there was provision for their languages in the school curriculum. They would not establish private schools through which they could ensure that their languages were taught to their children. They may have a political inclination to do so, but they would not be able to marshal a significant social effort to achieve such an objective.

It remains to be seen how much effort they would put, so far from home, into organising celebrations to mark Freedom Day on 27 April of each year. We would have to measure their behaviour in this regard from an assessment of the passion with which the home base marks such a day, and other public holidays. The noticeable diminishing passion with which such days are marked, the further away we move from the historic day of 27 April 1994, might indicate that the political significance of such days has yet to assume a social form with a momentum of its own, independent of its political origins.

Will the Africans in the black sub-group maintain the tradition of choral music with their colourful choirs singing and dancing on the spot? Will the sub-group fracture into ethnicities with Indian and coloured groupings emerging on foreign soil, wondering where they belong? Will the Indian sub-group melt away in New World reconnections in the county of Flushing?

This scenario and the questions it raises are intended to enable us to explore with some detachment the basis of our unity. Can that unity hold outside of the physical borders that compel us to stay together? To the extent that it holds, we might get a handle on the binding factors. To the extent that it cannot hold, we will need to discover factors that bind. This, I think, has been the central quest of this conference. Six years into democracy, we still lack a national consciousness. Our communities still need common values in order to create a unifying framework within which a democracy can operate.

I have speculated before (in 'The Lion and the Rabbit') that in addition to the physical borders that keep us in, forcing us into a national community, there are other potential forces of coherence that may have played a role in preventing us before 1994 from disintegrating into a civil war. We are linked together by a complex network of transportation and telecommunication; by chain stores and banks that we recognise wherever we go; by football teams that have fans across the land; by a calendar of schooling that gets all our children learning together at the same time, and many of us go on holiday when the schools are closed. Such activities impose regularity and predictability and ensure that we are never really too far from one another.

The latest binding factor is our new constitution. It sets out our bill of rights and the instruments of governance, and recognises our rich diversity. In sum, we do seem to have a set of factors in place that have the potential to define us. What we lack is a more compelling social experience of them. What does it take to bring this experience about?

I am mindful of the fact that for black South Africans, in particular, the struggle against apartheid had an immensely unifying effect on those abroad. South Africa dominated their dreams, their conversations, with a passion that bordered on obsession. Our country and the struggle presented themselves as the ultimate justification for being alive. It was a purpose that galvanised enormous energies.

Yet, when I pose questions today ('Who are we?' 'What drives us towards cooperative action?'), silence stares back at me. It is not the silence of emptiness; it is the silence of too much sound yielding little meaning. But these, I believe, are questions we have to answer, not because we, too, may think we need to have festivals and carnivals in foreign lands, but because the questions may force us to reflect on the process we are going through now: the process of becoming, of making sense of all the noises.

The answers might lie in the cycles of daily life in our communities. We need to observe closely what patterns of life yield predictability, offer stability and a sense of purposeful permanence.

The calendar of life in a typical township in the worst days of apartheid was all too short. It was a twenty-four hour calendar. It was designed to obliterate any sense of history beyond yesterday, any sense of the future beyond tomorrow. The township was little more than a dormitory, a place of limited social growth. It was the place to which you retreated to sleep after a long day of working for someone. You relaxed in the evening, and then procreated, and then set off to work again in an unending day-to-day cycle of activity where any experience of predictability was the measure of the day, the week, the month, and the year. There were very few events on a scale that involved communities of people in predictable and purposeful social cooperation of the kind that results in cultural calendars.

Cultural calendars arise when social activity over time evolves common values, common adherence to an evolved discipline of rule and regulation, and socially programmed anticipation that results in planning as a social activity, not something that bureaucrats do to or for people. Cultural calendars produce communal competences. They bring about a sense of predictability and stability. They provide social cohesion and security. From the perspective of the cultural calendar, days, weeks, and months become a series of signposts in the passage of social time, not the purposeless measure of life without value.

I want to reflect on a personal experience, which, it seems to me, speaks to the heart of this problem. Some nine months ago my father passed away at the age of eighty-seven. This is how I approached his death and the funeral ahead. Having been an administrator for many years, I instinctively began to draw a list of to-do's, and an action plan. Despite having lived away from home for many years, I would arrive with my plans and take charge of the situation. I was to be humbled on the third day. A funeral in the township can never be the result of anyone's plan. The bereaved become a mere reference point for a series of activities for which people emerge as if from nowhere to assign themselves tasks. The grave will be dug; the cow will be bought and slaughtered; the cakes will be baked; the home of the bereaved will be cleaned; the prayer meetings will be held; and on the great day of the burial, the mourners will come, and an army of uniformed caterers arrives to cook and feed the multitudes. And when the last of the mourners have departed, the bereaved remain behind exhausted but satisfied, grateful for having been members of the community.

Such social activity around death and burial is a combination of traditional practice and the need to survive in a harsh white world. The social competences of organising a funeral have been acquired and mastered over a long period. Because the occurrence of death cannot normally be predicted, these competences are activated whenever needed. Similarly, social competences of this nature are activated by the announcement of a wedding or some special festivity.

It will be observed that this kind of activity tends to be restricted to specific events that centre on individual families, and galvanise social, largely informal, support systems. While their social value is self-evident, they have yet to evolve effectively towards support for civic, impersonal events beyond the immediate personal dimension. We have yet to see a similar galvanising of social support, for example, for a functioning community school system, or for effective local governance. For these, a civic calendar has to emerge, triggered by the need for a coordinated social response to a series of community-defined needs. For this to happen, the social support systems we have seen will have to evolve from a survivalist orientation towards the positive ownership of the entire social and civic landscape.

This kind of ownership has yet to occur in any significant way. My sense is that we continue to experience the contemporary civic environment as imposed. It has yet to be a space for self-generated social initiatives such as would transform social effort into a series of reproducible, predictable activities that are then transmitted to future generations. We lost this kind of coherence at some point. We need to get it back over time. A civic calendar might look something like: the beginning of the school year; the election of civic leaders; the beginning of the business year of local government; the local trade fair; the sporting seasons; the choral music festival; a multicultural festival; the celebration of national public holidays.

I want to reflect on one more community experience. It concerns my hometown of Duduza, a township that has grown phenomenally in the last twenty years. Indeed, the East Rand townships of KwaThema, Tsakane and Duduza are growing towards one another into a huge mega township. Because of this, the movement of people from one part of the township to another began to be a problem. And here, one of the ways in which the apartheid landscape impacts on our capacity to assess our self-interest manifests itself. My concept of a transportation service is that of a service that takes me away from the township and back. If I want to go from one part of the township to another, I have to walk. A township taxi would not normally perform this service. A transportation system that served internal township transportation needs could not be conceptualised for some time. Of course this had much to do with size.

I am reminded here of an analogous situation: for a long time as a young student I could not conceptualise an African-language-to-African-language dictionary. An African language existed in relation to a European language, into which it was being translated. It was a relationship of dependence. It spawned a service, instrumentalist mentality. In contrast to this, a horizontal relationship between African languages, particularly in an urban setting, promised new possibilities and an enabling sense of autonomy that allowed African languages to grow formally and socially in relation to one another.

To return to Duduza: as the township grew a local taxi service began. Now you can see the small Mazda 232 cars, called *amaphela* (cockroaches), running up and down the streets of Duduza. At first, the established taxi services that use minibuses sought to flex their muscles and run the new service out of business. The community rallied behind the new service. They had recognised a service that considerably enhanced internal mobility, facilitating easier communication. The economic potential for this development, and the impact it could have on other aspects of township life, has not been fully realised. There has yet to evolve a civic culture that is able to capitalise fully on emerging opportunities and enhance the sense of communal autonomy. But what we do have are the makings of an internal economy that ought to be the focus of policy.

What I am attempting to highlight is the social context of values. I want to suggest that at stake is our ability to visualise and establish well functioning communities. The school, economic activity, civic authority and moral institutions form the hub of community life. We have to expose these relationships and rediscover their implications. We ought to be able to recognise forms of social behaviour that result in and embody values celebrated in our constitution. I am attempting to link the community and the school within a framework of social effort that would enable us to reinvent communities.

The beginning of the school year features first in the civic calendar in recognition of the centrality of education in building the ties that bind. More should be made of the first day of school, which involves the entire community in which the school is located. A series of activities building up to that day: acquiring uniforms, books and stationery, registration, etc. are socially cohesive forms of behaviour. Because of poverty and other forms of social dysfunction, purchases of this nature came to be seen as unavoidable commodities rather than as embodiments of responsibility, crucial to the survival of the community.

The schools as public institutions become the focus of the community's local social policy. How many schools should they have? What kinds of schools? How does the community ensure that its schools are adequately resourced? How do they ensure that the school attracts the best teachers possible? What are the languages of the community, and how do the predominant languages impact on the choice of the medium of instruction? What are community preferences in this regard? How does the school curriculum reflect community needs at the same time as it exposes children to national and international issues? How does the community ensure that all children in the community go to school?

The values of tolerance, accountability, equity, multilingualism, openness and dialogue make sense within such a context. It is a context within which we strive to achieve a fit between the formal structures of governance and lived life. I am arguing for an approach to values, education, and democracy that focuses on the building of communities, an approach that can be replicated throughout the land. Values, being inseparable from the social experience of their efficacy, are located there.

But the human landscape in South Africa is complex. How do we achieve bonding across community boundaries in a diverse, multicultural society? Since such boundaries may not necessarily be crossed physically, at least for some time, it is crucial that they be crossed deliberately in other ways. It could be through the curriculum, through the world of work, through the celebration of public holidays in public spaces, through opportunities for diversity to be celebrated. It should be noted here how Ndebele art forms are now 'owned' by most South Africans as a way in which we identify ourselves in the world. Ethnicity-based cultural forms tend to reverberate beyond their ethnic origins. The media infrastructure is most likely responsible for this phenomenon.

If our migrants of the year 2001 are unlikely to survive as a cultural entity in New York, how would those that arrive in 2050 rescue them? Hopefully, the new arrivals will do the things their earlier compatriots would not have been able to do. They will make demands on the public school system. They will make sure that their children learn their languages and their history. They will be known for their open-mindedness and brazen independence, passionate about the values of community life. They will set up restaurants with a South African cuisine. Their musicians will be sought after for the distinctiveness of the South African beat. Once a year they will do what everybody else does back home: come together in a national festival celebrating their diversity. A broad sense of cultural effort will have replaced politics as the single most important and definitive catalyst in value making.

Thabo Mbeki: comradeship, intrigue and betrayal

a vital leadership endgame

2001

While travelling overseas, my attention was captured by a headline in a British newspaper. It read: 'Mbeki launches investigation into assassination plot by ANC rivals'. Immediately below the headline were pictures of Matthews Phosa, Tokyo Sexwale, and Cyril Ramaphosa, all prominent public figures and leaders of the ANC.

I received this news with immediate and total incredulity. Why would these three remarkable men want to do such a thing? It didn't seem possible that they could even have contemplated such infamy. But then their public exposure on television by the minister of safety and security implied that there must be incontrovertible evidence at hand.

My incredulity grew, though, when it turned out, according to the report, that the minister of safety and security, Steve Tshwete, did not specify what the men had done. Even more so when I learned later that the centrepiece of evidence against the troika was testimony by a James Nkambule, a former ANC youth leader in Mpumalanga, who was reported to be facing numerous charges of fraud and had been expelled from the ANC. Meanwhile, Tshwete had called for an end to speculation on this entire matter to allow the investigations to take their course. This came after he had ensured that speculation was rife following his unsubstantiated branding of prominent public figures.

Why was I so resolutely incredulous and agitated? I have come to a preliminary conclusion that this mixture of feelings may be the beginning of a profound sense of disappointment. I have known all along that as we move further away from 27 April 1994 we will become increasingly normal and

---

Cape Argus, 3 May 2001

more ordinary, shedding the well deserved sense of specialness that we earned from our 'miraculous' transition. Nevertheless, I believed we had a choice: we could ensure that as we face the promise and chaos of democratic governance, as we face the prospect of our weaknesses and anxieties being exposed, as we fight our political battles within our parties, as we combat crime and racism, as we grapple with being misunderstood and demonised by a media ethos that is doing right while often armed with the perceptual tools of the past, as we struggle with our human capacity for dishonesty and pride, we will hold on to one thing that might keep our dignity intact. It is that if we should fall, it should not be too far down the scale of ennoblement. If we do slip down, it should be from a failure to succeed in the course of an extraordinary effort to be noble.

I am disappointed that we do not appear to have succeeded in defining the terms of our ordinariness. Our own brand of ordinariness ought to work at a higher level. Has the visionary drive that took us through a difficult transition begun to run aground and lose its energy? Known for our resourcefulness, are we running out of creative options? How quickly can we transform from a visionary into a manipulative State?

In this connection, I am not reassured by President Mbeki's statement: 'The whole topic sounds very dramatic but I'm not worried about it at all.' I cannot avoid the feeling that the president was giving the appearance of playing down something that he knew to be brewing in the national imagination, and that by seeming unconcerned he was deftly distancing himself from an intended effect. At which point I began to feel, as a member of the public, deeply distressed and manipulated.

Supposing it is found that these three men, now exposed and denounced (for the dramatic television exposure does carry with it a heavy implication of denunciation), are found to have in fact been plotting to oust President Mbeki from office, even to the point of planning an assassination. There would be little comfort for the president in such an outcome. The critical question would still remain: why would they have felt driven to such desperate ends?

Furthermore, President Mbeki is reported to have said that people have natural ambitions: 'Some people want to be president of South Africa. That's fine [but] the matter that's arising is the manner in which people pursue their ambitions ... We need to create a space so that all competitors can compete openly.' These are fine sentiments, but it is possible that there could be others who hold the view that not only does such space not exist but that there seems little chance it would ever exist under the circumstances.

Could there be something fundamentally disempowering in the exercise of leadership in the president's office? Is there no adequate vehicle for addressing transparently the important issues of succession? Or, is it possible that the issue may not only be that some people want to be the president of South Africa but also that there may be others who want to be the only president of South Africa within living memory?

God forbid the unthinkable scenario where conditions are being laid for the constitution to be tempered to make it possible for someone to be president of South Africa well into the unforeseeable future. It takes one leader to want to be the sole ruler in sight for a culture of this kind of leadership to sink in and reproduce itself, with devastating consequences for our democracy.

I have always thought that one of the greatest legacies of our struggle against apartheid is the gift of the leaders it bequeathed us. We even created a governance framework to allow for leadership. The provincial and local government models allow for leadership to be developed and expressed such that anyone who becomes a premier of a province or an executive mayor of a municipality or a mega city has the potential to be a minister of government or the president of South Africa.

From this perspective, it should be a source of pride for us that there are so many who have this potential. It should be a necessary aspect of our long-term national security that we have proven leaders in the offing who can be called upon to occupy the country's highest office with distinction.

Seen in this light, it is one of the most important responsibilities and attributes of a president in office to recognise, nurture and protect an inherited leadership asset that is arguably unparalleled in Africa and other parts of the world. We cannot afford to destroy this wealth of gifted people by subjecting them to humiliating denials of leadership ambitions, or by impugning their reputations. To do so in the course of normal political practice constitutes a threat to our long-term national security. Our future depends on our ability to produce and nurture leadership.

When we opted for a negotiated settlement, later to be supported by one of the most admired constitutions in the world, we opted to live and develop mastery in living with difference. In this situation, the disposition that leaders of all kinds bring to office is fundamental to the management of diversity. They must see the talents of others as a resource with which to strengthen their leadership rather than as a threat to be cast aside.

In this kind of complex environment, heroic leadership of the kind vested in a single individual is no longer a viable option. The source of President Mbeki's leadership must surely be the gift of his intellect, arguably a vital source of his authority. Rather than from any tendency to impose control, it will come from his recognition of the merits of talented colleagues who may have a different opinion and style but who willingly support him because they respect the authority of his mind, which remains open to their own contributions.

Our president must allow the authority of his mind, by which he can exercise dispassionate and sound judgement, to take precedence over the attractions of control.

But, from what one hears, the president also brings with him remarkable skills of diplomacy, problem-solving, and an enormous capacity for work. This formidable combination of attributes should make him more than the equal of many, enough for him to be fully confident of managing the demanding talents of others. We should ask for no less from him than that he be true to his gifts.

The endgame to this matter of comradeship, intrigue, and betrayal will be vital. Should investigations absolve the three men from blame and suspicion, their own reaction to such an outcome will either make or unmake them. It would be unwise to gloat and push the president into a humiliating corner. By the same token, if they are found to have been involved in illegal or unethical intrigue, the president will need to respond with such wisdom as will take us out of an extremely dangerous path.

One would hope that all these tested veterans of struggle and negotiation will opt for a truce out of which will emerge a covenant that restores creative leadership to the centre of our national life. We must triumph over the temptations of manipulative politics by restoring trust and confidence in the abilities of our leaders to take us, despite ourselves, towards the new politics and a future that makes us better human beings.

The 'Black' Agenda and South Africa's Universities

some sobering thoughts

2002

Reflecting on the making of his film *Lumumba*, the director Raoul Peck makes an interesting statement: 'I belong,' he says, 'to a reality that's shared by many Third World nations: we are not in control of our collective memory.' I saw in this statement an unexpected connection between the report of the National Working Group on University Mergers and the so-called 'black' response to it.

The reaction to the national working group's report has resulted in some tension within the higher education sector. It is a tension that replays apartheid's historic fault lines. It is not unlikely that part of the reaction of most black academics and education leaders, as reflected in the media, has something to do with the sense of powerlessness Raoul Peck describes. While that condition may be understandable, it could also be a fatal indulgence in South Africa today.

I begin from my understanding that all universities in apartheid South Africa were white institutions. This speaks not to the colour-coded categories of human bodies that were required by law to go to and congregate at their designated institutions. It speaks, more fundamentally, to the dreadful politics that brought those institutions into being in our country. They were all part of the long and complex history of colonialism and white supremacy in South Africa.

In the post-April 1994 environment, where political agency has shifted from 'white' to 'black', black people now in power carry the ultimate responsibility for the success or failure of higher education in South Africa. It is in carrying out that responsibility that they cannot avoid having to make difficult decisions.

The negotiated nature of our transition to democracy ensured that there was no violent overthrow of the old order by a new one. As a result, many political, social, economic, and educational institutions were inherited intact by the new order. The goal of changing them to reflect new and urgent national realities called for a resort to various strategies that depended on prevailing conditions at respective institutions. Many factors determined the pace and quality of change.

Often, agents of change at an institution are confronted by the continuing momentum of institutional culture that was set in place long before they came onto the scene. What elements of that culture are they willing to retain, which ones should be cast away? These are questions they face daily. Sometimes, the changes they succeed in bringing about are dramatic, but more often they are slow. This is a common experience across the higher education sector.

Knowing this enables agents of change to devise transformation strategies that respond to the local environment at the same time as they endeavour to measure the impact of their efforts against progress in the rest of the sector and, beyond that, environmental changes in the rest of the country. The common denominator, however, must be consolidation and deepening of the 'black' interest in the national life of South Africa.

If this understanding makes any sense, then all South Africa's universities are in the process of becoming 'black'. By 'black' I am again not referring to human colour coding, but to the historic centring of the majority interest in national life. And it is that interest that is the driver of a national transformation project. To ensure success in the transitional short to medium term, it makes a great deal of sense to pay particular attention to the legacy of available strengths rather than a legacy of weaknesses.

This approach locates the central challenge of historically white institutions. Their contemporary relevance lies in their ability to address with conviction how the majority interest informs the content of their primary mandate: building on some of their inherited strengths to provide the highest possible quality of education for our new democracy.

This point is made from the perspective that it is not too difficult to see that, in general, our academic strengths are, with a few exceptions, not located in historically black institutions. It is not, therefore, in the universal interest of the black majority to seek to destroy existing strengths, merely because of their historic location, in the understandable desire to create new ones. To do so would simply be suicidal. This point, the national working group's report makes very clearly.

As a political duty, in the 1980s and early 1990s, many historically disadvantaged institutions admitted inordinately large numbers of black students to broaden access. The resulting pressures on infrastructure, teaching and administrative capacity were enormous. With the promise of liberation in the offing, it was not unreasonable for these institutions to have expected they would be rewarded with massive redress funding by the new democracy.

Unfortunately, the combination of infrastructural decay and unrelenting student and worker activism on many campuses resulted in almost permanent damage to the academic capacity of many institutions. The sudden deracialisation of the entire higher education sector led to dramatic drops in enrolment in historically disadvantaged institutions and to an accentuation of their negative image. Lastly, competing national agendas around health, housing, primary education, etc., heightened the competition for scarce financial resources.

The fact is, historically disadvantaged institutions have, in the main, failed in the last seven years to define and effect radical internal institutional changes such as would have seen them discover and embrace new intellectual and academic commitments. This failure is not a judgment but a descriptive reality.

It is reasonable to assert that the combination of a history of political activism on many 'black' campuses and the continuation of an educational environment perceived to be comparatively substandard continues to wreak havoc on those campuses' ability to turn the situation round. This combination resonated with a vengeance recently when some vice chancellors of historically disadvantaged institutions threatened to take to the streets once more in response to the report of the national working group. Resorting to the mobilising power of mass action ironically accentuated the vice chancellors' powerlessness. The substitution of street activism for intellectual leadership did not augur well for those institutions.

What we have then is not only the failure of institutional redress to materialise, but also the failure of the institutions concerned to demonstrate that resources will not continue to be wasted on institutions that have yet to succeed or reveal any real potential to become places of serious scholarship.

At issue here is not merely a question of resources or capacity but also a certain condition of futility. This condition is seldom acknowledged and confronted squarely.

More significantly, the fact that they continue to market themselves as historically disadvantaged means that these institutions are unwittingly indulging in negative branding. Students of today and of the future will want to associate themselves with positive effort and new institutional identities.

Of course, not all historically disadvantaged institutions fall into this picture. Some continue to make heroic efforts, and are recording some significant successes. They need to be rewarded. Others show no signs of change. They may need to be closed, in the form in which they currently operate, that the freed sites of learning may be used in new ways to meet pressing education needs.

The lesson in all this is that if the black interest, as I have defined it, is not mainstreamed and projected nationally, beyond individual institutions, it will only retreat into numerous ghettoes. I am certain that many will agree that the black interest has definitively gone beyond the ghetto.

If we come with such a perspective, then the current higher education environment becomes amenable to a creative reordering into various configurations. And here we confront the central weakness of the report of the national working group. It prescribes mergers as a one-size-fits-all solution. In reality, its brief should have been much broader.

The logic I have been exploring is simple: if the historically white institutions are perceived, from a certain 'black' perspective, not to be ideal places for meeting and satisfying 'black' education needs, then historically black institutions are in an even worse position.

It makes very good sense to consolidate our efforts where our current strengths lie. The result might be that historically white institutions evolve hybrid cultures, and become increasingly diverse, without necessarily offering definitively new directions but striving towards them as a condition for defining their relevance. Whatever the case might be, *for now we have to accept their indispensability*. To do otherwise is to bury our heads in the sand.

Every major historic era builds its kind of university. The different phases of white supremacy in South Africa produced their kinds of institutions. Some institutions have been so successful in carrying out their political mandate that few traditions of serious teaching and research of special significance have survived in them. This is so despite any heroic political role they may have played in the struggle for liberation.

All of which leads us to an interesting speculative question. When, if need be, will the new democracy see its new public university? Can it come out of the ashes of apartheid's institutional tragedies? Can thinking creatively about the possibility of such a university pull us out of some of our current conceptual traps?

For now, if there are many who feel 'not in control of their collective memory', they may wish to consider the wisdom of at least being in control of the means of getting to that phase where they will be in control. In my view, those means do not include embracing current weaknesses at the expense of current strengths, for that would only ensure that they remain not in control in perpetuity.

AIDS and the Making of
Modern South Africa

responding to a pandemic in a time of complexity

2002

During the long years of exile when Oliver Reginald Tambo built the external wing of the ANC into a formidable organisation with worldwide respect, he developed an intriguing relationship, in the popular imagination, with his peer in prison, Nelson Mandela. While Mandela, although imprisoned and stowed away, represented a future desperately hoped for, Tambo represented the complex realities of unfolding possibility. And while the release of Mandela signalled the arrival of the future, our historic election of 1994 signalled the achievement of effort embodied in Tambo. Hope and the possibilities of effort converged into historic triumph. Tambo's work was done, and Mandela began an entirely new journey of actualising the future.

The world has become a very dangerous place to live in, particularly in the last six months. With war drums beating a discordant note in a world thirsty for peace and security, friendship between peoples and countries around the world with shared values is something to be preserved, nurtured, protected, and celebrated. In this regard, we must stand firm against countries that glorify war. The world must never be intimidated by images of overwhelming, state of the art, military might. Such might, we should never forget, is an inferior asset in the total value and moral scheme of the world today. It belongs on the bottommost rung of the very last, if primitive, resort. That is why Oliver Tambo's level-headedness, conciliatory approach, and integrative vision should more than ever be remembered, affirmed and invoked.

Oliver Tambo Memorial Lecture, Dublin, Ireland, 21 October 2002. The lecture is organised annually by the Irish-South African Society.

I write on this difficult topic for a number of reasons. First, subjecting myself, if with somewhat of a taste for self-inflicted suffering, to the pressure of having offered to speak on it, I saw this topic and the occasion of this lecture as offering me an opportunity to reflect personally, with much more focused intent, on the meaning of AIDS to South Africa.

There is inherent risk in this. I am not medically trained to speak authoritatively on the subject. That being the case, and given the range of national controversies on the issue in South Africa, I also saw this opportunity and challenge as an occasion for me to reflect on how one might interpret the responsibilities of citizenship in a new democracy such as ours. The tension, as I see it, is between notions of truth and advocacy, on the one hand, and, on the other, the capacity of those notions to expose fault lines that can induce a sense of vulnerability to fracture in a nation that still deeply craves compliance, ostensibly voluntary, to a unifying consensus on the radical project of nation building.

To reflect on this topic is to reflect on, among other things, how currents in world opinion see a particular country; how that country sees itself; and how it, in turn, sees the world. Expectations flow in both directions. Sometimes they coincide; sometimes they diverge, or are poised in opposition. It is to stare also at the heart of contemporary global tension: the complex interplay between global and local interests.

I want to pick up on the metaphor of the relationship between Tambo and Mandela: the creative tension between the drive for the future and the challenges of an unfolding reality that is often difficult, even impossible, to anticipate. This metaphor is at the heart of South Africa's struggles with the present in anticipation of the future. It is about how notions of the future legitimise or delegitimise strategies for solving current problems. It is at the heart of how we understand and build our democracy. The heated, often painful, ebbs and flows of controversies around the AIDS pandemic in South Africa have revealed in interesting ways the dynamics of our transition to democracy, captured in this metaphor.

The euphoria began with the release of Nelson Mandela and peaked on 27 April 1994 when all South Africans who could vote, voted for the first time. 'A Better Life For All' was the ANC's election slogan. With the election of the ANC, South Africa saw its first truly democratically elected government in its entire history come into power. The future had arrived. The provincial system of governance and its local authorities would kick in, ensuring broad citizen participation in democratic governance. Houses would be built for the homeless. Land, unjustly expropriated from the oppressed, would be reclaimed. The early years of schooling would be free. Jobs would be created. The newly enfranchised black citizens would enter the economy at higher levels. The rights of workers would be protected. Access by the black citizens to the country's best institutions of higher learning would be accelerated. Above all, pregnant mothers would receive free medical attention. Through primary health care, clinics would be built all over the country to ensure universal access to health services. Indeed, the end of the struggle for liberation signalled the beginning of another, potentially more difficult, more daunting struggle: to make the future happen.

All systems were set to go until AIDS, hovering rather uncertainly at the periphery of the national consciousness, reared its head, threatening extinction at the *very* moment that freedom affirmed life and promised infinite possibility. By 1989, ANC exiles who would be returning home soon had begun to be anxious. They had seen the disease wreak havoc in some of the countries of their exile in Africa. That is why, in 1990, the organisation convened an AIDS conference in Maputo. Chris Hani, head of the ANC's guerrilla forces, Umkhonto we Sizwe, who was assassinated by white supremacists in 1993, encapsulated the looming anxiety in the collective imagination of an organisation poised to make the future happen. 'We cannot afford,' he said, 'to allow the AIDS epidemic to ruin the realisation of our dreams.'

Other ANC initiatives followed. In particular, the party, now in government, assembled an advisory panel headed by current minister of foreign affairs, Dr Nkosazana Zuma, to devise 'an AIDS plan for the new government'. More wish list than blueprint, it prescribed $64 million worth of education programmes, mass media campaigns, free condoms and support programmes for patients with HIV. It recommended the creation of a national AIDS commission, modelled in part on an approach in Uganda that was then beginning to be hailed as a success. The anti-AIDS effort would be run from the president's office 'to give it a high profile and bureaucratic authority with government ministries such as the labour department, which would be more likely to accept direction on strategies in the workplace for dealing with HIV'. This was in 1993.

A year later, a controversy raged in the country about an AIDS awareness play contracted by Dr Zuma, then minister of health, to the tune of R3 million. The efficacy of this particular initiative was not only doubted, even given the relatively small budget of Dr Zuma's department of health, but government contracting procedures were, allegedly, circumvented. Nor did Dr Zuma, it would seem, seek the advice of independent AIDS activists and professional actors and playwrights experienced in community awareness campaigns. This was also one of the first major controversies in the new democracy to highlight the problem of a predominantly white-owned media taking to task a new black government.

But this was not all. There was to be yet another controversy. In January 1997, South Africans got to know that three white researchers in Pretoria claimed to have discovered a drug called Virodene that could cure AIDS. The claims on behalf of this drug, including references to patients said to have been cured, were reported in South African newspapers. So dramatic was this 'discovery' that Dr Zuma prevailed on the cabinet to receive a briefing from the three researchers.

The magic cure had come, discovered nowhere else but in South Africa, a new democracy that came into being having defied all predictions of violent disintegration. The miracle of the peaceful birth of a new democracy, inspiring the entire world, would be followed by the miracle of a cure for AIDS that would indeed ensure 'A Better Life For All'. Not only would South Africa inspirationally contribute to world peace through its peaceful political transition but this remarkable new country, led by a responsible government, would also save the world from a devastating pandemic: AIDS.

It was not to be. The researchers were found by the South African Medicines Control Council not to have used proper procedures to establish the efficacy of the drug. Furthermore, it was discovered 'that its active agent was an industrial solvent'. The miracle drug was totally discredited. Quarraisha Karim, the first director of South Africa's national AIDS programme, seeks to describe the underlying politics, the psychology, and sociology behind the drama of this drug, when noting that: 'There was this sense that this drug would be the thing that offset the perception ... of Africans as substandard and less than capable. All eyes were upon [the ANC] and the expectations were very high and they were really trying to find their feet but they didn't want to exercise caution. This was driven by this need to show the world: "Yes, Africans can do this. We can do this." Virodene became our redemption.'

What this brief narrative shows is that the ANC's concern about AIDS pre-dates the new democracy, prior to their becoming a government. They recognised its potentially devastating effects on South Africa. It is clear to me that it would make no sense to evaluate the behaviour of the ANC towards the pandemic outside of the history of its heroic ascendance to power, and its desire to prove that it was doing everything possible to fight the disease and establish its bona fides to a hopeful population. Making the dream of freedom real is an understandably compelling motive force.

There was no black South African in those early years of the new democracy who did not walk with an upright and sprightly gait in a new world of infinite possibility. In this regard, the disappointment around Virodene introduced, very early on in the life of this new democracy, one of the first reality principles. While governance procedures for inducting new parliamentarians, new provincial authorities, the new cabinet and the new president were spectacular events conducted in public and embodying and celebrating the heroism of ascendance to power, contracting procedures and the testing of medicines represented the intricate, rigorous, if mundane and unspectacular, aspects of governance. They had to absorb the reality that compliance to detail could make or unmake a government. This salutary experience of an entire government was to be replicated in many new black entrants into the opportunities and traps of corporate life, too quickly judged as corruption.

In retrospect, while the noise in the white-controlled media could justifiably be regarded as racist in its underlying perspectives, it was nevertheless quite correct for it to hold a relatively inexperienced government to account on the key issues at hand. Any suspicions of underlying racism should not obscure the cardinal virtue of reminding government of its responsibility to prescribed process. An unrestrained and unreflective spirit of heroism could easily eat into the fibre of good intentions and steadily, over time, degenerate into incipient incompetence and corruption. Indeed, heroic discretion, time bound and event specific, and exercised under a sense of political entitlement, can engender its own momentum and introduce a regime of corrosive randomness.

174

But while certain aspects of the exercise of journalistic questioning were useful, South African media also inserted into the public domain a virus of bias and distrust of the new order that replicated itself in the body politic in geometric progression. Lacking an appropriate context against which to formulate an objective assessment of the performance of the new government, the media initially portrayed the minister of health, Dr Nkosazana Zuma, as a bungler. This strategy was useful because Mandela himself was untouchable. On his departure, Thabo Mbeki was to bear the brunt of criticism directly. Moreover, this criticism was then distributed to his entire cabinet. If everything below Mandela was wrong, then everything below Mbeki was wrong, beginning with him. In no time, the image of a government of bunglers combating AIDS gained currency and lingered like a bad smell around anything that Mbeki and his government tried to do.

I believe it was this perception that influenced Mbeki's rhetorical strategies in his April 2000 letter to world leaders on AIDS in Africa. The letter opens with a painstaking documentation of the many initiatives and strategies adopted by the ANC government since its election in 1994. It is a sustained, if pained, effort to underscore bona fides, to demonstrate concern, political commitment, and planned intervention. It had little effect. The virus of bias and distrust, working in the manner of economist Brian Arthur's principle of increasing returns, had overwhelmed media rationality. The social virus of bias and distrust took on the characteristics of mass prejudice reminiscent of the hunt for the witches of Salem, recreated by Arthur Miller in *The Crucible*. What I am referring to here is the mass condition of irrationality, where irrationality becomes its own logic, a perverse reality that feeds on itself.

The principle of media vigilance over government behaviour, eminently vital on its own, was a useful façade of rationality behind which lurked rearguard anxieties over loss of power by a once dominant social order, where those that once thrived in it felt vulnerable, uncertain, and insecure about the future, and were still in control of the means of reflecting, commenting on, and influencing the formation of public perceptions and opinions.

The departure of Mandela exacerbated these anxieties. Ironically, foreigners, particularly Europeans and North Americans, enthralled by a country declared 'an example to the whole world', did not take kindly to a bungling fool who had stepped into Mandela's 'giant shoes' and was busy destroying their image of a country once ruled by a noble figure. Mbeki, an ordinary, specific African, who, relatively unknown, replaced Mandela, the universal black man, was seen as a disconcerting symbol of risk.

What does one make of disparaging comments about Mbeki's surfing the internet for information? *Time* magazine reports: 'Mbeki is believed to have encountered "dissident" thinking ... during a late-night Web-browsing session, and it's hardly surprising that he may have been searching for an intellectual escape route from the implications of his country's nightmare.' 'Believed'? Lack of specificity on an issue that can be confirmed as either true or false leaves us hanging in the domain of rumour and damaging innuendo. A single encounter, 'during a late-night Web-browsing session' leaves us with a picture of random, drowsy stupidity. The article then drives the point home: 'There's certainly something to be said for Mbeki's vigorous intellectual independence. He won't be told what to do by anyone.'

'But what is the best way to respond to Mbeki, or indeed to any non-expert who endorses a contrarian scientific position?' asks the sober voice of Steven Epstein writing in the *Washington Post*:

> The problem is that to pose the question dismissively – 'Why don't those ignorant people simply accept the conventional wisdom endorsed by the vast majority of experts?' – misses an important point: Throughout the history of the AIDS epidemic non-experts have challenged expert pronouncements about AIDS – not always for the better.
>
> Patients, sometimes scouring the internet much like Mbeki, have confronted their own doctors with printouts of cutting-edge research that the physicians didn't always know about. Activists, with no formal schooling in virology or statistics but with a hard-won, seat-of-the-pants grasp of scientific principle, have pressed for changes in the design of clinical trials that have led to the enrolling of more patients. People are becoming less inclined to embrace an unthinking obedience to the authority of experts; the very bound-aries between non-scientists and experts are becoming harder to pin down. At least in areas like medical research, where scientists pronounce on topics as intimate as our own bodies, we should expect – and, I would argue, respect – the active participation of the

uncredentialed. In this regard, simply to dismiss Mbeki's foray into medical topics is problematic and unhelpful.

Steven Epstein ponders on a crucial contemporary reality. The internet, the great contemporary leveller, has profoundly democratised access to knowledge. Why shouldn't a president of a country who, in exercising his/her responsibility to govern wisely, not surf the internet to extend his own store of knowledge and information so that he can develop informed views, from the front, about one of the twenty-first century's greatest phenomena: AIDS? Why shouldn't such a president pose Socratic ironies? Presidents, we are told, must act and not intellectualise, particularly when people are dying. But surely AIDS must be the ultimate disease of the post-modern world. It must arguably be the most knowledge-intensive disease that has, in an unprecedented manner, galvanised the world's best scientific minds. But it is precisely for this reason, unfortunately, that it cannot be left to scientists alone. For AIDS is the disease of theologians, priests, lawyers, judges, philosophers, linguists, sociologists, anthropologists, historians, musicians, novelists, journalists, economists, environmentalists, urban planners, policy makers in every area of human endeavour – and of politicians.

I have searched for the definitive statement by Mbeki in which he denies the link between HIV and AIDS. I have not found it. What I have found are statements that go beyond the implications of this link, probing for the implications of a deductive relationship between the link and certain curative strategies. References are made to Mbeki's evasiveness when asked direct questions about this link. What I have found is not evasiveness, but, rather, a steadfast and intelligent refusal to be trapped in a web of unstated assumptions behind the questions of an interviewer who already had an answer to his own question; a refusal to be the object of a desire to get him to recant fallacies he had not proclaimed.

In his letter to a head of state, which apparently embarrassed the Clinton government, and angered influential elements in the American public, Mbeki makes some undeniable statements:

> [A]s Africans we have to deal with this uniquely African catastrophe [in] that: ·

- contrary to the West, HIV-AIDS in Africa is heterosexually transmitted;
- contrary to the West, where relatively few people have died from AIDS, itself a matter of serious concern, millions are said to have died in Africa; and
- contrary to the West, where AIDS deaths are declining, even greater numbers of Africans are destined to die.

It is obvious that whatever lessons we have to and may draw from the West about the grave issue of HIV-AIDS, a simple superimposition of Western experience on African reality would be absurd and illogical ... I am convinced that our urgent task is to respond to the specific threat that faces us as Africans. We will not eschew this obligation in favour of the comfort of the recitation of a catechism that may very well be a correct response to the specific manifestation of AIDS in the West.

I make these comments because our search for these specific and targeted responses is being stridently condemned by some in our country and the rest of the world as constituting a criminal abandonment of the fight against HIV-AIDS.

I cannot find anything to seriously quarrel with in Mbeki's reasoning here. Isn't his a call for creativity in dealing with the manifestations of a disease in a specific context, compared to its different manifestations in another context? Surely, this is commonsense. So where is the problem? It must be that dominance can impose its own forms of blindness on those living within its protective universe. It must be that the latter context just referred to is located at the centre of political and scientific authority, which decrees hegemonically that the world shall be known according to that authority's own laws of perception and reasoning.

It could also be that a cure that comes from a drug means that the drug has to be manufactured and sold. Where, far off in a continent of dark people languishing in poverty and disease, there are millions of potential buyers seeking to ward off death, a drug can be an infinitely lucrative business – so lucrative and so morally problematic that the moral and ethical dilemmas at play are too stark to be squarely faced. Blame and demonisation

178

can be resorted to as tactical diversions. Power can metamorphose into truth, and truth into power. The lesson seems to be that the authority of science, ensconced within certain regimes of politics and economics, can also be deployed imperialistically, even at the expense of its most prized methodologies.

I am not the only one to have had doubts about certain aspects of the onslaught against Mbeki. Susan Rice, US assistant secretary of state, in response to Mbeki's letter reasoned in the *Washington Post* that:

> It was clearly impassioned in parts, but I thought much of its substance was quite logical and quite compelling. I mean, he clearly acknowledges the severity of the HIV-AIDS problem in Africa and in South Africa in particular, and he goes through a persuasive description of the efforts that have been undertaken by his administration ... I don't read Mbeki's intent as trying to pit south versus north on the issue. He's making a pretty simple point, which is 'This is a hell of a serious problem for Africa, and we don't want to be constrained in the universe of solutions that are available to us.'

This is what I saw too, or understood. I did not see Mbeki as expressing a preference for the dissident view, only a desire to understand more its possible implications for a broader strategy. Nor did I sense a rejection of the predominant view. What I did record then, as I do now, is someone seriously articulating and acknowledging complexity, and a desire to understand it and its full implications. What is wrong with this? Why should such a desire evoke so much controversy?

President Mbeki established an AIDS advisory panel. His method was painfully scientific. If you want to understand an issue as fully as possible, bring together people with contrasting views. This does not mean that you accept any of the views before hand. To do so, would be to prejudge the issue and undermine the value of your methodology. You suspend judgement in order to create conditions designed to produce more data. In the case of the panel, because Mbeki included those declared dissidents with discredited views, he was himself declared a dissident, or was said to be giving credence to dissidents.

I took some time to read the report of the panel. It is interesting to contrast the recommendations of the two camps on the panel. The initial proposals are as follows:

> Recommendations from panelists who do not subscribe to the causal linkage between HIV and AIDS:
>
> It was recommended that the South African government commit to the following:
>
> 1. Suspend the dissemination of the psychologically destructive and false message that HIV infection is invariably fatal and assist in reducing the 'hysteria' surrounding HIV and AIDS
> 2. Suspend all HIV testing until its relevance is proved, especially in the African context, given the evidence of false positive results in the tropical setting and the fact that most assumptions and predictions about AIDS in Africa are based on HIV tests
> 3. Continue to improve social conditions in South Africa
> 4. Continue to decrease poverty
> 5. Continue to control infections and sexually-transmitted diseases
> 6. Continue to increase the nutritional status of the population.
>
> Dr Gayle and Prof Abdool-Karim, representing panelists who endorse the causal link between HIV and AIDS, reinforced the importance of the following initiatives for the South African government:
>
> 1. Continue strengthening the surveillance of risk factors such as the behaviour of youth
> 2. Surveillance of HIV prevalence in antenatal clinics, blood banks and among workers
> 3. Conducting incidence surveys
> 4. AIDS surveillance at health facilities
> 5. Keeping death registers
> 6. Standardisation and evaluation of diagnostic criteria and their completeness for reporting purposes
> 7. Surveillance of antenatal syphilis
> 8. Laboratory reporting
> 9. Health facility reporting.

I find the contrast between these recommendations most fascinating. They are a study in the contrast between bold advocacy of the unconventional, on the one hand, and the confident prescription of known rules, on the other; between broad social awareness and specific disciplinary focus; between imagination and expertise; between politics and scientific procedure; between intuition and rule. Neither of these opposites carries inherent value. The relevance of each is contextual.

But I got something else from the report. I came away with a view that the HIV-AIDS causality argument actually presents us with a high probability scenario. High probability is not definitive. It suggests the high expectation and predictability of a certain outcome. The key point is that such high predictability can be reasonable grounds for a government policy to be developed and implemented to combat a pandemic, despite the existence of some data deployed by the 'dissidents' that denies definitiveness and closure to a high probability scenario.

This latter data, because of the power of a high probability scenario, may be found to be a nuisance to the dominance and currency of the statistically winning scenario. In the context of power play, its conclusions may even be declared heretical. It is in the potential for this situation to reverse power relations in the light of how history may play itself out that leads Umberto Eco to posit the notion of the 'force of the false' in opposition to 'the force of truth.'

'To demonstrate that the false,' he writes in his book *Serendipities: Language and Lunacy*, '(not necessarily as in the form of lies but surely in the form of error) has motivated many events in history, I should rely on a criterion of truth. But if I were to choose it too dogmatically, I would risk ending my argument at the *very* moment I begin it.' Thus, support for a dominant view is potentially vulnerable to the charge of gullibility. This is particularly so when the dominant scientific view takes convenient refuge in philosophical positions that can be deployed in the service of political advocacy.

Thus a dominant scientific view can assume the constitutional correctness of its position under 'freedom of expression' where the scientist who holds the view perceives that there is a political threat to that value. That is why scientists can often be tempted to admonish politicians to stick to politics and leave science to scientists: a profound denial of free speech to politicians who may have a different view about scientific findings and the power of those findings to define truth and influence political action. A scientist of liberal orientation may assail a politician of the 'new' South African order for questioning a scientific view, because that very questioning may raise doubts in the mind of a liberal scientist about the competence of that politician to govern. Black politicians who have the guts to question the findings of advanced science may be deemed a danger to democracy. The scientist, at that particular moment, confuses his/her role as a scientist with the role of being a citizen. In the former role, he must endeavour to explain, and explain, and explain: in the latter, he must declare his interest.

The methodological desire to provide irrefutable outcomes may be the object of experimental science, but there is ample evidence to suggest that such irrefutable outcomes are not only not always possible but that where they may occur their validity is not immune to collapse in the face of new evidence. Thus, acceptance of a finding as true, even in experimental science, is not entirely free from the need for the kind of humility that emanates from recognition that definitive closure around our understanding of natural phenomena is not always possible.

This recognition requires that we approach the quest for new knowledge with a mandatory open-mindedness and generosity of spirit.

Early this year, I invited a small group of academics at UCT to help me think through the AIDS crisis in South Africa. Like many South Africans, I found the controversy around the pandemic confusing and painful. I presented to this multidisciplinary group a series of problems and questions I had been asking myself, in no logical order of importance. These questions indicate the nature and extent of my own agonies.

I list them from the document I prepared, presenting them as issues that may turn out to be some of the defining features of our time.

- HIV/AIDS has been designated an 'unnotifiable disease'. This was deemed desirable, it would appear, in order to protect the human rights of an HIV positive person, who could be subjected to various forms of discrimination if his/her condition were known. The question here is: how do we balance the rights of the individual against the broad societal right to information about the probable extent of a pandemic whose potential long-range

impact on the capacity of nations to survive is deemed to
be immense? The extent of the impact is sometimes described in
apocalyptic terms. Some highly influential commentators have
gone so far as to describe it as a major security issue of the day.
But, how do we make an informed and accurate assessment of the
extent and impact of the pandemic?

- This matter seems related to the issue of reporting AIDS-related
  deaths. It would appear that most doctors mention only the direct,
  immediate cause of death, even though the primary reason may
  have been that HIV/AIDS had so weakened the immune systems of
  the body that reportable causes of death took fatal advantage of the
  situation. What are the probable effects of this requirement on
  doctors, on our capacity to study and know the pandemic? Is there
  any probable threat to scientific enquiry? Are doctors not being put
  in an ethically invidious position?

- Furthermore, from my layman's reading of the recent Medical
  Research Council report on HIV/AIDS prevalence, it seems
  possible to argue that HIV/AIDS does not constitute a major and
  serious threat to society because the prevalence statistics, based
  on the reporting restrictions on HIV/AIDS-related deaths, could
  be read to indicate as such.

On balance, it is difficult to avoid the sense of a society (despite its
admirably enlightened view on human rights) burying its head in
the sand. Does the right to confidentiality, where millions of people
have the same problem, not translate into public hypocrisy? Does
not such confidentiality reinforce stigma? Will the stigma not
dissipate with public acknowledgement and acceptance of overwhelming threat?

Now that I have mentioned the MRC report, another thought
related to it crosses my mind. During the controversy around this
report involving the government, the MRC and AIDS activists, it
became difficult for me to separate methodological questions
around statistical modelling from arguments over administrative
procedures regulating relationships between the government and
publicly-funded research agencies. Allegations of impropriety

around the 'leaking of the report' became clouded with debates around the scientific validity of the report, prompting the question of who validates scientific results. Is it politicians or scientific peers? At some point, the conduct of Statistics South Africa became a matter of concern for me. In the middle of an atmosphere of political clamour, Statistics South Africa's public criticism of a scientific report made them seem to be taking a political position in support of 'their' government. The potential danger to science here was manifest. The credibility of SSA was threatened by its perceived political conduct, in which it could be interpreted to have been attempting to cast doubt on the credibility of its target, a scientific report, by non-scientific means.

Both the SSA and the MRC stood to lose considerably from these incidents. Serious questions need to be asked around the nature of relationships between publicly-funded, knowledge-producing institutions, which also serve government. How do they navigate between scientific and political seas?

One consequence of SSA's seemingly political intervention was to allow doubt to be cast on the scientific credibility of researchers, two of whom were from UCT. The potential for the interference of politics in teaching and research at a university became an issue of serious concern for me. I did not see, though, a deliberate intention on the part of government, to interfere. There was nothing in its conduct that suggested the threat of a major philosophical shift on such matters. Rather, the political urgency of the moment may have produced behavioural reactions whose probable side effects, if not checked, could solidify into behavioural attitudes with corrosive effects over time.

- *The Sunday Independent* editorial of 4 February 2002 bears the heading: 'ANC AIDS policy defies reason!' The issue under its scrutiny is the supplying of Nevirapine to HIV-positive pregnant women. Indeed, if this drug has been found to be effective, why is the ANC government not making it easily available? What are the government's central arguments on this issue? It is in my attempts to find answers to these questions that things seem to get clouded. Depending on what one reads, the drug has been

184

tested, or it has not. It may be very toxic, or it may not. The associated issue of the efficacy or otherwise of breastfeeding may be decisive, or it may not. Health Service infrastructure may be adequate or it may not. What is the actual position? If the drug has not been properly tested internationally, in all these contexts, then the government's hesitance in having the drug distributed widely would not be entirely unreasonable.

- One is also puzzled about the situation concerning the treatment of AIDS sufferers – are we not in an obvious national emergency, analogous to the anthrax crisis recently in North America? Can we not produce anti-retrovirals at lowest cost as a national effort, and treat all patients according to best practice? Would this not decrease the rate of new infections? Is it really not possible to do this with the available infrastructure and patient support? Has Brazil succeeded in this, or not?

- The controversy around the distribution of this drug also brings up in newspapers serious ethical charges on this issue against President Mbeki's leadership.

For example, President Mbeki, who appears to have read extensively on HIV/AIDS, is portrayed as someone who ought to stick to politics, and to leave scientists and AIDS activists alone. Moreover, he is portrayed as thinking that the devastation that HIV/AIDS purportedly wreaks on Africa is no more than a racist plot to maintain the image of Africa as a diseased, backward continent. Once this image has been restated and reinforced, he seems to think, multinational drug companies can position themselves to make enormous profits on the sufferings of a despised continent. Is that what Mbeki really thinks? If so, what arguments does he marshal to support such a position?

What has President Mbeki actually said about the connection between HIV and AIDS?

What has led to the image of an uncaring leader who intellectualises in the face of death? The political behaviour of Mbeki as a leader has become a central public focus.

Two images of a leader have emerged against which his behaviour is explained and evaluated. One of them is that of Mbeki as a

Coriolanus figure driven to his own destruction by a tragic dog-gedness. The other is the image of a Joan of Arc driven by notions of divine conscription, who has been sent to South Africa to rescue the country with his gift of intellect. He intellectualises while South Africa dies, convinced that his truth will one day be appreciated and South Africa saved, if there is anyone alive to be saved.

The sum total of these images is a picture of an insensitive leader who is either wilfully or naively presiding over the death of his people.

How accurate is such a picture? How do we go about assessing its accuracy? Has the picture itself been sufficiently scrutinised? What social or political conditions produce such pictures of political leaders?

Whose story do such pictures tell? Could they also be telling us more about the creators of the images than about the subject of their portraits? If, as a result of his extensive reading and thinking on the issue, Mbeki comes to the conclusion that it does not make sense for health workers and activists to focus on a single aspect of a disease which has a complex range of possible causes, is he wrong? Is he being 'worked on' by a clique of clever manipulators?

Yet another question! Could President Mbeki be faced with a genuine leadership dilemma? It could be framed in the following way: 'If I allow Nevirapine to be distributed according to popular demand, people may die because the drug is really untested. If I don't allow it, people will still die, because they will not have taken the drug and the disease will take its course.' Either way there are severe ethical costs. How genuine is this dilemma? Is the 'we can't afford the orphans' allegation really serious?

- These days there are unconfirmed reports that this matter is causing a serious rift within the ANC as well as within the tripartite alliance. There is a change of heart in the offing, we are told. This seemed confirmed by Mandela's comments the day before President Mbeki's state-of-the-nation address to Parliament earlier this year. But the president's address indicated no such change of heart. Instead, what emerged from his state-of-the-nation address was his now characteristic insistence on the need for a more complex approach to the AIDS pandemic. Are these rumours the wishful thoughts of the media? Are they capable of being confirmed or denied?

- Finally, how do the various manifestations of HIV/AIDS in South Africa reveal signs of new cultural meanings? Do we have the skills to read such signs and discover their meanings? The raping of infants and children? Who are the perpetrators? Are they predominantly from a particular social class? Could their behaviour be interpreted as a response to their sense of the apocalypse and how it could be staved off? Is there a middle-class or elite response? Could it possibly take the shape of rumour and counter-rumour? Could their strident criticism of political leaders be their own way of displaying their own kind of desperation? Could their own fear of the disease make them vocal, if at times self-righteous, critics of a cautious government? What is the demographic composition of this elite? Where are these demographic components positioned in relation to one another?

In this discussion document, I was intrigued by an overriding question: what country are we becoming in the wake of the unfolding national saga of HIV/AIDS? Given that there is no aspect of our lives untouched by it, how will our response to this disease impact on an emergent national character? Such thoughts have led me to the conclusion that the discourse around an issue so sensitive and complex should not be let to run its own course in the public domain without a rigorous intellectual intervention.

I sought to explore the possibility of a public intervention in the form of articles that would boldly yet sensitively address as many as possible of all the relevant issues around AIDS, if we could identify them.

However we may see it, AIDS is a complex disease. There is no aspect of our lives it does not touch. The very act of species reproduction could, in a brief moment of intense pleasure, metamorphose into a fatal act of species extinction. Methods for combating the pandemic range from state of the art scientific research to morbid beliefs that sex with a virgin will cure the disease, leading to a wildfire of child rapes. Here the route to extinction is less obvious. Foregrounding an ultimately futile act of male selfishness, it works like this: grown women transmit the HIV virus; virgins suck it away like a straw to their own deaths. The final terrible logic is that a country with deflowered virgins carrying the virus of death will ultimately perish and male rapists, suffering under the illusion of being cured, will finally have no women to dominate. This scenario is the stuff of myth: AIDS producing its own mythology.

We may well come to understand AIDS, the disease of the era of the knowledge economy, as the ultimate inducement for humanity to cultivate ecological consciousness: an almost definitive requirement of the contemporary global consciousness. It is a disease that forces post-modernity to confront the phenomenon of species mortality. And because fighting it calls for far more than the administering of drugs, it compels us to define health in terms of the global condition. Mbeki's comprehensive view of the pandemic demonstrates the workings of an ecological mind. Responding to the AIDS pandemic potentially places South Africa, where wealth and poverty exist side-by-side, at the cutting edge of global awareness.

In this connection, the contrast with the United States may be instructive. The United States of America as a civilisation at this point in its history is not structured to cultivate ecological thinking as a foundation for a national or global value system. It is not configured for an interconnected world beyond the instrumentality of economic and military imperatives it has determined by and for itself. Self-centredness as a quality of national consciousness is antithetical to global ecological connectedness. We who are ravaged by AIDS know just how crucial human connections are and how we need to develop the attribute to seek them out. We have come to know that connectedness with the human family is the basis for the world's salvation.

Viewed in this manner, AIDS is fundamentally not only a catastrophe but also an unexpected opportunity. It presents us with the challenge to master living under the threat of extinction. It suggests that, to survive it, we must renew ourselves and perfect new ways of thinking, feeling and living. The foundations of such a life are the mastery of imaginative thinking, access to the broadest and most rigorous education, mastering long-range planning and the ability to model a fully functioning society in the face of population loss, learning to thrive from patience and urgency all at once, foregrounding social research for a sustainable society, a capacity for active tolerance and compassion, mastering the skill to be socially connected. Living with AIDS should mean nothing less than the fundamental engagement with the quest for social rebirth. By the time the virus disappears, an ecological disease (in the sense of a disease not of the environment as such, but one that engenders complex awareness) will have enabled us to lay and consolidate, in South Africa, the foundations for a new civilisation.

What I have attempted to do is to reflect on a recent national and international issue involving a president of a country and a disease. My thoughts indicate that this issue and the way it was largely responded to did not reflect with dignity the workings of the global mind as it was filtered through powerful global media. I have opted to plead for the primacy of rationality and humility in the conduct of a vital human matter. No one typifies these values more than Oliver Reginald Tambo.

Higher Education and a New World Order

towards leadership without control

2003

The continuum of change within the higher education sector happens primarily within individual institutions; among them in their regional and national contexts; and within the larger and more complex environment and national transformation.

I seek to understand and engage in a dialogue about what possibilities there are for higher education globally to participate actively, confidently, and creatively in the evolution of a 'new world order'.

Let me foreground yet another aspect of this global possibility. We learn from Howard Philips' history of the University of Cape Town that the new South African Union government of 1910 'with its emphasis on English-Afrikaner reconciliation, was keen to implement an idea first mooted by Cecil John Rhodes in 1891, to establish a national, teaching university on his estate at Groote Schuur, where English and Dutch-speakers could mingle during their student years, thus laying a foundation for future cooperation.' Is it not remarkable that Rhodes' dream of inter-ethnic cooperation should, at this time in world history, combine with Mandela's dream of reconciliation, the latter encompassing a much more complex human environment? The combination resonates with new possibilities not only for South Africa but for our entire world.

The recourse to the names of Rhodes and Mandela in the current state of the world forces us to contemplate the phenomenon of leadership. Since 11 September 2001, we have been anxious, looking for signs that we are headed in a direction away from the grand gestures of war-making towards the more intricate, more difficult, and more courageous acts of building

---

Keynote address, Rhodes Trust centenary celebrations, 31 January 2003

190

ever-expanding global communities of understanding. This is not a grand, unattainable desire. This is no romantic notion of the world. It has become the very cornerstone of our survival. What may seem far and distant is actually located within us as individuals, in our institutions, and in our countries. We experience the desire at various levels, in various articulations of it in our day-to-day lives.

Some sixteen months ago, I grappled with this issue with heads of academic departments at UCT. I was driven by the thought that we could not express a desire for a new national or world order the features of which were not a reality on our campus. I would like to share with you some of the thoughts I expressed.

What the world needed in the aftermath of September 11, it seemed to me, was not another war but a new kind of leadership, the principles of which are located somewhere in the realisation that no one country, no matter how powerful, can alone prescribe how the world can be redeemed. Any such country in today's world, that doggedly conflates the global interest with its own interest and drums up a war effort in the service of that interest, will succeed only in provoking global insurrection involving numerous countries around the world who will not be keen to be the subjects of a new empire.

This is not to deny the special importance of the world's most powerful countries, and the leading role they can play. It is merely to suggest that a more mature approach can get us to leverage many of the world's achievements and the opportunities they present towards a more accommodating world system. It is in this regard that I made a connection between the United States and South Africa. Given the enormous power of the United States in the world, it may not be out of order to make connections between the ways in which that country is governed and how it seeks to influence the governing of the world.

To what extent, for example, has the endurance of bipartisan politics in the United States made it impossible for its governance system to evolve towards a formal accommodation of the multiplicity of American cultural voices? Indeed, if the internal political system has been unable to evolve in this way, how can the great power, without home-grown experience, respond with wisdom to the multiplicity of the world's voices beyond its borders?

The current crisis has revealed at the global level some interesting displacements which I describe in the following way: notions of alliance will need to give way to notions of community; notions of national interest to notions of global interest; notions of dominance and control to notions of shared leadership and empowerment; notions of war to notions of conflict resolution; notions of identity to notions of relationship; notions of secrecy to notions of openness; notions of the secular to notions of the sacred.

In the short time of our new democracy, we have come a long way in South Africa towards negotiating the transition between the value sets. We have come a long way from predictions that our country would go down in a racial bloodbath, which did not occur. But we still have quite some way to go.

The bloodbath did not happen because we allowed ourselves first the opportunity to imagine and then to undertake the impossible. That meant allowing for the necessity for enemies who recognised a common interest to negotiate a mutually acceptable settlement. This happened despite all the terrible things we had done to one another in the past, which would normally predispose us to react according to the logic of vengeance.

But we recognised, too, that a negotiated settlement, valuable in its own right, was a mechanism to prevent mutual destruction. It did not remove innumerable inequities embedded in the social and economic conditions we inherited. This situation generated its own set of displacements, comparable to the ones I have suggested. They took on a South African specificity.

Confrontation gave way to negotiation; vengeance to reconciliation; superiority of racial ego to shared vulnerability; despair to hope; amnesia to memory; arbitrariness to the rule of law; unfair historic advantage to corrective discrimination; ignorance to awareness; prejudice to open-mindedness; simplification to complexity; self-centeredness to relationships.

I have vivid memories of the many humiliations of growing up in a racist society where one's existence was a constant legal problem in a world relentlessly hostile. I encountered very few kind faces on the pavements of South Africa's cities and towns. Yet, if I wanted to survive I had to go there where the means of livelihood and all the conveniences and commodities were to be found. In this way, I soon learned to embrace contradiction and difficulty. Life was a constant series of tactical accommodations. I learned that, despite the unequal relations of power that characterised South African life, I could come to terms with the reality that life was about giving and taking, whatever the condition of society, and that the tragic flaw of the powerful was their inability to recognise and acknowledge what value they got from those they deemed unworthy.

There were other lessons too. Where poverty abounded, one learned to appreciate people for who they were, rather than for what they had. Power relations were less predatory as shared suffering imposed values of community. On the other hand, we also knew that those that claimed superiority were not that superior. The unaccountable acts of hostility by the average white person often rendered them objects of condescending amusement. We always wondered if they could stand the pain to which they subjected others. We doubted it. That is why today, I think, many of them experience change as dispossession, even though they have been dispossessed of very little.

Of course, I was not the typical poor and dispossessed. It was left to my parents to experience that in their upbringing. I was a township boy with parents whose successful struggle to be educated made them township social elites: that South African phenomenon of a middle class without property and severely limited access to capital. And because it was a middle class that could not escape by law the physical conditions that their education prepared them to abandon, they developed the skill to form genuine relationships across a variety of social strata. This was no romantic situation. It involved constant behaviour adjustments that could have been ethically genuine or tactical rationalisations.

I share these experiences as a way to suggest that millions of South Africans came out of conditions that prepared them to respond with a marked sense of urgency in negotiating the transition from the old world values of confrontation, war, conquest and oppression to the new world values of dialogue, negotiation, and freedom, defined not as boundless possibility but as the courage to face uncertainty with hope in a constitutional democracy. Indeed, not only South Africans but also much of the so-called Third World have been socialised by a particular set of historical experiences not to see the 'other' as a potential threat that could or should be eliminated. Rather, the unknown 'other' offers the possibility of new experiences.

The global system of higher education does not appear to have reacted to the events of September 11 with any significant degree of zest or coherence. Silence, apprehensiveness or uncertainty appear to have characterised the general reaction. As was to be expected, the range of American academic opinion was expressed through the pages of the *Chronicle of Higher Education*. One major view was a critical concern that the understandable surge of American patriotism, combined with government militaristic clamour and increased internal security measures in the United States, posed a serious threat to civil liberties. While the bulk of academic opinion, in this regard, called for increased American introspection, a small conservative voice warned that a less than principled support for the call to 'war against terrorism' could amount to unintended support for an onslaught against the homeland, threatening those very civil liberties.

However, the most significant and coherent view that also emerged is captured in an important 2002 publication by the American Council on Education titled *Beyond September 11: A Comprehensive National Policy on International Education*. In this publication, influential higher education and scholarly associations in the United States express broad support for a new policy on internationalisation that would lead to increased 'international and foreign language expertise and citizen awareness' in the United States. It was a call for a fundamental review of the curriculum to reflect a greater focus on international studies. As a reaction to the fear that overwhelming American power has led to self-satisfied American ignorance of the world, this intervention foregrounds the importance of the university curriculum as an instrument in bringing about a major attitudinal change towards the world in Americans. This view searches for the roots of the problem in the nature of relationships between the United States and the non-Western world. It prescribes more knowledge as an antidote to world conflict.

While there is no doubt that this position has enormous value, it does not sufficiently take into account that there is a disjuncture between the broadly humanistic traditions in the American academy, on the one hand, and, on the other, the predatory nature of American foreign policy which may rely on academic research but locates it and interprets it within the paradigm of control and self-interest.

Secondly, this position could be more a statement about the relatively low impact of academia on moral and ethical issues than a statement on economic matters in which knowledge is applied to enhance productivity and profitability. The economic utility of higher education has become a much more dominant feature of higher education than its ability to enhance social consciousness such as would impact on the public's ability to exercise fundamental moral choices. The educative function of higher education has become subsumed under more dynamic, more compelling, economic imperatives.

This tendency is borne out by the trend towards the establishment of international consortia by institutions of higher education that are driven by the goal of maximising competition for students in the global market. This trend is fundamentally a response to diminishing financial resources for higher education institutions within national economies. The model for such consortia is the ubiquitous multinational company. Driven by notions of the knowledge economy, by the omnipresent virtual world of information and communication technologies, powerful universities form academic conglomerates to produce global workers who take a range of online courses in business to make themselves more serviceable to a global economy.

The reflective capacity of higher education has given way to marshalling the human intelligence towards economic productivity. This view does not in any way seek to diminish the rigour involved in curriculum planning and instruction. Nor does it suggest that economic productivity and profitability are not desirable. It suggests that reflection has significantly given way to instrumentality, and that this has potentially disastrous effects on the evolution of contemporary civilisation towards more humane forms of global awareness.

If there is any relevance for higher education in this situation, it would be in the realisation that the progressive instrumentalisation of the human intellect, which has assumed a global dimension, represents a serious decline in the ability of humanity to re-imagine the world. Higher education consortia that are not informed at their core by such an understanding contribute to the marginalisation of their own reconstitutive possibilities as centres of learning and creativity.

An act of synchronicity brought to me, by email, a telling statement of the problem. An essay by David James Duncan found its way to me through a writer friend's mailing list. Entitled 'When Compassion Becomes Dissent', the essay, published in *Orion* in early 2003, opens in a most remarkable way:

> I have been serving my country, this deceptively serene Rocky Mountain autumn, as a visiting instructor of creative writing at the

University of Montana. I lead two classes, each three hours long, with twenty students all told. My students are not 'aspiring writers' exactly: they're the real thing, and in two months' time their collective intensity, wit, and talent have lifted our joint undertaking into the realm of arduous but steady pleasure. Yet, as the semester unfolds and we listen to President Bush and his various goaders and backers wage a rhetorical war on Iraq and prepare an increasingly vague national 'we' to lay waste to Saddam Hussein, the mere teaching of creative writing has come to feel, for the first time in my life, like a positively dissident line of work.

Creative writing requires a dual love of language and of life, human and otherwise. The storyteller then sculpts these raw loves with acute observation, reflection, creative struggle, allegiance to truth, merciless awareness of the foibles of human beings, and unstinting empathy toward human beings even so. Not only have these strategies foundered in the post-9/11 rhetoric of the Bush administration, they look to me to have been outlawed by two recent federal documents: the '2002 National Security Strategy for the United States' and the 107th Congress's 'Patriot Act'.

Duncan goes on to subject these texts to the same intense proofreading he applies to the rough drafts of his students. His conclusions are damning. Judging the texts as laden with puffed-up rhetoric, hypocrisy and half-truths, he concludes that he would have advised the writers of the texts to 'throw them away and start over'. There follows a sustained and moving reflection on the capacity of creative writing to fundamentally undermine the authorised superficiality of public pronouncements made by elected public figures in which deception is elevated to fact through rehearsed postures of conviction. Such performances of conviction do change opinion polls significantly, pushing them up and confirming to the leader the illusion of his declared truths.

The strength of creative writing lies precisely in the shared social knowledge that it does not pretend to be true. Yet, it is an imaginative invention that has the capacity to get closest to human truths because it engages our thoughts, our feelings and emotions, our memories of loss, disappointment, despair, joy, compassion and the unverifiable certitudes of intuition. Truly, at that point, in a public environment of posture and declaration, in which only the public declarer knows the truth but does not declare it, creative writing becomes profoundly dissident. Duncan goes on to reveal how a systematic reading of public documents is important:

> I hope to heaven I'm wrong, but the $73 million Dick Cheney's cohorts at Halliburton have in recent years invested in oil infrastructure in Iraq despite the presence of Saddam casts a hell of a shadow over my hope, as do the words of Senator Richard Lugar (Republican, Indiana) of the Senate Foreign Relations Committee, who during the July/August 2002 hearings on Iraq said, 'We are going to run the oil business, we are going to run it well, we are going to make money, and it's going to help pay for the rehabilitation of Iraq because there is money there!'

Is this information true? If it has existed somewhere in the public domain, why has it apparently not caused profound public unease? The point here is that this critique, such observations, are not a comment on an individual president. Rather, they are a comment on the state of a particular political culture, one that has enormous capacity to legitimise itself, and on how far it has evolved. If, indeed, we are being prepared for war on such undeclared grounds and those grounds may actually drive the motives of decision-makers, then, given the balance of factors on the behaviour of these decision-makers on other issues that seriously concern the survival of humanity at this juncture, we have to ask: is it possible that we are witnessing the beginnings of the decline of a civilisation? The extent of human suffering we may be about to witness, against the probable banality of the real intention behind it, is sufficiently indicative of a serious crisis of civilisation.

Then, we have to ask: how do we begin to prepare ourselves for a new world? Much of the literature on leadership and management has emerged from studies of the corporate experience. These studies have yielded a rich body of literature. They suggest that, although the pursuit of profits has remained the primary purpose of corporate entrepreneurial activity, there has developed also an admirable corporate concern with ethical conduct, with notions of empowering leadership that seeks to create, at the site of production, a vital sense of community in which the rewards of work are manifestly more than monetary.

Unfortunately, the trials and tribulations of the vice chancellorship as a form of leadership have yet to receive as rigorous attention. The literature suggests that infusing something of the collegiate ethos of universities into the dynamic, purposeful culture of industrial production has humanised considerably the corporate working environment. This has made universities in comparison seem like lumbering dinosaurs that take ages to make the simplest decision. This is why they have followed rather than led the experiment with organisational transformation. It is small wonder that the corporation, with its ability to deploy enormous resources, has become such a dominant feature of the world that it can structure thinking in such a way as to make its workings assume the inevitability of a natural law.

Starting from the position that there are considerable redeeming features in certain aspects of the global corporate culture, higher education globally has to decide whether it still believes in the inherent value of academic freedom, which has traditionally given it that autonomous space to seek the truth, to promote human values. If we have been able to preserve, to various degrees of success, freedom from State interference in teaching and research, why do we seem so uncritically willing to hand it over to global trade?

Not too long ago, in a fundraising situation, a prospective corporate donor asked me to characterise UCT in a single sentence that would capture his imagination. I was mortified, anxious that I would not be able to do so, and that no funding would come. A colleague had the presence of mind to confront the issue squarely by pointing out that a university did not produce a distinctive commodity that could be reproduced a million times according to market demand. Maybe, we are on our way to doing that. But universities produce knowledge, ideas, from varied disciplinary perspectives. Those disciplines may cooperate around specific projects and then dissolve when the project is over. We produce graduates who, at the exit point, are as differentiated as they were when they entered. Hopefully, they leave with a quality of awareness, insight, and compassion qualitatively different from when they arrived, and which, hopefully, they will struggle to describe.

The university as an institution is, next to religious institutions, one of the most resilient of institutional types. When the world's largest corporations have come and gone, universities will most likely still be there, teaching and researching as best they can. For now, the corporation, with its government and military support structures, has eclipsed them. They have no choice but to rise from their slumber. The context in which they have to function now, in which they have to rise to a state of pre-eminence, is extremely complex but very urgent. It is a world characterised by extremes of poverty and wealth; environmental degradation; debilitating local wars and ancient conflicts.

Higher education cultures of the world are extremely diverse. They range from the well-endowed systems of Europe and North America to the struggling systems of Asia and Africa. Institutions with a long history that renders them part of the world's heritage exist side-by-side with new ones, which distinguish themselves by their energy and confidence in being new. But all remain distinctive as institutions of a particular kind, poised at this moment to reinterpret the human condition by urging us closer towards a consciousness that enables us to sense the world through nuance: a combination of intelligence and sensitivity.

Within the system of higher education in our country, we feel this sense of urgency keenly, that it is not enough to have bodies of students and teaching and administrative staff on our campuses. They must come out heavily networked to make a difference in our nascent democracy. Our optimism makes us feel we could be at the cutting edge of a new value system of leadership without control.

199

The 'War on Terror' and the 'African Renaissance'

on identity and citizenship today

2003

T he expressions contained in the title are a feature of public political language today: 'war on terror' and the 'African renaissance'. It seemed, though, that their easy availability in the public domain constituted a problem as I began to write. I had thought I could easily get my teeth into these concepts and the range of issues they point to. What seemed easy on the surface became extremely elusive as I assessed exactly what thoughts I had on the matter. I faced a rather terrifying void.

But then I drew some consolation from the sudden realisation that I was actually not the only one to experience this disconcerting reversal of expectation. Two powerful countries, one a leader, another a follower, recently attempted to convince their respective populations and the rest of the world that they would clinically breeze into Iraq before lunch, conquer and liberate, and then head back home intact, in time for dinner. It turned out that the script for actual war is far more difficult than the script for imagined war.

I am thinking that this disjuncture between dream and reality has assumed a special form at this time in world history. It has resolved itself into a disjuncture between essence and banality. Mediating between these two poles of contemporary culture is technology; something that has the capacity either to ennoble or to debase. Here's what I mean:

Many years ago, I remember seeing a film called *Brother John* in which Sidney Poitier was the eponymous hero who returns to the small southern town of his birth. He carries about him an air of dignified detachment. Travel beyond the United States, having exposed him to diverse and enrich-

Inaugural Ukuza Lecture of the British Council, Spier, Stellenbosch, 4 April 2003

ing experiences, has made him calm, reflective, deliberate in his actions and wise in his words. He finds that his old town is trapped in a time warp. A lingering provincialism still sustains small-minded acts of racism and a low-intensity sense of social purposelessness among its black victims.

The definitive moment in the film for me is when Brother John stands on a hill overlooking the town, and the camera, following his visual perspective, zooms in on a dump of scrap metal and other kinds of garbage. In the middle of his kingdom, this dump of discarded things, is a grown white man with a shotgun. He is intently shooting at something: rats. He finally finds one and shoots it many times after he has killed it. The scene, which is not more than a couple of seconds, then fades out, having made a devastating commentary.

This scene in which a technology of destruction is used overwhelmingly against a relatively defenceless, living target has been played out in many parts of the world, particularly in the second half of the twentieth century. Since the discovery of nuclear weapons, the extent of the deployment of human inventiveness and genius towards the invention of technologies of destruction has no historical parallel. Because of the ghastly destructive power of nuclear weapons, much ingenuity has been channelled towards the invention of smaller weapons whose destructive power keeps pushing beyond the outer limits of their size towards that of nuclear weapons without themselves becoming nuclear weapons. Let's call it the art of pushing the limits of containment.

Vietnamese rats were the first to be used for the testing of such weapons on human targets. We first heard then about napalm bombs, cluster bombs, and the expression 'carpet bombing', a phrase suggesting the overwhelming randomness of destruction. The latest rats are Iraqis, in what President Bush has billed 'the first war of the 21st century' which, having been started by him, enables him to enter history. Palestinian rats are next. The Israelis routinely test on them the latest American gadgetry of destruction. The technological capacity to kill a thousand times what is already dead has been a common feature in the onslaught on human rats. The latest onslaught has been relentlessly on display on our television screens in the last three weeks.

It began when the American general who is conducting this war, and whose name I happily do not remember, told his soldiers: 'As soon as

President Bush gives the order, it will be hammer time for Saddam.' He was referring to a bomb apparently nicknamed 'the hammer', otherwise known as MOAB, the 'mother of all bombs'. Its destructive power reportedly approximates that of a small nuclear weapon without itself being a nuclear weapon.

The expression 'hammer time' should be seen in the context of similar expressions generated by this war: 'shock and awe', 'regime change', 'targets of opportunity', 'surgical strikes', 'precision guided munitions', 'smart bombs', 'arsenal of tactics', 'operation Iraqi freedom', 'operation decapitation', 'coalition forces', 'coalition of the willing', 'crossing the red line', 'war on terror', 'embedded journalists'. It is the language of terse encapsulation that ironically strains towards the economy of poetry but, unlike poetry, yields not insight but cleverness of the kind that supremely admires itself. The expressions underscore the phenomenon of a war without a transcendent goal or cause. It is a war obsessed with its own techniques.

This is a war that follows from the driven logic of inventing the ultimate means of destruction. The resulting weapons, accumulated over years of well-funded military research, reach a point where, straining to be tested, they become predisposed to attracting banal causes. It is difficult to see anything substantial in this war beyond the display of weapons and the manifest obsession with describing their effects. What we have in the end is an elaborate war game in which a sequence of objectives is acted out: how to start a war, how to conduct it, and how to execute a plan for rehabilitating a target destroyed many times over.

I believe that with this war we witness the end of an era as far as war is concerned. War as national glory is over. It is replaced by the notion of war as technological self-indulgence. Thus ends the history of the glorification of war. For we see no heroism in this war; no display of individual or group acts of bravery and courage. We witness only the deaths of rats and how they are killed a thousand times over: ordinary men, women and children clinically described as 'collateral damage'. We see the destruction of valuable public infrastructure. We see smouldering bodies of cars and trucks along public roads.

It is difficult not to remember Afghanistan, where food and bombs, thanks to the invading Americans, tumbled from the Afghan skies simultaneously. Kill and feed. Kill and liberate. (These are expressions missing from the collection mentioned earlier, and should be added.) We saw then, as we do now, not the glory of war but the banality, obscenity and vulgarity of wilful high-tech destruction.

It could have been the concomitant intention of the 'coalition forces' to induce fear among observing nations through 'shock and awe' effects. This war was meant to be a demonstration to all of us around the world of what the power of the Americans could do to us if we did not take note and do their bidding. Unfortunately for the Americans, it is not fear that has been evoked in me. I feel rather a huge loss of respect for a country I have admired. This war evokes revulsion.

Compare for a moment the 'civilised', high-tech bombing and killing of civilians in Iraq with the crude and random hacking of limbs of civilians in Sierra Leone not too long ago. Both these acts of war are intended to 'shock and awe'. Despite the cloak of 'high-tech civilisation' in the one case, there is no moral difference between the two.

What this war has exposed is a great country that may have reached the limits of its moral imagination. Its enormous capacity to imagine and then unleash destruction may have outstripped its capacity to visualise, as a civilisation, a new moral order beyond its current, considerable achievements. Drunk with wealth and destructive power, it can only maintain what it has achieved at home and endeavour to meet its insatiable appetite for 'the good life', as it sees it, through military adventures abroad.

Indeed, what 'the first war of the 21st century' has signalled is the onset of the decline of a great civilisation. The signs are definitely there – the flurry of activity around UN arms inspectors, Security Council resolutions based on technical agreements rather than trust, and threats to 'go it alone'. They reveal the emergence of a manipulative state in which the desire for violence overwhelms the public capacity to discern falsehood in argument. A powerful country in a state of decline validates its arguments through force. We witnessed the same kind of behaviour in South Africa from 1976 onwards: the manipulative intelligence of state machinery that can no longer be sustained by argument. Of course, the United States may take more than a century to finally peter out. But it has begun its inexorable journey in that direction unless it does something to radically alter itself.

This war has also dredged up potentially serious historical fault lines. Is it accidental that Britain, Spain and Portugal, old centres of the colonial project, are the most vocal behind a new war of conquest? Hopefully the French are not watching wistfully on the sidelines, wondering if they have not made a mistake in not getting involved. How should we understand this? Have the old powers yielded to the reflex memory of the rat killing of imperial times? I think not. I think that a memory lapse has occurred that has allowed a strategic understanding of history to be put aside in the face of American resolve to retreat from the multilateral, global community project of the last sixty years.

On the face of things, America's is a tactical retreat to assert dominance. But a dominance based on an old value system of military superiority is, ultimately, unsustainable. It is unsustainable because in the twenty-first century, the measure of courage is likely to be displayed in conflict resolution rather than in conflict generation. The twenty-first century is the world of the Kyoto Protocol; of sustainable development; of anti-racism; of the World Criminal Court; of the banning of anti-personnel mines; of nuclear disarmament. The United States' exercise in global leadership has been to spurn these efforts.

It is in this that Prime Minister Blair has let many down. He failed to provide an alternative leadership. He needed to display the new global value of courage by pulling out of a war I believe he knows to be inordinately nonsensical. He had an opportunity to display the courage to face the British people and the global community and say, 'I jumped into this rather impulsively. I am getting out of it now.' Instead, he chose to act out consistency and resolve.

My reference to this post-modern partnership of old colonial powers, led by a new power with anti-colonial origins, is intended to be a transition in my thoughts as I begin to grope towards the second part of my topic: the African renaissance. I want to start with the general proposition that it is possible to read the British colonial project as having been, ultimately, a global, modernising agent; this, despite the trauma visited upon conquered peoples. American ascendance to global leadership, essentially anti-colonial in spirit, took the notion of human freedom to higher levels.

Unfortunately, through its foreign policy, which has been essentially antithetical to its internal national democratic project, the United States steadfastly snuffed out the democratic experiments in other countries it did not approve of. So, its intervention in Iraq is not new; only, it has never intervened this crassly, except when the rats of the island of Grenada were overwhelmed and President Reagan, in a classic Hollywood ending, said about the invasion of a small island by a superpower: 'We got there just in time.'

The point I wish to make is that in the context of the long history of human evolution, particularly in the last three hundred years, which saw unprecedented human movement across the globe, we are all seriously implicated in one another's histories. In that process, the notion of the global village has progressively become real.

In her very recent, remarkable book *A Human Being Died That Night*, Pumla Gobodo-Madikizela, an associate professor at the University of Cape Town who served as a commissioner on the Truth and Reconciliation Commission, writes about her experience of interviewing the man known as 'Prime Evil', Eugene de Kock, who was one of apartheid's most accomplished killers. It is a deeply affecting story in which she confronts the emergent realisation that, after all, a human being is lodged inside this killer. The book is a journey into that discovery and what it implies for forgiveness and reconciliation in South Africa.

Early in the book she asks some disturbing questions: 'If showing compassion to our enemies is something that our bodies recoil from, what should our attitude be to their cries for mercy, the cries that tell us their hearts are breaking, and that they are willing to renounce the past and their role in it? How can we transcend hate if the goal is to transform human relationships in a society with a past marked by violent conflict between groups?

'This question may be irrelevant for people who do not have to live as a society with their former enemies. But for those whose lives are intertwined with those who have grossly violated human rights, who sometimes even have to live as neighbours with them, ignoring the question is not an option.'

Now, it is risky to jump from the dynamics of a country to the world community of countries. But I will take the risk. I restate the point about how implicated we all are in the world in one another's histories. I restate the reality of a truly shrunken world, connected in so many intricate and intimate ways. There are countries that have treated other countries as brutally as Eugene de Kock treated his victims. But, through the United Nations, friend and foe have been compelled to sit together, subject to a common set of rules and values. That is why a 'coalition' of war bringing together old colonial powers at this time in world history looks so gross. Which is the next country that the coalition will gang up against? Are we re-opening the world to a free-for-all condition of violence and destruction, in order to re-write the world map?

We cannot and should not return there. The millions of people around the world who have stood up against war do not want us to go back there. This desire takes us beyond the notion of the African renaissance towards a more compelling one: global renaissance. There is so much good that the United States of America is capable of doing. With the challenge of poverty and disease around the world so enormous, it is surely obscene for a country of such enormous wealth to pour more money, and yet more money, into a needless war. Unfortunately, wealth and military power do not necessarily go hand-in-hand with high moral purpose. Perhaps the former Irish president, Mary Robinson, is right: the next superpower is global public opinion. Perhaps, the nation-state is indeed a primitive entity that must now give way to a more transcendent system of global governance.

For the rats, the powerless peoples around the world who have known vulnerability, one thing is clear: they have a responsibility to dream the new world. In this they will not be alone. They will be joined by millions of Americans, the British, Spaniards, Portuguese, others all over the world: people who are being let down by their governments.

Finally, there is another reason why the United States' quest for global dictatorship is not sustainable. The historical evidence shows that empires rise and fall. If the end of any new empire is assured, why should it be accompanied by so much violence and destruction? To prevent this we need shared global leadership. The greatest question is: can the United States conceptualise and commit to an overarching global interest which in some vital ways may override its own national interest, in the service of that very same national interest? What we need is global sustainability beyond the notion of empire. Which country or countries will take us there?

Thinking of Brenda

the desire to be

1996

I first heard Brenda Fassie sing on a languid, sunny, spring Saturday morning in the Roma valley of Lesotho. It must have been in 1984. It was one of those mornings when the world demonstrates the notion of slowness. There was the blue haze in the horizon, rural smoke rising slowly against the sky until it seemed as if the sky was floating. I remember the distant kra-a-a-k of a white-necked raven gliding somewhere in the sky, and the trees so still, as if they had sucked in through their leaves all the motion there ever was. That was the scene I saw when I finally got out of bed after waking to the sounds of 'Weekend Special' on Radio Lesotho somewhere in the house.

The music had reached me while I was hovering between the states of waking and sleeping, suspended between re-emerging consciousness and the continuation of sleep. I had not heard the song before, nor did I know who was singing it, but I will never forget the pounding thrill of it, the rhythms that I felt certain could keep a party going endlessly. And that is exactly how it turned out to be at many of the parties in Maseru those years. Much later, in the *Sowetan* in 1999, Elliot Makhanya was to capture what many felt: 'Brenda Fassie is a unique creative energy and an overwhelming talent ... Fassie has been singing for just over two decades, but every time you listen to her, it seems as if she has just begun.'

There are few controversial characters in contemporary South Africa who stand out like Brenda Fassie. Besides her musical talents, she has some highly marketable qualities. For example, there is a great deal of outrageous brazenness about her that newspapers simply love. That they quickly

---

A version of this essay was presented at the National Arts Festival, Grahamstown, in 1996. It was first published in *Chimurenga*, 2002, and then updated and published in *This Day*, May 2004.

recognised what a musical catch they had in their hands came through in many headlines. At first, the headlines reflected the genuine discovery of a major musical talent: 'There's no stopping Brenda' says *Bona* magazine in April 1984, soon after Brenda's dramatic entrance into the entertainment industry through her hit song 'Weekend Special'.

But even back then there were signs of another media prize: Brenda's mouth. 'I have been through a lot of difficulties paving my way to success,' she told *Bona*. 'Now that I have reached this stage in my career, I am not going to turn back. My ambition is to become a number one musician in this country and ... well ... make a lot of money.' Here was a rags-to-riches story that landed in the hands of the press like a bird. The profiling of Brenda as a musician shifted dramatically from her music towards the drama of her private life.

There is a telling sequence of pictures in the supplement to *Drum* magazine of December/January 51/91, depicting township life over forty years as captured by the magazine's photographers. There are many pictures of musicians and dancers, particularly in the 1950s and 1960s, who are shown performing on stage. Dancers, in particular, are captured in dramatically frozen motion. In contrast, Brenda Fassie, a dynamic contemporary performer, is shown in her wedding dress, on her wedding day, with Yvonne Chaka Chaka, her senior bridesmaid, mopping the bride's brow on a 'steaming hot Durban day'. Chicco Twala, her producer and manager, is shown leaning against his Mercedes-Benz with his huge double-storey house in the background. At the bottom is a head-and-shoulders picture of Mbongeni Ngema, accompanied by a comment on how he 'is now a wealthy playwright and music producer who counts among his friends Quincy Jones and Oscar-winning actor Denzil [sic] Washington'. Further, the headline runs, boldly: 'Affluence and confusion strike a chord in the 90s'. The music and performance of these artists are downplayed in favour of gossip about their private lives.

Indeed, in 1987, three years after Brenda had broken into the musical scene, she was on the cover of *Drum* with half of the picture, in which she is seated on the floor, dominated by her exposed right thigh, knee and boot. The other half is her smiling face. Her face radiates a mix of innocence and calculated sexuality. 'Brenda – I can't buy me love' goes the cover headline.

The story inside has a juicy heading: 'She's looking for a lifetime special!

Brenda tells all on Chicco, a lesbian fling, and one-night stands.' And Brenda, the star of 'Weekend Special', rises to the occasion and rattles on about men and love, building on what was to be her characteristic style of self-exposure: 'I know that most of them are just lusting after me. They don't love me. They just want to go to bed with me.' And then follows her characteristic sudden shift in focus as something strikes her: 'I can also seduce a man if I want to.'

Later on in the same interview, she pronounces: 'It was a good experience,' referring to what the article calls 'a lesbian fling'. 'I was just curious. I wanted to know how they make love to other women.' Just an experiment, which, it turns out later, has been a defensive method to maintain self-respect. If the public has a problem with lesbians, Brenda was merely experimenting. She was not one herself. But because a part of her really is, she has to protect herself against herself and protect her self-esteem to herself: 'I am always nice to the lesbians. I don't snub them. I hope I will never become a lesbian.' This is a verbal distancing effect for the public, and is designed to facilitate and maintain an internal coherence. And so, Brenda keeps 'telling all' to the excitement of *Drum* magazine and many shocked readers whose appetites are whetted for more stories, more of Brenda's musical hits and more appearances at festivals, where they will endure long hours waiting for her to appear.

'One malicious columnist,' complains Brenda, 'wrote that I look like a horse. And some people say that I am ugly.' Revealing another talent for the art of reversal, she continues, 'I don't want to be beautiful. My ugliness has taken me to the top. I have proved that I have style, and all that glitters is not gold.' Once, she was asked why she hadn't been to the United States, where she could build on her fame. She retorted that Michael Jackson did not come to South Africa to be famous. Very early, Brenda firmed up her mouth as one of her best assets.

Covering the next major episode in her life, *Drum* magazine is found standing diligently on Brenda's side in March 1989 when she does indeed find her 'Lifetime Special' in Nhlanhla Mbambo. 'Mass hysteria as Brenda says "I do"' announces the cover of *Drum* with a picture of the smiling couple dressed in white. *Drum* dubs it the 'pop wedding of the year'. However, in August 1990, *Drum* announces the dramatic end of Brenda's marriage with another cover story. It shows us another picture of the couple. This time they are dressed in black leather clothing. There is no smile on Brenda's face. She is looking pained and sad, but also decidedly petulant; her husband is trying to smile. The headline goes: 'Brenda and hubby: our marriage based on jealousy and infidelity'. It is not long after this announcement that the couple makes up. But, marital bliss is not for them. After a separation announced in November, the *Sowetan* announces on 10 December: 'Curtain falls on Brenda's marriage'. And so it does.

❑

Since 1984 when she broke into the musical scene with 'Weekend Special' Brenda Fassie, Ma-Brrr, and her music have lived through some of the most significant changes in the history of South Africa. Today, she still 'Wows audiences', as a typical *Sowetan* headline would put it. In all that time, she floated into our personal and public lives as sound and rhythm. As sound, she has come at us in two ways: music and speech. In a way, whether she has been on-stage or off it, hers has been a continuous performance. That is why, in this connection, it seems inappropriate to separate her public from her private persona. They are one.

It is useful to recall some of the major public events through which we travelled with Brenda Fassie, and during which, for sixteen years, she has been at centre stage. Some of these events are captured so well in a book called *Mandela, Tambo, and the African National Congress*. In the summer of 1984–85, the time that we were listening and dancing to 'Weekend Special', a

> ... new pattern of protest grew [in South Africa]. It consisted of stay-at-homes, roving demonstrations challenging the police patrolling the townships, and attacks on the businesses, houses, and persons of Africans charged with collaborating in the new Community Council system. Local grievances became the vehicle for protest against the apartheid system as a whole, spreading from township to township through a population thoroughly mobilised by student participation in school boycotts and broader involvement in the anti-constitution campaigns. At the same time, the existence of national bodies such as the UDF provided new means for coordination or protest, epitomised in the Transvaal stay-at-home of November 5–6, 1984, in which an estimated 800 000 participated.

Beyond that, the struggles progressed through several other phases. We witnessed the state of emergency, necklace killings, economic sanctions, rent and rates boycotts, the calls for 'liberation now, education later', increasingly successful ANC guerrilla attacks against the apartheid state, the release of Mandela, the constitutional negotiations and the historic elections of 1994, ten years after 'Weekend Special'. And now that we have entered the phase of democracy, governance and delivery, Brenda is still there, continuing to make an impact.

In all this time she has hungered for love, made money, got married, divorced, confirmed her bisexuality, wrecked her life through drug addiction, during which she experienced one of her most painful moments: the death of her lover Poppy, seemingly from a drug overdose. Through a difficult struggle, thanks to Chicco Twala she recovered and is falling in and out of love once more, while continuing to make new music, which continues to enjoy enormous popularity. As an interviewer, Immanuel D'Emilio, observes in *The Namibian*:

> Controversial songstress Fassie has an honours degree from the University of Hard Knocks, but she never let traumatic life events get in her way of having a good time. Now that she has made peace with her odious past, she's embarked on a mission to regenerate her reign as the inimitable queen of the South African music industry. Her Highness spoke to me about love, drug addiction, loss and power of fame.

Although the tone of D'Emilio's writing is exploitative and disparaging, it shows how the media, in reflecting the ups and downs of Brenda's life, took advantage of her. But it is Brenda's own words that ring loud: 'I am a born again musician', she announced to the *Sowetan*. Remarkably, these ups and downs are reflected in many of the lyrics of her music. Her life and her music are inseparable. What could it all mean?

❑

For one artist to remain at the centre stage of South African popular music for sixteen years is a phenomenon that has to resonate with special meaning for the times. Allister Sparks makes an interesting observation of crowds at political rallies in the 1980s in his book *The Mind of South Africa*:

Here the anonymous individuals of a humiliated community seemed to draw strength from the crowd, gaining from it the larger identity of the occasions and an affirmation of their human worth. Their daily lives might seem meaningless, but here on these occasions the world turned out, with its reporters and its television cameras, to tell them it was not so, that their lives mattered, that humanity cared, that their cause was just; and when they clenched their fists and chanted their defiant slogans, they could feel that they were proclaiming their equality and that their strength of spirit could overwhelm the guns and armoured vehicles waiting outside.

Similarly, in the apparent futility of daily life under oppression, Brenda seems to succeed in giving meaning to the daily details of life by affirming them in song. When her audiences recognise those social facts, and sing along, imprinting them anew in their minds, and dancing to the rhythms that carry the picture or message-bearing words, they participate in a vital process of self-authentication and regeneration.

'*Zimb' izindaba ...*' begins the song 'Kuyoze Kuyovalwa' on the CD *Abantu Bayakhuluma (People Talk)*:

> *Mina ngihamba ngo-7*
> *Kuyoze ku clozwe*
> *Izikhiye zilahleke*
> *bese bayavula vele*
> *kuyoze kuyo valwa-ke*
> *Sihamba ngo 7*
> *Thina siyalala la*
> *Thina siyahlala la*

[We're not leaving this party. We'll be here until daybreak. They may close and throw away the keys, but will surely open again until daybreak.]

This mock defiance of hosts is partly a result of known characters, who never take hints and overstay their welcome. But it is also an expression of pure pleasure: how fun it is at the party. However, hosts must be warned, the party-goers may just stay until daybreak. The popular format of 6 p.m.-to-

6 a.m. festivals (dusk-to-dawn) replays this potentially anarchic social game at an immensely grand scale.

'Lyrically, Fassi's [sic] songs are a mish-mash of the latest township lingo, sometimes barely comprehensible even to locals, but they stick in the minds of her listeners,' says a report on Brenda Fassie in *World Music: The Rough Guide*. 'Mish-mash' suggests confusion. Not necessarily. What Brenda does, and this seems in part an ingrained pattern of behaviour, is bring together unusual juxtapositions that make sense only in context. For example, the bumper sticker on her car reads HULLO BU-BYE, KOKO COME IN. This may look like incomprehensible 'mish-mash' to the socially uninitiated. But it is a free-spirit expression of the social energy in the endless comings and goings in the township, the meetings and the partings, and the opening and the closing of doors. It is a dramatic validation of common experience.

Perhaps the most controversial act of validation is Brenda's outspokenness on the taboo subject of sex. The problem, for society, comes precisely at the point where, for Brenda Fassie, the wall between the private and the public totally collapses. What could be more outrageous in public, coming from a popular star, than to utter this very private of sentiments: 'Some men cry because I sing; I sing when I make love, I sing for them', as she told *Vrye Weekblad*. This obliteration of the divide between the private and the public is at the bottom of her verbal ungovernability. Indeed, if the State is to be rendered ungovernable, and if that ungovernability is a factor of not only the intention to be free, and if the act of rendering the State ungovernable is itself an act of freedom, then Brenda's voice enters the public arena as ungovernable, the ultimate expression of personal freedom. While she may shock, she is at the same time admired, not for her courage (for this is not courage at play) but for being representative of the value of expressiveness. She made real in the personal domain the public political quest for an abstract notion of freedom. She brought the experience of freedom very close.

Indeed, long before the issue of sexual preference became a burning constitutional issue, Brenda had widened the doorway.

But there is yet another way that Brenda touched a significant chord in a national context. Here we are looking at the impact of the politics of culture in creating a national identity. I had occasion to reflect recently on binding factors that could explain why it would be difficult for the South

African state to disintegrate in conflict. In the essay 'The Lion and the Rabbit' I observed in 1999 that:

> [A]n increasingly familiar commercial and industrial landscape has progressively drawn the population into a unifying pattern of economic activities. A replicated landscape of major commercial chains throughout the country has, over the decades, become a feature of how the land is imagined. Spatial familiarity of this sort renders the land familiar, less strange and more accommodating wherever you may be in the country. This kind of familiarity may have a binding effect, which cuts across the particularising tendencies of geographic and ethnic location. Linking the country is a complex network of a communications system, which promised accessibility of every part of the country to every citizen. This sense of universal accessibility was sensed as an achievement even before Codesa was underway.

In this context it is remarkable how extensively Brenda toured the country to sing and entertain. Particularly noteworthy are the festivals held in the homelands. Between September 1991 when she performed at the Mphephu Resort, in Venda, and December 1994, when she performed at Phuthaditjhaba Stadium, in Qwaqwa, Brenda Fassie visited all the homelands put together nineteen times. In a hectic schedule, she could move from homeland to homeland in one weekend. In this way, her music, given the political context of a difficult struggle, helped to consolidate a view of culture as social affirmation. Secondly, it contributed to the consolidation of a sense of South African musical space, familiar to millions across the land. Some symbols changed in the process. Stadiums associated with bogus independence became sites for a social assertiveness heavily suggested in Brenda's style.

❑

So who is Brenda Fassie? In Sesotho, I would say *Ke sebopuoa* (God's own being).

Charl Blignaut, of the famous interview in the *Vrye Weekblad* headlined 'In bed with Brenda', ponders the conduct of his subject during the interview. As we have noticed, she strays from answering questions while she digresses on minor intrusions. 'Over the years,' Blignaut writes,

> I have come to the conclusion that there is no way to write a Brenda interview without its being personal. That's because there really is no such thing as a Brenda 'interview'. Every self-respecting hack who's been around the block has done the 'Waiting for Brenda' or 'Trying to keep up with Brenda' piece. You don't 'interview' Brenda, you experience her. You could be the recipient of her venom or of her devoted attention. Most likely it'll be both – with switches happening when you least expect them. Then again, maybe it's just me. As I said, it's personal.
>
> One minute she's outside crying on the balcony because you've really upset her and hurt her career, the next she's feeding you her lunch. And that's probably because, like any serious pop star anywhere in the world, Brenda Fassie has a love-hate relationship with the media. I've interviewed other famously difficult people like Naomi Campbell and Boy George and have remained reasonably calm. But, without fail, each time I prepare to interview Brenda, I'm deeply on edge for days. Because no matter what you're thinking, you seldom know what she'll do next; you're never quite ready for her. The point is that Brenda Fassie, whether she's topping the charts or lying in the gutter, is every inch a star. She makes her own rules.

There are two observations I would like to make about Blignaut's experience. The first is how he may not have fully realised the extent to which Brenda subjected him to the rules of her own life. When he says that interviewing Brenda is a 'personal thing', a feeling that he expresses through a public medium, he lives, for a moment, in Brenda's world in which the personal and the public not only coexist but seem to merge.

Secondly, I doubt that Brenda really has a special 'love-hate relationship with the media'. While she would never be totally indifferent to the media, her swings of mood are not necessarily a calculated desire to be outrageous, to wound and then to make amends in order to keep the lines of communication open. They are part of the fabric of her life. One moment she berates

Yvonne Chaka Chaka for living in the suburbs, the next moment she declares her a true friend.

When Brenda gets angry, it is because anger is natural. When she becomes compassionate, it is because compassion is natural. But whatever the case might be, you never sense hatred. But affection, even love, is never absent. You find it, however tenuously, even in the most outrageous statement. Being the kind of person she is, essentially trusting, Brenda is likely to experience many moments of vulnerability, and be wont to feel sharply the pain of disappointment. '*Akusese mnandi, yo/Monday Buti yo/ Ungishaya ngaphakathi*' (It's not pleasant anymore/ Monday Blues/The pain of it, I feel deeply within). She tries to come to terms with the pain of being let down and transcends it through song. It is a quality of innocence that lies at the core of her life. It makes no sense to be angry at the storm or, in contrast, to declare love for the sun. They are both facts of life indifferent to how you may feel about them, even though it may be comforting to imbue them with human attributes.

American journalist Donald G M McNeil Jnr, confirms this impression when he reflects on the inappropriateness of comparisons between Brenda and Madonna. 'In interviews,' he says in *A Common Hunger to Sing*,

> [T]he comparison to Madonna seems ridiculous. Madonna is a study in calculation; Fassie is all impulse. She cannot sit still, leaps to answer phones that are not hers, peremptorily sends people out for things like artificial fingernails and ice cream bars. She brags that she'll tell anybody who her sexual partner was the previous night.

On the other hand, Mark Gevisser in the *Mail & Guardian* concludes: 'She is a textbook tabloid commodity: her fix, and her downfall, has been notoriety, not cocaine.' Not quite, I think. Her fix, not really a fix because it is who she primarily is, is her innocence, which may have courted notoriety as a method of expression, bumped into along the way. If Brenda had discovered something exciting about being a nun, something about which, as a musician, she could say some outrageous things and swing her pelvis on the stage in the process with the kind of zeal some born-again religious people can demonstrate, she would have played around with saintliness as a method of expression. At bottom is the desire to be. Unbridled freedom, though, like the political strategy of ungovernability, can burn the one that wields it.

If this has been a personal, imaginative embrace of Brenda, I have also now made the personal, public. I think the Truth and Reconciliation Commission was also about making the private, public. I think that only if we attempt this pouring out of personal feeling and thinking into the public domain will a new public become possible. We cannot tell what kind of public it will be, but we do need to release more and more personal data into our public home to bring about a more real human environment: more real because it is more honest, more trusting, and more expressive.

And so, the journey that began in my bed on a languid spring morning in 1984 in the Roma valley in Lesotho is far from over. Twenty years later, I am in a free country and Brenda Fassie is dead. But we have her music.

Learning to Give Up Certitudes

vulnerability in our mutual need

2004

I have from time to time reflected on the human condition through the prism of literary art. As a South African who is black, a man, a husband and father, a teacher who has interacted with many students, teachers and researchers over the years, I affirm this value regularly as a tribute to those who learn and teach, as well as exercise leadership.

By a remarkable coincidence, this year South Africa celebrates ten years of democracy. While our country feels new, my university proudly feels old and, hopefully, wise and mellow. But, we feel so intimidated by the passionate youthfulness of our country that we are doing everything we can to reinvent ourself, and if we cannot succeed in actually looking young, we may at least try to feel so.

I look at more than two hundred years of democracy in the United States, and wonder how its communities feel at this point. Do they feel old and wise and mellow? Or have they had more than two hundred years of passionate youthfulness? These are not the kinds of questions to ask young people who, in the glory of their youthfulness, despite being young, are enjoying yet another birth today. Being old is far from their thoughts right now. Yet, I would like to invite you to try to be old, not in age, but in the ability to stretch the imagination back into history because I am fascinated by what ten years of one country and more than two hundred years of another means about what could possibly connect them.

Ten years ago my country achieved its freedom from tyranny and oppression. But we did not attain our freedom in the usual way. Our road towards liberty could be described as counter-intuitive. This means that in a world that had become conditioned to think of conflict, particularly

---

Commencement address, Wesleyan University, Middletown, Connecticut, 23 May 2004

between black people and white people, as something that ends in victors and vanquished, the winner taking all, it was strange not to have had a racial war and, secondly, that the contending races negotiated themselves out of conflict in favour of an outcome with two victors and no losers. Very strange! What kind of people give up power? What kind of people give up the possibility of winning it?

What most of us recognised in South Africa, at the very last moment, was just how much we needed one another. We realised that violent confrontation promised only mutual destruction and a long life of shared misery. It was a choice we made. It was a choice against habit: the habit of seeking to march into the final battle. But there is something deeper about the choice of abandoning habit. It is something we have not fully reflected on.

South Africans have been reflecting on the impact of the last ten years on their lives. Rightly, they have pointed to achievements that were beyond our imaginations. Within ten years, millions of people have their own houses, clean water, electricity, telephones, and universal early schooling. Major institutions of democracy such as Parliament, the Constitutional Court and other courts of law are used to resolve disagreement and conflict.

While these achievements are real and substantial, the deeper revolution in South African society is not sufficiently appreciated. It is that we have not explored fully the implications of our counter-intuitive solution.

I like to think of this matter this way: consider the white leaders who had been telling their followers by word and deed, and through the way they organised society into the contrasts of black and white, power and powerlessness, wealth and poverty, that they had a divine right to be superior to black people only for these leaders to declare almost overnight that that view was wrong all along. How do you turn around in this way and retain credibility? Such leaders faced the fear of loss of credibility, of being thought to have betrayed their people, to have cowardly lost their nerve and become weak at a crucial moment.

Many whites did feel betrayed. Many experienced confusion and tremendous anguish when, overnight, they lost their specialness. We remember one who in a fit of anger and frustration took his gun and shot any black person he came across, killing many. Remarkably, many others recoiled in horror before what they suddenly recognised in themselves. What they saw of themselves reflected in that gory drama they found revolting. They were later to vote overwhelmingly in a referendum for a new future without violence.

On the other hand, consider the black leaders, symbolised by Nelson Mandela, who told their followers over decades of struggle that the white man understood only one thing: the language of violence. Freedom would come only at the barrel of a gun. Then one afternoon, on the very day that Mandela was released and tens of thousands of people waited for him to announce the beginning of the war, he told them, instead, about responsibility, reminding them about higher goals of freedom. It set the conditions for negotiating with the enemy. How do you turn around in this way and retain credibility?

What these events dramatised in an intriguing way was how two camps recognised mutual vulnerability through exposing themselves to considerable risk. In doing so, both sides resisted the attractive, historic habit of being 'tough'. Being tough would have meant going to war at whatever price because both would have convinced themselves that truth was on their side. Thankfully, our leaders realised that being tough in this kind of way had caused much misery in the history of humanity. Caught in the clutches of danger, they discovered a new meaning of toughness as something much harder to do. They discovered that being tough lay not so much in going to war but in choosing to avoid it.

I believe there have been remarkable benefits from this that were profoundly human. South Africans gave up one-dimensional ways of thinking about one another. They gave up bias, stereotype, and preconception. In giving up historically determined certitudes about themselves, they sought to become far more tolerant, more open-minded, more accepting of personal or group faults. And that, for me, has been the greatest South African revolution: the transformation of deeply held personal and group attitudes and beliefs.

Perhaps, to get a sense of just how far we have come, we must recall what it was like living in South Africa just before we gave up war and violence as a solution to our problems. We remember how arrogant and self-righteous members of white society and their apartheid government were in those days, and how these attributes of behaviour made them blind to their cruelty and the extent of it. They projected invincibility, as if things would be the way they wanted them to be to the end of time. Being the most powerful military machine in Africa, they had terrorised the entire sub-continent into submission. The South African sun would never set. South Africa had become a manipulative state obsessed with mechanisms of its own survival. Its military capability had far outstripped its capacity to be accountable to a higher moral order. South African identity became inseparable from, and even reducible to, its weapons of war.

South African whites had the sense that they could stand up to the whole world, defy global opinion and do whatever they liked in the pursuit and promotion of their self-interest. In this they subjected their own citizens to the kind of control and brutality they meted out to others. In dealing with those they regarded as of lesser human quality than themselves, they were accountable to no higher morality. I remember that, far from earning my respect, they engendered fear. But it was a fear that went with deep loathing.

It all seems like a dream now. Within a short time, the false sense of invincibility gave way to a deeply liberating sense of vulnerability, and even humility. That was one of the defining moments of our transformation: this embracing of uncertainty and vulnerability, which went at the same time with the certitude that the past was unsustainable.

I have reflected much on this. What seems to happen in this situation is that, at the point at which you recognise mutual vulnerability between yourself and an adversary that will not go away, you signal a preparedness to recognise that there might be new grounds for a common humanity, whose promise lies in the real possibility that you may have to give up something of what has defined your reality, handed down from a past that cannot entirely meet your best interests now and in the future. It is the humility that arises when you give up certitudes around what was previously the uncontested terrain of your value system and unsustainable positions derived from it. It is the willingness to embrace vulnerability of the kind that faces you when you learn to unlearn because there is so much more that is new to learn. Your new sense of comfort comes from the confidence that others, who are on the opposite side, are doing so too, and are also experiencing vulnerability. It is about the capacity to abandon certitudes acquired through a history of habit.

It is a delicate psychology that is at play here. Its full potential is possible only through a newly discovered foundation of trust. It is about how to reconstitute identity, meaning, and credibility during that fragile moment when you and your adversary are both in danger of losing them all. It is about recognising that both of you are caught in a situation of profound need for each other. But it is never easy to reach such a position, and if it can be so difficult for individuals, consider how difficult it must be for entire nations. Few are the moments in history when nations were in a position to accept that they could be wrong; that a value system that stood them so well through centuries may no longer be sustainable. In this, nations would rather go to war and be humiliated by unintended outcomes that showed them just how much they ignored an inner voice of caution, or were forced by pride to ignore it.

Things have not been easy for us. Peace persists, but it has not been without pain. The divide between the wealthy and the poor is still great (often seems to be increasing); although the combating of crime and corruption is beginning to have desired effects, the levels of crime are still unacceptable; the spatial landscape of apartheid persists, and so does the uneven distribution of opportunity. With everyone having lost face, we are all finding new faces as we willingly struggle with the problems along the way.

These reflections arise from my challenge to young people to stretch their imagination back into history to try to find what could possibly connect a ten-year democracy with one that is more than two hundred years old. Well, what is it?

We still recall with excitement in South Africa, the pains, traumas, and finally the pleasures of giving up a past. I believe that, for the young people of the United States, the connection is their capacity to recall how exciting it was to do so, more than two hundred years ago. Where do they sense themselves to be at this juncture in our common world? Is there reason to contemplate another birth? Is there need for some great leap to be taken? One of the greatest fears of political leadership is the fear of losing it. The question is: has the fear become so inordinate that it has become a real threat to the future?

So much that has happened to the United States since 9/11 when the world was truly in solidarity with that country. But something seems to have happened in the aftermath that has made the world seem much more troubled, more divided. Since then, I experience the world with increasing fear. I see the world becoming more and more divided. I sense that the situation we are in, from a global perspective, is not fundamentally different from where my country was ten years ago. I sense that the world needs a leading nation, or groups of nations, that can reassure, inspire hope, and offer fresh perspectives and new directions. I ask myself what that nation or nations could possibly be. I do not have an unambiguous answer. One moment I know it, the next moment I do not. Of one thing I am certain, though: the evolution of global awareness has led us to yearn for a world that needs to value highly multiple visions of itself. We need leadership to get us there. Where will it come from?

One thing is certain: war and conquests in the twenty-first century suddenly look distressingly primitive as instruments for conducting the affairs of the world, no matter how advanced the weapons of war. We need a new value system for resolving world conflicts. In that value system, the mechanisms for the resolution of conflicts and disputes would be founded on the principle that it is possible and even desirable to achieve mutually affirming solutions: to have mutually respectful victors and no losers. The value system based on the single, predetermined solution, often one that is imposed by force of arms, will not result in mutually affirming outcomes, but can generate powerful human emotions that lead to perpetual global dissonance, anxiety, fear and despair.

I do have faith in the power of humanity to reinvent itself. In this, every young generation offers that possibility. That is why I am so happy when the young move out into the world, confident that they will contribute to societal renewal through their infectious enthusiasm and zest for life. Universities continue to bring out young people who can think about our world in new ways. South Africa and the United States can play a vital role in facing the challenge to renew a world that sends out many messages to us about just how much we need one another. We can no longer afford to be blind in continuing to ignore those messages.

Acts of Transgression

on entertaining difference and managing vulnerabilities

2004

The identification of human suffering requires, therefore, a great investment
in oppositional representation and imagination ... to think emancipation and
the struggle for emancipation is both an act of social transgression and an act
of epistemological transgression.

T his most apt quotation from Boaventura de Sousa Santos appealed to me as intriguingly disturbing. I was struck by my reaction to this quotation, remembering that the expression 'investment in oppositional representation and imagination' could have signified, not too long ago, an easy identification of myself with such investment. It had immediate targets, easily identified and located out there, external to myself. Transgressions, whether against a social, political order or against dominant ideas supportive of such order, were easily accepted and accorded immediate validity and legitimacy. That was the context of struggle where the lines of conflict were clear, with a limited range of doubt.

Now I find that reading such a statement sets up an uncomfortable ambiguity. Suddenly, I experience the erstwhile target out there as something intimately inside of me. Opposed positions, which in the past were elements of an external drama, I now experience as located within me. This, you will admit, constitutes a terrain of immense confusion. But it is a confusion, I suspect, that all who had agreed to participate in this momentous historical moment experienced to varying degrees. I submit that this is a confusion we all need to embrace.

The confusion may have something to do with the fact that South

Voices of the Transition: the politics, poetics, and practices of social change in South Africa.
(eds. Edgar Pieterse and Frank Meintjies), Heinemann, Sandown, 2004

Africans may recreate the comfort zones of old solidarities even when such solidarities may have been rendered unworkable in a new situation in which new roles cut across those very solidarities. In effect, those who elected and those who were elected on 27 April 1994 assumed a common knowledge and expectations of how governance and the mechanisms of administering a new society would work themselves out. In reality, such assumptions of shared understanding may have contained some elements of illusion.

April 1994 brought about a complete displacement of white people by black people in the centres of political power. When this happened, we did not fully appreciate to what extent the inherited structures and workings of government and the world of business could generate significant discontent among the newly enfranchised.

So the shock of Santos's quotation is that it forced me to confess that I increasingly experience the need to transgress. I want to shatter the illusion of old solidarities, by insisting that our past solidarity should not carry the implication that I will agree with every government edict. I want to say, there is a danger here that mutual expectations of uncritical solidarity in our new society may diminish the quality of decisions and actions to be taken. I want to say, let's stop complaining about racism: let's rule. I want to say, let's not make promises to the poor that we cannot fulfil. I want to say, we must be resolute against public displays of stupidity that pass as revolutionary talk. We must be resolute against fraudsters who, it now turns out, fooled us into thinking highly of them during heroic, less thoughtful times.

But in a democracy, what prevents one from staking a claim on freedom of speech and then proclaiming it? Here you will have to remember the story of the caged animal which, when the cage door was opened, could not leave to take its freedom. I confess to feeling anguished by the thought that my transgressions, committed in the belief that they represent a process of democratic self-actualisation, could be mistaken for betrayal rather than correction. This new world of my own, the space that is South Africa, is one that I am strongly committed to. It has given me an historic sense of belonging such as I have never experienced before. I should steadfastly resist the urge to stay in the cage.

However, it is not immune to the need for transgressions of the kind Santos invokes, and I am capable of being not only the author of such transgressions but also of claiming entitlement to speak my mind when I perceive wrongdoing and to be taken seriously without being slandered in return. And so it is that sometimes I have spoken, sometimes I have said, let me give them another day. That day then becomes another, and freedom is compromised.

But perhaps the worst part of the dilemma is the suspicion that mistaking a genuine transgression for something it is not could indicate the extent to which the tendency towards suspicion of dissent as something analogous to betrayal, during the days of struggle, may not have been completely abandoned. Such a tendency can impose severe constraints on public debates in which contrary views are branded rather than engaged with. Such a situation prevents contestants from discovering and establishing new discursive identities. When that happens there will be times when contestation is experienced as not occurring between the new and the new but between the new and lingering forms of the old that have not been abandoned

The desired condition is the necessary and legitimate contest between the new and the new. This will flourish when we succeed in opening fully the bottle of old solidarities in order for the multiplicity of voices, previously kept in firmly during the struggle by a cork, to escape like the legendary genie. It is this multiplicity of voices that should be the focus of a new, liberated politics.

All this suggests that the reality of new and contesting voices should be accepted as one of the primary foundations of a thriving democracy. And we should acknowledge that such a foundation exposes us all to risk and vulnerability. This is vital, for it would bring more honesty into the public arena. Mutually declared doubts are always empowering. They create grounds for new opportunities and solutions. They allow for new and fresh solidarities to be created. They allow for a robust public forum that does not brutalise. Disagreement that affirms contestants allows for more ideas to emerge and the possibility of creativity to increase geometrically. Two examples will suffice.

We are learning that the desirable policy of black empowerment contains pitfalls that were not sufficiently anticipated. Black people in business and government, who are now experiencing enormous financial and political power, can be severely compromised by received and unsustainable structures of authority and reward incentives. The conflict between material needs (from a past of deprivation) and inherited rewards, on the one

226

hand, and political legitimacy, on the other, can weaken individual moral resolve. This may transform a competent and proven struggle stalwart into a common corrupt official.

The inherited system and its structures of operation have the capacity to engender and spread moral anguish. But these may be perceived to be so difficult to dislodge that the only way out is to rationalise our way out of the dilemma by granting moral legitimacy to them. This is analogous to the way theft from the rich was given a political justification in the past. The capacity of an enduring inherited system to undermine a new order may lead the new order to invent and invest in measures that incrementally undermine its own legitimacy. It is a process of delegitimisation that can begin within a ruling party and then spread to the rest of society.

Those in government, driven by the understandable pressure 'to deliver', may expect compliance from comrades in the various structures of governance. This may not be because the policies and measures to implement them make sense, or because sufficient effort has been made to secure buy-in, but because the new officials assume that loyalties of old should kick in when required. In doing so, they may fail to recognise the shifting grounds of relationships, which are structural and role-defined, not personal. Former activists who could spot a bureaucrat a thousand miles away are unable to recognise the bureaucrat in themselves. This is not because they are conceptually unable to do so, but because the pressure 'to deliver' tends to suck them into a kind of tunnel vision.

❑

The second example involves the relationship between political power and social enablement. A new democratic government puts itself in danger, in the medium to long term, if it does not embrace multiple positions within itself. Such multiplicity may pose difficulties in the management of opinions, but almost always ensures a higher quality of decision making. Each position in a field of multiple positions deserves to be understood before being discarded.

It might be argued, for example, that the ANC has always entertained difference. True, the 'broad church' metaphor has been used to describe this character of the ANC. The metaphor also resonates in the expression 'the ANC family'. But the metaphor describes an important field of affective unities that worked in the form of ever widening circles of inclusion, crucial in the act of resistance. Increasingly, the affective, as a principle for ensuring broad unity, may need to give way to the professional. The 'broad church' cannot deliver on its own. The need for internal coherence is no longer required to prevent the threat of infiltration by apartheid state agents, but to professionalise the actions of those in power. Disagreement within the party should not be regarded as a threat.

I define the professional as a mechanism for achieving praxis in a legalised and regulated environment. The laws and regulations must be the product of a particular political vision. They may have their origins in voluntary and visionary association, but they evolve towards compliance and enforcement in order to actualise the broad vision. The professional-isation of decision making demands more variety of opinion, including counter opinion, as a principle, in order to ensure the best decisions. Every instance of strong dissent should not be viewed as a political challenge. Strong dissent on issues does not necessarily constitute opposition. Deployed in a context of strong decision making, dissent may actually affirm political loyalty. There is a need to err on the side of stretching the boundaries of tolerance.

In a new democracy that is still seeking to consolidate public comfort with the new order, publicly humiliating dissenting individuals is not a creative way of resolving internal differences. Attributing dissent to disloyalty too soon suggests insecurity and intolerance rather than internal coherence. It suggests a reflex imposition of party discipline in place of understanding. These negative outcomes are not intended, they arise from problematic choices which may become formidable obstacles. This may be seen as an early hint of organisational decay rather than a demonstration of organisational integrity. By 'decay' I am not referring to the effects of old age or some creeping sense of irrelevance but, rather, to the ability of the democracy to actualise itself.

In a policy environment supported by law and regulation, pressing for compliance and enforcement is understandable. But compliance and enforcement do not always, on their own, yield the required results. A government in power will need to create a safe space in the public domain where its own internal contestations can, from time to time, be played out without the fear of being compromised politically. The government can then withdraw into the formal sphere of power play and turn understandings into decisions without risking massive fracture. This space can be an interface between public policy players and an array of civil society players.

Such a safe space need not become a formal structure like the National Economic Development and Labour Council. Formal structures soon lead to expectations of binding outcomes. Non-binding outcomes represent a coalescence of understandings that may be more durable than signed declarations because they activate the integrity of moral commitment. The safe space can be found through multiple forms of cross-sectoral engagements, public debates and seminars. These safe public spaces legitimise the creativity inherent in differences of opinion. This approach would enable a government in power to manage the creative tension between the 'broad church' and central authority by extending circles of inclusion within a professionalised ethos, as I have defined it.

Of course, part of the problem is dealing with the notion of 'opposition'. The logic I have been pursuing strongly suggests that we should anticipate the arrival of a moment when there is no longer a single, dominant political force as is currently the case. The measure of current political maturity will be in how we create conditions that anticipate that moment rather than ones that seek to prevent it. This is the formidable challenge of a popular post-apartheid government. Can it conceptually anticipate a future when it is no longer overwhelmingly in control, and resist the temptation to prevent such an eventuality? Successfully resisting such an option would enable its vision and its ultimate legacy to our country to manifest itself in different articulations of itself, which contend for social influence.

The aim of this conceptual approach is to enable the current government to manage its own anxieties, and make choices with some confidence. It is a way of focusing and reflecting on current strategies, testing them for long-term aptness and durability. I have been concerned to understand some of the springs of certain emergent forms of discomfort in our transition that need attention before they fester into incurable sores. The subject is a complex one. But articulating the concerns is absolutely important in its own right. The thing to do is to let the concerns critically play themselves out in the public domain.

Jacob Zuma and the Family

how Zuma's bravado brutalised the public

2006

As the early stages of Jacob Zuma's rape trial unfold, I am intrigued by Deputy Judge President Mojapelo's explanation of why he was unable, 'for personal reasons', to preside over the case. He is reported to have considered it 'highly unethical' for him 'to try his former comrade for rape'. This position suddenly revealed to me dynamics of the Zuma drama that have been elusive.

Judge Mojapelo precariously balances personal loyalties and the public interest where these converge in politics. For him, personal loyalties, having merged with political sympathies, may have led him to the view that he would not be perceived as impartial.

At issue here are webs of social and political relationships that may bedevil professional conduct. It is how Zuma resolves such conflicting loyalties that may explain his apparent disregard for the broad public in his dramatic appearances before his supporters immediately after two of his recent court appearances over rape allegations. He just seems unaware of the rest of us. His single-minded focus is his political home: the ANC and the broad alliance.

It is a complex political home with a strong private dimension to it forged over many years of exile, and is capable of exerting a powerful public impact. Particularly in exile, the ANC evolved into a strong political community bound by powerful affective ties. The metaphor of the ANC as a 'broad church' often goes with that of the ANC as 'a family'. These metaphors refer to intimate and intricate relationships forged out of oppression; out of common dangers faced; joys shared over marriages, births, and personal triumphs of various kinds; grief over deaths of comrades in combat, assassinations, suicide, sickness or old age.

Sunday Times, 6 March 2003

Even gossip about affairs and the anguish of divorce is a string that deepens bonds. It provides the validating intimacy of shared personal secrets which sooner or later everyone in the network knows. Few beyond the network ever get to know. The organisation was an ever-expanding network of social siblings, nephews, nieces, uncles and aunts, and 'family ties'.

There must be many in the ANC who now look at Zuma and all his problems with deep pain. It must cut even deeper in the realisation that they are compelled to resist the family instinct to rally around him. It must have been in recognition of that instinct that even the president of the republic, Thabo Mbeki, had to throw a reassuring gesture towards his brother and comrade when he recognised the presence in Parliament recently of Jacob Zuma. More than an act of political management, it was also a gesture of personal reassurance: a psychological hug. Zuma can choose to be influenced by it and behave or, should he consider that the stakes are too high, he can ignore it altogether and defy its affective intent at the next rally outside the court, when he will rhythmically, in body and in song, call for *umshini wami*, 'my machine gun'.

Zuma is angry with the family. He wants to force it into a state of tension and anxiety; unsettle it through public displays of power. Feeling betrayed, he threatens to reveal everything at the right moment. This way, he secures the attention of the family. Nevertheless, despite his anger, I can see no likelihood of hatred between him and the family; only various degrees of unhappiness.

It is for this reason that in this battle the rest us are an anonymous mass despite strong notions of public morality in the country. It is the force of this morality that has many of us wanting to see even faint signs of pain and agony on the face of a public figure facing a charge of rape. The more Zuma postures his power to affront the family, the less he seems to have it.

The family anxiously knows this too. It is a paradox located at the core of Zuma's tactics. The conflicting loyalties between family and a constitutional public result in a psychological blind spot in which the public is invoked only to embarrass opponents; not because it is itself seen as aggrieved. The ability to see the public as aggrieved would almost certainly have resulted in different strategies and tactics. Instead, this blind spot, accentuated by the personal nightmare of his fall from grace, has distorted Zuma's sense of judgement.

He has yet to give us a convincing indication of his understanding that Mbeki, in the aftermath of the Schabir Shaik corruption trial, had little choice in deciding to uphold the rights of the constitutional public above historical, affective loyalties. When he did so, Mbeki pointed his party in the only sustainable direction it can take into the future.

The responsibility to uphold the rights of the constitutional public points to the unsustainability of the family ethos in the transaction of state business. In a constitutional democracy of increasing complexity, it can have devastating consequences. It can paralyse judgement and encourage indecision, until indecisiveness begins to define the very image of government. It can lead to easy assumptions of correctness and certitude. 'Family members' may experience increasing opportunity at the same time as they do not equally feel the pressure of professional and ethical constraints imposed from within the family. The instinct to protect one another must now be unlearned. The family ethos must transform in the direction of a robust public and professional culture. Where the ANC has called on everyone and every institution to transform, it is time it, too, did so.

But the family ethos should never be totally discounted. It can be invoked to humanise public life. That is why Zuma must now call off his supporters. His ability to do so will expose him to yet another test. What are the limits of his capacity for self-mastery? This latter attribute is vital for whoever aspires to high office. It will enable him to spare me, and others among the public, the pain and revulsion I felt when I saw him on my television screen, calling for *umshini wami*. Was he knowingly and defiantly inviting me to make horrible connections between the AK-47 and the invasive penis? The public morality issues at stake are as graphic as this.

That is why, as he sang and danced with his supporters, images of South Africa's raped mothers, sisters, daughters (some, infants), nieces, aunts, and grandmothers, raced through my mind, torturing me. Are their pain and the broad sense of public morality of little consequence in the settling of 'family' scores?

Msholozi, we presume your innocence until proven guilty. We owe this to you, with all the respect you deserve. In turn, please spare a thought for the rest of us.

Leadership Challenges

truth and integrity in an act of salesmanship

2006

C ommon intuition would have us assert that influence flows from the bigger towards the smaller. In reality, it is not always so. We have many examples in history of how powerful people conquered others, only to submit to the superior culture of the conquered. This is testimony to the strength of culture. It is not how big a country is that finally matters, but how successfully it has organised its national life. It is the power of organised living that survives. And this is the power of the counter-intuitive and it has immense possibilities.

South Africa is at a critical point in its still new democracy. There are indications that the value of public engagement highly prized by someone as counter-intuitive as Morena Moshoeshoe through his *lipitso*, or community gatherings, and now also a prized feature in our democracy, may be under serious threat. It is for this reason that I am awed by all those in our country and elsewhere who daily or weekly, or however frequently, have had the courage to express their considered opinions on some pressing matters facing our society. They may be columnists, editors, commentators, artists of all kinds, academics, and writers of letters to the editor, non-violent protesters with their placards, and cartoonists who put a mirror in front of our eyes. Even when they venture into sacred territory, as some cartoonists recently did, they are only reminding us that even the sacred can be abused for ends that have little to do with sanctity. It is their way of helping us, perhaps more profoundly than we realise, to preserve that very space of sanctity in our lives. They deepen our insights by deepening our understanding. It is fitting to celebrate their courage.

Inaugural King Moshoeshoe Memorial Lecture, University of the Free State, 25 May 2006
Edited version first published in *City Press*, 28 May 2006

They remind us that leadership is not only what we do when we have been put in a position of power to steer an organisation or some institution. Leadership is what all of us do when we express sincerely our deepest feelings and thoughts; when we do our work, whatever it is, with passion and integrity; when we recall that all that mattered when you were doing your work was not the promise of some reward but the overwhelming sense of appropriateness that it had to be done. The awareness of consequence always follows after the act, and then the decision to proceed.

As we celebrate these people of courage, we should also remember the actual threats they face from those who incite others, through hate speech, to commit violent acts against people who express dissenting opinions. It is not with courage that they incite but with their recourse to the narcotic protection of the crowd. Let us remember that our constitution does draw the line on what is permissible.

Section 16, subsection (1) of our bill of rights prescribes under freedom of expression:

- freedom of the press and other media;
- freedom to receive or impart information or ideas;
- freedom of artistic creativity; and
- academic freedom and freedom of scientific research.

However, 'the right' in subsection (1) does not extend to

- propaganda for war;
- incitement of imminent violence; or
- advocacy of hatred that is based on race, ethnicity, gender or religion, and that constitutes incitement to cause harm.

Bloemfontein has a special history among South Africa's cities. I suppose it is no accident that it became a famous railway junction. Its geographical location became one of its major assets. In those days of the railway, well before the time of the highways, railway junctions got people from all corners of the country to converge at a geographically convenient spot, either as a destination or as a resting place before an onward journey. Some railway junctions evolved into major centres of business. But Bloemfontein became something else. In time, people congregated here to confer, to debate, and to decide. It was in such an environment that prominent political, education, religious, legal, and traditional leaders gathered to create the African Native National Congress in 1912, the precursor of the ANC.

Let us just recall some of these remarkable people who established the ANC on 8–11 January 1912. There was John Langalibalele Dube (1871–1946), who was to be elected the first president of the ANC. Sol Plaatje (1879–1932) became the general-secretary of the new movement. There was Pixley ka Isaka Seme (1880–1951), credited with having been the intellectual spirit behind this founding moment. These were remarkable people, who were not only honoured by the positions they were elected into but, in turn, enhanced the dignity and stature of those positions, such that there was dynamic complementarity between the office and the attributes of those that filled it.

I would like us to recall that there was a significant influence from Lesotho at this founding conference. Morena Letsie II was not present at the conference. He was, however, prominently represented by Morena Maama and the king's secretary, Phillip Modise. In a most remarkable circumstance, Phillip Modise was made, on the second day of the conference, the ninth elected chair. This connection between Lesotho and South Africa enables us to play a little more with our metaphor of the railway junction.

Lesotho, under Morena Moshoeshoe, attracted people from various parts of our sub-continent. They had fled from the devastation that came to be known as *lifaqane*, as Shaka consolidated his kingdom through military conquests. While historians may give various explanations for these momentous events, there is general agreement that the resulting wars shook the social foundations of many societies in southern Africa. It was in this context that Moshoeshoe exercised leadership. How do you create order out of the surrounding chaos? More urgently, how do you sustain such order? Moshoeshoe must have sensed the pressure of external events pushing inwards towards him, and further sensed the limitations of confronting the pressures on their own terms.

He created a junction of sorts where those arriving would owe allegiance to the overarching values of peace and social justice while maintaining their languages and culture. Over time the cultural plurality became itself a binding value. Moshoeshoe was able to prove that diversity can be a binding attribute, in an environment in which it could otherwise be expected to be divisive. This seems a key principle of leadership for Moshoeshoe, and is not an easy one to grasp. You achieve the most unity among distinctive entities where you give relatively free play to their distinguishing features. This principle does not sit easily with our intuitions.

As in the case of railway junctions, geographical convenience for Lesotho was vital. As it turned out, the mountainous character of Lesotho presented a formidable barrier to a casual or a determined aggressor. In particular, the strategically chosen Thaba Bosiu became the quintessence of defensive capability. For example, in the aggressive environment of the *lifaqane*, Moshoeshoe introduced the notion of defence. At a time when nations enhanced their sense of security by attacking others, he introduced the idea of securing what you have. It was a radically different kind of mindset.

In addition to purely military considerations, securing what you have must also crucially depend on achieving the voluntary allegiance of citizens. Again, Moshoeshoe's method was counter-intuitive. Whereas conventional wisdom would have a leader wield his power to secure compliance, you are likely to have more compliance where it is voluntarily given rather than prescribed. The latter has only short-term value. In a situation as uncertain and insecure as the time of the *lifaqane*, you needed, paradoxically, citizens with a greater sense of personal autonomy. Such citizens are more likely to be resourceful than those who are held on a leash. Of course, voluntary allegiance is hard to achieve. It tests to the limit the ability of a leader to be patient and work the way of humility.

There is a remarkable story of how Moshoeshoe dealt with Mzilikazi, the aggressor who attacked Thaba Bosiu and failed. When Mzilikazi retreated from Thaba Bosiu with a smarting ego after failing to take over the mountain, Moshoeshoe, in an unexpected turn of events, sent him cattle to return home with, bruised but grateful for the generosity of the victorious target of his aggression. At least, he would not starve along the way. It was a devastating act of magnanimity which signalled a phenomenal role change. 'If only you had asked,' Moshoeshoe seemed to be saying, 'I could have given you some cattle. Have them anyway.' It is impossible for Mzilikazi not to have felt ashamed. At the same time he could still present himself to his people as one who was so feared that even in defeat he was given cattle. At any rate, he never returned.

The unusual way he dealt with Mzilikazi and other aggressors mirrored Moshoeshoe's relations with his people. It is likely that Moshoeshoe surmised: the people around me, secure in a protective space, have survived social dislocation elsewhere. They may easily reproduce in the new environment the culture of aggression engendered by the dislocation they have experienced. That could have rendered vulnerable the safe space that Lesotho could be, and became. It was not enough to secure the physical space; it was equally vital to create and secure a new psycho-social space through robust law and custom, and participative governance. A new value system was required in which learned behaviour was turned round.

The way of Moshoeshoe strongly suggests that the application of old rules to new situations will almost always compound the problem. The leadership challenge is in being able to recognise that there is a new situation at hand, and that what needs to be done may involve doing what, in another context, could be considered problematic.

❏

I look at our situation in South Africa and find that the wisdom of Moshoeshoe's method produced one of the defining moments that led to South Africa's momentous transition to democracy. Part of Nelson Mandela's legacy to us is precisely this: what I have called counter-intuitive leadership, and the immense possibilities it offers for re-imagining whole societies. In the book *South Africa's Nobel Laureates*, I have observed of this kind of authority that:

> The characteristic feature of this type of leadership is the ability of leaders to read a situation whose most observable logic points to a most likely (and expected) outcome, but then to detect in that very likely outcome not a solution but a compounding of the problem. This assessment then calls for the prescription of an unexpected outcome, which initially may look strikingly improbable. Somehow, it is in the apparent improbability of the unlikely outcome that its power lies. The improbable scenario is soon found to evolve its own complex solutions. A leader then has to sell the unexpected outcome because he has to overcome intuitive (and understandable) doubts and suspicions that will have been expected. In

237

this act of salesmanship, truth and the absolute integrity of the leader are decisive attributes.

Allister Sparks in *Tomorrow is Another Country* recalls one of the defining moments of the transition from apartheid to democracy when Mandela met some key generals of the South African Defence Force:

> Mandela, with his characteristic candour when the stakes are high, is reported to have given the generals his frank appraisal of the situation everyone faced:
> 'If you go to war,' he told the generals, 'I must be honest and admit that we cannot stand up to you on the battlefield. We don't have the resources. It will be a long and bitter struggle, many people will die and the country may be reduced to ashes. But you must remember two things. You cannot win because of our numbers: you cannot kill us all. And you cannot win because of the international community. They will rally to our support and they will stand with us.' General Viljoen was forced to agree. The two men looked at each other ... [and] faced the truth of their mutual dependency.

In a similar vein, I have observed that this critical moment calls for greater appreciation of the odds and possible outcomes and I quote here at length from *South Africa's Nobel Laureates*:

> Nothing could be clearer; nothing more devastating in its logic and the clarity of inevitable implications. Mandela's technique is to concede to the relative strength of an adversary, a concession that buttresses the latter's self-confidence. But the implications that follow the logic of the battlefield are devastating. They promise a low-value outcome too stark to disregard. They guarantee a pyrrhic victory of little worth to both sides. It is at that point that mutual interest emerges and is further affirmed by an agreement to explore a different path.
> The histories that led Mandela and his colleagues, on the one hand, and on the other, General Viljoen and his colleagues to converge physically in that house in Houghton, and even more

significantly, to converge in understanding, are divergent. But that divergence is superficial. In reality, the political boundaries that define South Africa, its economic landscape which, in its capitalist manifestations is more than a century old, the complex human movements across the land in which languages and cultures interacted intimately, all point to increasingly common perceptions South Africans developed over time, of an overriding reality more experienced than consciously acknowledged. So, more than the discussants at the meeting 'facing the truth of their mutual dependency', they were giving recognition and legitimacy to unifying tendencies that were taking shape over time.

The dynamics of that meeting in a house in Houghton are significant in another sense. I would submit that it is highly unlikely that General Viljoen could have given Mandela's assessment of the situation with a similar degree of clarity, conviction, and authority. This is because General Viljoen and his colleagues have been socialised to defend white privilege won by conquest. Such a culture engenders inward-looking behaviour. Where it is as powerful as South Africa's white society was, it turns other cultures outside of it into instruments of its self-defined goals. It limits the capacity of its defenders to empathise with and to even imagine a common interest with outsiders.

On the other hand, Mandela's clarity of thinking, strong sense of purpose, his moral and visionary authority, are all definitive of an ascendant value system. General Viljoen and his colleagues submitted to this authority because it convincingly included them in its articulations. They recognised the leadership of someone they had oppressed to have the wisdom and integrity not only to seek a future that preserves their lives, but one which also promises new kinds of fulfilment. Only the oppressed have the human capacity to free not only themselves, but their oppressors as well.

A number of events in the last twelve months or so have made me wonder whether we are faced with a new situation that may have arisen. An increasing number of highly intelligent, sensitive, and highly committed South Africans, across the class, racial, and cultural spectrum, confess to feeling uncertain and vulnerable as never before since 1994. When indomitable optimists confess to having a sense of things unhinging, the misery of anxiety spreads. It must have something to do with an accumulation of events that convey the sense of impending implosion. It is the sense that events are spiralling out of control, and no one among the leaders of the country seems to have a definite handle on things.

There can be nothing more debilitating than a generalised and undefined sense of anxiety in the body politic. It is a situation that breeds conspiracies and fear. There is a sense that we have a very complex society that seems to be evolving rather simple, centralised governance in the hope that delivery can then be better and more quickly driven. The complexity of governance then becomes located within a single structure of authority rather than in the devolved structures such as were envisaged in the constitution, which should interact with one another continuously, and in response to their specific settings, to achieve defined goals.

The autonomy of devolved structures presents itself as an impediment only when visionary cohesion collapses. Where such cohesion is strong, the impediment is only illusory, particularly when it encourages healthy competition among the provinces, for example. In reality, such autonomy is vital in the interests of sustainable governance. The failure of the structures to actualise their constitutionally defined roles should not be attributed to the failure of the governance mechanism. It is too early to say that it has not worked. The only viable corrective way will be in our ability to be robust in identifying the problems and then dealing with them concertedly.

Let me now characterise a combination of circumstances that seem to lead to the sense of unravelling. I would like to engage them in the form of questions. I resort to questions in order to avoid identifying and referring to difficult and painful events in a manner that could suggest that the mere reference confirms the problem implied. I want to avoid saying 'Look at the election violence in Khutsong and the continuing unrest there' as if you will understand what I mean when I say you should look at Khutsong. I have found that it is such knowledge assumed to be shared that leads to despair, for it conjures a reality so overwhelming that it is fatalistic.

Let me ask some questions.

Nothing could have been more frightening than when a plot by the

Boeremag was uncovered and some members of the organisation were apprehended. The general feeling then was that, in the total scheme of things, they were not such a threat. One hopes, though, that the vigilance of the State continues. In the course of the trial it was announced that some members of the Boeremag had escaped dramatically from a maximum security situation. As far as I am aware, they have not been recaptured. Lingering questions remain which feed into other questions raised by other unresolved, threatening events. How extensive is the probable security fracture within the security and law enforcement agencies? What has been done to close the gap? For a matter of such importance, the public does not know very much. The scant communication may dangerously convey the message that either nothing is being done, or the State is failing in this matter. The sense of insecurity and vulnerability is accentuated.

We have seen some gruesome, needless killings recently. Why were two young girls abducted, raped, and then killed? A little girl's home was broken into and, not satisfied with raping her minder and taking some family possessions, the assailants went on to murder her. Why? Why is it that, increasingly, the perpetrators are young men? Evidence suggests that these are not isolated events.

Why did the matter of municipal demarcation lead to the situation in Khutsong? The problem seems to continue unabated. There were a number of similar, seemingly local, uprisings in small localities around the country, a fair number in the Free State. What have we learned about these uprisings, which took place about the same time? What were they really all about?

What should we think about the seemingly unending cycle of labour stoppages around the country? The recent, ongoing strike action has been, by all accounts, particularly brutal, so brutal that it is difficult to imagine a union celebrating victory eventually after so many deaths. What kind of victory could this ever be? This situation is not helped by trade union leaders who declare that they do not condone violence, and then go on in the next breath to express their understanding of it by invoking its apartheid origins. When they do this, they seem to convey their inability to hold their members to account. They seem helpless. Or are they?

I should mention the one event that has dominated the national scene continuously for many months now. It is, of course, the trying events around the recent trial and acquittal of Jacob Zuma. The aftermath continues to dominate the news and public discourse. What, really, have we learned or are learning from it all? It is probably too early to tell. Yet, the drama seems far from over, promising to keep us all without relief, in a state of anguish. It seems poised to reveal more fault lines in our national life than answers and solutions.

The common thread among these events is the sense of an unending spiral of confidence-sapping problems with a beginning and no visible end. Individually they may have little to do with one another, having only cumulative effects. Are they elements of a cumulate message that a new situation may have arisen?

There may be a strong suggestion in all this that, perhaps, we have never had social cohesion in South Africa definitively since 1913 when the infamous Land Act was passed. What we certainly have had, over decades, is a mobilising vision. Could it be that the mobilising vision is cracking under the weight of the reality and extent of social reconstruction, and that the legitimate framework for debating these problems is collapsing? If that is so, are we witnessing a cumulative failure of leadership?

In the context of the public drama we have been witnessing, there is the real sense that none of our leading organisations seems in control of the situation. We seem to be on autopilot, where good work continues to be done by dedicated public officers almost as if they are saying, our work will speak for us. But the continuing good work and the continuing sense of crisis run in parallel, sending conflicting messages. Few are the voices that give some authoritative reassurance. I am making a descriptive rather than an evaluative statement. I do not believe that there is any single entity to be blamed. It is simply that we may be a country in search of another line of approach. What will it be?

For example, we may very well witness a call to unity, where the counterintuitive imperative would be to acknowledge disunity. A declaration of unity where it manifestly does not seem to exist will fail to reassure. We have seen much in the public domain that suggests that many within the broad alliance think that the mobilising vision of old may have transformed into a strategy of executive steering with an expectation of compliance. No matter how compelling the reasons for that tendency, it may be seen as part of a cumulative process in which popular notions of democratic governance are apparently devalued; where public uncertainty in the midst of seeming crises induces fear which could freeze public thinking at a time when more voices ought to be heard.

I am a speculating member of the public, looking for answers. It seems to me that what we need is a confidence-building mechanism by which we could acknowledge the situation we are in, whatever it is. We need a mechanism that will affirm the different positions of the contestants while validating their honesty in a way that will give the public confidence that real solutions are possible. It is this kind of openness, which never comes easily, that leads to breakthrough solutions of the kind Moshoeshoe's wisdom symbolises. Who will take this courageous step? What is clear is that a complex democracy such as South Africa's cannot survive a single authority. Only multiple authorities within a constitutional framework have a real chance.

I want to press this matter further.

Could it be that part of the problem is that we are unable to deal with the notion of 'opposition'. We are horrified that any of us could become 'the opposition'. In reality, it is time we began to anticipate the arrival of a moment when there is no longer a single, overwhelmingly dominant polit-ical force as is currently the case. Such is the course of change. The measure of the maturity of the current political environment will be in how it can create conditions that anticipate that moment rather than those that prevent it.

This is the formidable challenge of a popular post-apartheid political movement. Can it conceptually anticipate a future when it is no longer overwhelmingly in control, in the form in which it currently is, and resist, counter-intuitively, the temptation to prevent such an eventuality? Successfully resisting such an option would enable its current vision and its ultimate legacy to our country to manifest itself in different articulations of itself, which then contend for social influence. In this way, the vision never really dies; it simply evolves into higher, more complex forms of itself. If the resulting versions are what is called 'the opposition', that should not be such a bad thing – unless we want to invent another name for it. The image of fly-ing ants going off to start other similar settlements is not so inappropriate.

I do not wish to suggest that the nuptial flights of the alliance partners are about to occur; only that it is a mark of leadership foresight to anticipate them conceptually. Any political movement that has visions of itself as a perpetual entity should look at the compelling evidence of history. Few have survived those defining moments when they should have been more elastic, and that because they did not live to see the next day.

I believe we may have reached a moment not fundamentally different from the sobering, yet uplifting and vision-making, nation-building realities that led to the constitutional negotiations at Kempton Park in the early 1990s. The difference between then and now is that the black majority is not facing white compatriots across the negotiating table. Rather, it is facing itself: perhaps really for the first time since 1994. It is not a time for repeating old platitudes. Could we apply to ourselves the same degree of inventiveness and rigorous negotiation we displayed up to the adoption of our constitution? It is the time, once more, for vision. In the total scheme of things, the outcome could be as disastrous as it could be formative and uplifting, setting in place the conditions for a true renaissance such as could be sustained for several generations.

Morena Moshoeshoe faced similarly formative challenges. He seems to have been a great listener. No problem was too insignificant that it could not be addressed. He seems to have networked actively across the spectrum of society. He seems to have kept a close eye on the world beyond Lesotho, forming strong friendships and alliances, weighing his options constantly. He seems to have had patience and forbearance. He had tons of data before him before he could propose the unexpected. He tells us across the years that moments of renewal demand no less.

The State of Journalism
and the Country
asking the right questions

2006

Recently the South African National Editors' Forum celebrated its tenth anniversary. The forum has become a major institution in the current national landscape. Its strong presence helps to strengthen our democracy. This is even more so since we are repeatedly told, and as is borne out by the increasing number of court actions, that certain things must be tested in court before they can be released to the public. I hope the strength of the South African National Editors' Forum might, on its own, impact positively on the 'saleability of our country'.

My optimism is based on the belief that it is possible for market confidence to be strengthened by the corrective capacity of robust public opinion. Indeed, we must prevent the situation where our courts become instruments of a new kind of censorship. We must insist that the market of opinion find its own balance. Testing the limits of compliance is always about extending and strengthening expressive capacity. Cultural institutions of every kind exist partly for that reason: testing the limits of compliance. Media that do not do so are frankly of limited value to our society.

But playing such a role goes with enormous professional responsibility.

I had some run-ins with the media (newspapers and radio) during my interesting times at the University of the North, now the University of Limpopo. Recognising the enormous potential of the media to participate in, and help in defining and redefining the key challenges we faced, I once appealed to an editor to send back with a free hand the journalist who had written a patently biased and, I should say, irresponsible report on a set of

Keynote address, South African National Editors' Forum, Durban, 20 October 2006

events on campus. In view of the earlier problem report, I drew up some questions as a possible context for the journalist's fresh effort.

'Come back', I said, 'and help us answer some of the following questions. What kind of institutional conditions, in a transitional period of reconstruction, produce dysfunctional behaviour that insists that it is revolutionary? How do we use institutional systems to repair human conduct? Can we? How do you effect a fundamental institutional paradigm shift beyond rhetoric? Isn't it so that such a shift would allow the campus community to see problems always within context?

'Can a historically disadvantaged institution with its enormous inherited problems ever make it, given the impossible choices we have to make as a new nation? What would it take for it to succeed? What forms of government and community intervention can make a decisive difference? How do you revive intellectual activity where rhetoric and threats of disruption have become substitutes for intellectual effort; where the failure of personal effort is hidden behind the irrational accusations of others; where transformation seems to have degenerated into disruptive protest and endless talk about the future in response to a litany of well-known aberrations of the past? How and when do we move from the art of making demands to the art of honing our professional skills to achieve our goals? How, in the view of the newspaper, did the white paper on higher education address such problems with sustainable solutions?'

I believed that with answers to such questions, the context of evaluating the success or failure of institutional effort would become infinitely richer. The newspaper, in this instance the *Mail & Guardian*, of course, never returned, and never published my challenge to them. I felt that a journalistic and intellectual opportunity had been lost. The media became one feature of unconscious social behaviour I had to live with and factor into my institutional practice and decisions.

I believe that there are many institutions in South Africa that do not need to be told constantly that they are bad, and that people running them are corrupt. I believe that we would all be better off if the mirror put before us would somehow assist us to understand how and why some organisations were badly run, and how officials in them came to be corrupt.

It may be that this kind of probing journalism, which does not set out to look for easy angels and devils, is deemed not to sell newspapers. I beg to disagree. The corollary of a policy to develop a black middle class is journalism that pushes that new middle class to the limits. The members of the new middle class operate in a very complex and conceptually demanding corporate and public sector world. It is too simple to label some of them and their actions corrupt and leave it at that. The intellectual appeal of journalism that probes such matters will find its own market. I have to say that we are increasingly seeing this kind of journalism. It appeals not only to fear of the exposure of sanctionable actions but to the desire to do well through the corrective effect of increased understanding.

I listen to 'The Editors' on SAfm regularly on Sunday mornings. Last Sunday, at the end of what was a most engrossing discussion, the CEO of the SABC contrasted the relatively small circulation of the *Mail & Guardian* with the huge national footprint of the SABC and implied that the *Mail & Guardian* expressed small, marginal opinion. I wondered about this as it struck me that the *Mail & Guardian* could actually be seen as analogous to SAfm. Did Advocate Mpofu imply then that we should ignore SAfm in favour of the KwaZulu radio station UkhoziFM? I am sure he didn't, because he understands the role of each radio station within the spectrum of public interest in our country. It would be a false comparison if the size of audience was judged to equate with the impact of opinion. Media respond to and create their own markets. There is a growing market of readers and listeners who demand more thoughtful programmes and articles.

Now, I believe that there are many personal tragedies that occurred when the new black middle class being created found itself in corporate and public sector environments with remuneration, benefits, and incentives cultures that eroded the best moral resolve, at that very moment that they also promised to help meet enormous material needs. The pervasiveness of this problem can be seen from random samples: Travelgate, involving Parliament; fraud in local and provincial government; and abuse of State resources for special interests. The pervasiveness of this problem should warn us that we are most probably not just dealing with corrupt people but, perhaps more tellingly, with corruptive conditions. We have concentrated too much on exposing individuals without a simultaneous exposure of undermining context.

I further believe that it is this kind of context that can enable us to understand why senior public officers heroically accompany suspects to their court appearances, and convicted fraudsters to prison. Could it be that the collective sense of being misunderstood, despite the possible acknowledgement of wrong doing, may lead to a desperate and defiant closing of ranks that only exacerbates the problem? Unfortunately, this sense that there is no understanding of the totality of predicament occurs at the same time as the internal capacity of an organisation such as the ANC to provide robust internal corrective measures appears to have declined significantly. Instead, the ANC gives the impression of being an organisation that considers itself under siege and looks like it could implode. It defends itself no longer with its ideals, but with unconvincing acts of solidarity. Even where and when it seeks to invoke its ideals, the credibility of its purposefulness appears to have been seriously impaired.

This situation may tell us that the image of the post-struggle politician or trade unionist in South Africa has taken a hard knock. Once held in awe as liberators, they now seem on the verge of being merely tolerated. The awesome debates of old seem to have become the bickering of the moment. General conferences that used to inspire and point the way are now remembered for the shouting down and humiliation of State officials. How can we ever forget the manner in which President Thabo Mbeki was recently embarrassed before a visiting head of state in an empty stadium? I felt ashamed watching the television broadcast as it dawned on me that the event in question surely went beyond inter-party or intra-party wars. If there was ever a time for 'unconvincing acts of solidarity', this was it. If there was a moment in contemporary South African politics that lacked maturity, this was it. I felt let down by an organisation South Africans had entrusted with their dignity. What we have before us begins to look like the emptying out of public discourse and political process. What will fill the void?

For many involved in politics, particularly where mere organisational affiliation has conferred authority, this progressive waning of organisational authority will impose heavy demands on personal competence and integrity as sources of authority. This situation prompts many questions:

- Do we really understand the causes of rampant corruption and crime?
- Does our inability to provide convincing responses to this question imply more serious questions about the state of power

and its distribution in the body politic?

- If the current sources of authority seem to be floundering, where are the new sources of authority to be located?
- Where are the new sources of public influence?
- Can old organisations re-invent themselves, or will they fracture into new ones in the competition of new visions?

The point of my exploration, though, is not to explore the current state and future of political organisations but to suggest that we have before us, from a journalistic perspective, a situation analogous to the one that saw me appeal to a newspaper to come back to the University of the North for another unhindered look. Are we not in a situation of such complexity that it needs to be understood far more than simply characterised, and judged by implication?

For my part, I find that I am increasingly impatient and exasperated by more news of struggling organisations and corpses of dead reputations. I have come to expect that the historic forest through which we are looking for a direction is likely to be littered with such corpses. They tell me nothing new anymore. Instead, they may have become the new frontier of conceptual constraint that has to be pushed back towards newer boundaries. Without this, they fill me with gloom and pessimism. I see them and I do not understand fully how they come about. I want to know why they keep appearing. It is no longer enough to speak the truth to power through fresh revelations. I want to know: exactly what is *that* truth? We need to do more with more revelations.

The corruptive conditions I am invoking seem pervasive. Could they be the real threat to our future, not crime and corruption, as such? They are accentuated by continuing poverty existing side-by-side with policy-driven, instant enrichment. According to newspapers, some cash-in-transit robbers justify their actions by invoking political betrayal, thus imbuing robbery and killing with the legitimising tendencies of political motive. We do not understand fully the moral anguish of this situation. We have yet to grapple fully with the unintended consequences of some of our policies and decisions in the new democracy.

The anguish of our situation is captured not only in the social traumas we see but also in the extent of our inventive capacity to overcome them, even conceptually. For example, I am worried by important discussion documents of the ANC that still call for a 'national democratic revolution' with its 'motive forces' and 'strategies and tactics' in a discourse that nostalgically takes me back to the exciting, radical earthiness of the political language of the 1960s and 1970s. Distressingly, it all now comes across as lifeless repetition. I am worried about what seems to reflect a disjuncture between an old conceptual situation, with its own language relevant to its times, and an environment of new conceptual challenges that cries out for a new language. Is it possible for the conceptual journey of an organisation to be trapped in time?

What is the capacity of the new journalism to unravel this situation through a new engagement with its society? For sure, we need a new public space that allows for new bona fides; that allows for vulnerabilities to be expressed, shared and addressed; that replaces the brazen heroism of old with the fragility of a bubble that can yet withstand huge atmospheric pressures. The comparison between a nation and a bubble is fundamentally counter-intuitive. But the power of the metaphor lies precisely there: in its seemingly improbable wisdom. We are capable of being an indestructible bubble: strong because we are sensitive, thoughtful, and resourceful. Some answers to our dilemmas seem to lie there. But we have yet to face that new space of promise. When will we return to the table to bare our souls once more? Who will take the lead?

The Year of the Dog

a journey of the imagination

2006

It is many months since Jacob Zuma was forced to relinquish the position of deputy president of South Africa. Then he was tried for rape and acquitted. After these remarkable events which got many South Africans wondering about the future of our country, I would like to invite you on a short journey of the imagination. The temperature has gone down somewhat and now we can calmly reflect.

Imagine that you are witnesses to the beating of a dog. Imagine that you are watching Zizi Kodwa, described in newspapers as the 'spokesperson of the ANC Youth League', outside the court where Jacob Zuma was recently on trial. Kodwa was reported to have called for 'the dogs to be beaten until their owners and handlers emerge'. My name, according to reports, was one of four on a list of these 'dogs'.

Imagine Kodwa leading a crowd that has found a dog to beat and is surrounding it. They carry an assortment of weapons: fighting sticks, knobkerries, sjamboks, metal pipes and pangas. They are about to carry out a revolutionary task: 'hitting a dog so hard that its owner and handler' must emerge and plead for mercy on its behalf.

The surrounded dog is terrified, helpless. There is no escape. Its eyes wide open, it watches the crowd inevitably closing in. Suddenly, the crowd pushes Kodwa to the centre, where he towers over the dog. He knows he is being given the privilege of the first blow. He acknowledges the honour as he lunges with his fighting stick. It is a powerful blow. It cracks a rib. The dog howls in pain.

The howl drives the crowd into a frenzied yell: *'Bulalan'inja!'* 'Kill the dog!' The crowd weighs in randomly, indifferent to the dog's pain as its howls and yelps pierce the calls for its death.

Finally, its spine broken, the dog lies on its side, a bloody mess, still trying to raise its head, until a well-aimed knobkerrie blow smashes its skull. This silences the dog forever. The crowd continues, without a sound, to pound the dead dog's body. You hear only the dull thud of blows on the marshy body. What you have just witnessed was not a beating, but an execution.

The crowd then break into a triumphant cry, brandishing weapons in the air. They dance briefly around the dead dog and then begin to move away. Kodwa leads them dancing and chanting: '*awu leth'umshini wam*'. They have just performed a service to South Africa, in the first decade of the twenty-first century.

You have just witnessed, in your imagination, the enactment of righteous brutality. It is the kind that follows belief preceded by unconsidered declaration. Once unleashed it never stops until its objectives have been carried out. You are probably glad that what you have just witnessed happened only in your imagination. But be warned: the reality around you can be as stark as the world of your imagination, sometimes surpassing it. Let me take you down memory lane.

Remember the Native Land Act of 1913 when tens of thousands of Africans were thrown out of their lands 'like dogs'? Many years later, influx control laws were passed and Bantustans were created; hundreds of thousands of African families were uprooted and moved around 'like dogs'. Today, there are farmers who, having exploited them for decades, still throw out black families into the wilderness 'like dogs'.

Do you remember the pass law 'offenders' crowded in apartheid prisons 'like dogs', many of whom were then carted off 'like dogs' to work on white farms as free prison labour? Remember? White farms, mines, factories, construction companies, wherever 'labour units' were required in large numbers, were experienced as places of abuse where people were made to feel 'like dogs'.

Remember 16 June 1976, when thousands of schoolchildren where shot at 'like dogs'? And how, in turn, 'other dogs' from the hostels were sent by the State to attack township dwellers 'like dogs'? It all led to Boipatong, where balaclava-hooded men, bussed in, split the heads of babies with pangas 'like dogs'. We still bus in people 'like dogs' as 'voting fodder' or as 'demonstration fodder', sometimes just outside the court.

Remember the lonely and gruesome torment of Maki S'khosana, described as the first victim of 'the necklace'? Stunned by kicks and blows and stones 'like a dog' as the tyre was being placed round her neck?

Remember the old women of Limpopo who were killed 'like dogs' because someone said they were 'witches'? Or the man who beat a worker 'like a dog' and then fed him to lions? And consider how, just recently policemen acting on our behalf were killed 'like dogs' by criminals using AK-47s – the weapon glorified as 'imshini wam'.

You can see why the word 'dog' is never far away in the imagining of violence and abuse in our society. You can see how often we have treated people and things as if they were 'just a dog'. 'Nja-mgodoyi!', starving dog, is an insult that lays the ground for the beating of someone. 'Voetsek!' many of us say to people we unwittingly consider 'dogs'. 'Dog' is a pervasive metaphor regularly used to justify righteous brutality.

So, when Kodwa invokes the image of dogs being hit, he is showing how well-schooled he is in the archaeology of denigration and brutal punishment. How many times will he have witnessed the beating of dogs (people) in his neighbourhood as he grew up? Could he have been such a victim himself? Did he accumulate his own list of victims, and himself become, in time, the dog that hits others?

Come with me on another journey of the imagination. Imagine Kodwa has a dog and has experienced a profound conversion – like Saul, the persecutor in the Bible, who became Paul, a defender of Christians. Imagine that all those Kodwa addressed outside the court have their own puppies. Imagine that everyone has been bussed in with their dogs to the courthouse. Imagine Kodwa addressing them:

> Comrades, we have had enough of violence! For too long we have used the dog as a symbol of abuse. This must now stop. The dog, comrades, is a special animal. It is intelligent. It is loyal. It is courageous. It is dependable. It is capable of empathy. It cares. Perhaps if we stop brutalising the dog, if we stop brutalising ourselves whenever we invoke the cruel image of the dog we have created, we may recover our own humanity, which we lost along the way of our history. It is time for us to step out of our violent history. Let's honour the dog. Let's declare 2007 The Year of the Dog!

Imagine the crowd chanting: 'Viva the Dog!' They call for everyone to receive the gift of a dog. And they sing and dance:

Awu leth'inja yami
Uthath'umshini wakho
Ngiyayithand'inja yami
Thath'umshini wakho, bo
Ngiyayithand'inja yami

('Bring me my dog/Take your machine gun away/I love my dog/Take your machine gun away/I love my dog!')

They are all hugging their dogs, and this is how Kodwa and his crowd appear on the front pages of South Africa's newspapers and on TV. Kodwa's puppy is happy. It is excited to be loved by him. It keeps licking his chin. He tries to turn away, to no avail. 'What the hell!' he says, and decides to let the dog lick to its heart's content. Why shouldn't he enjoy being tickled by the rough softness of a puppy's tongue? Imagine! How wonderful! Imagine people loving their dogs! Imagine happy dogs licking the chins of their owners and handlers who will never again call for any dog, of whatever description, to be 'hit hard'. Imagine, with each dog loved there is one less beating, one less killing of someone by someone else somewhere in this beautiful country. Imagine all the people … loving all their dogs!

Snap out of your dream again. Perhaps you are now ready to make a declaration to your fellow citizens: 'A child is not a dog to be beaten. A woman is not a dog to be beaten or raped. Workers in factories, farms, mines, or anywhere else, including domestic servants in plush homes, are not dogs to be exploited. The 'learned ones' are not dogs to be 'hit hard' for not eulogising a leader who erred and for appealing to him to think of a different approach.

The South African public is not a dog that cannot make up its mind about a television documentary on the president of the country. South Africa's economy is not a dog to be plundered by fraudsters of any description. South Africa's towns and cities are not dogs to be trashed whenever we are on strike. Workers who do not agree with a strike are not dogs to be pushed to their deaths out of moving trains. Commuters are not dogs to be insulted and humiliated by minibus taxi drivers; nor are they dogs to be dodging bullets between warring taxi associations. Patients are not dogs to be abandoned to pain and death by striking nurses. Learners are not dogs to be abandoned to their ignorance by striking teachers. People living with AIDS, desperately hoping for a cure, are not dogs on which all kinds of dubious theories and medications are tried out.

Foreigners, particularly Africans from other African countries, are not dogs to be insulted, beaten and killed. Councillors are not dogs to be hounded out of their neighbourhoods after their houses have been set on fire. Yes, even the word 'dog' is not a dog on which to pin the meaning of all versions of cruelty and death. Declare all this and more to the world around you.

And then ask.

How did we come to view as debased an animal known for its intelligence, empathy, loyalty, dependability, courage, protectiveness, sensitivity and caring? Considering that so many of us own dogs, which depend on us, why do we continue to own what we seem to despise so much? How come an animal we own has become such a pervasive symbol of our own violence? How did we turn it into a symbol of abuse? Or could it be a symbol of our own failure to take care of it, and that it is comforting to know that we have something more piteous than ourselves?

But let me return to Zizi Kodwa. With the best will in the world, I cannot bring myself to believe that when he stood outside the court calling for '[the] dogs to be beaten until their owners and handlers come out into the open' he was aware of the full, brutal implications of his call. He could not have been aware of the full history of violence he was invoking; the kind of violence his own political movement has been fighting, and continues to fight by building a new society through our constitution.

I like to think he yielded to the seductiveness of a thoughtless moment. I like to think of him as a well-meaning young person who erred. I like to think he must have some remarkable qualities of leadership in him that got him to the position of leadership that he occupies in the ANC Youth League. It must be. I like to think he is a good young man with a future ahead of him, who might do better with wiser mentors. I like to think he should not have mentors who glorify guns on public forums twelve years after our country was freed.

I hope I may meet him one day, reasonably confident that doing so will not bring about my violent end. After all, I do not have an 'owner or handler' who will emerge to claim me during my ordeal. No one, throughout my writing life, has ever instructed me to write what I have written. That means I could very well be 'hit hard' like the dog of our imagination, until my last breath. But I like to believe that Kodwa, in his calmer moments, does not wish me such a horrible end.

I would like to have a conversation with him, to reaffirm with him that our democracy is still about dialogue; about expressing genuine outrage; about changing one's mind in the light of better argument; about accepting both the joys of victory and the pain of defeat; about the rule of law; about the difference between right and wrong; about orderly, efficient and caring government; about rights and responsibilities; and about the quest for beauty and intelligence, creativity, hope, kindness, humility, cooperation, friendliness, trust, conviction, respect, and courtesy in our living environments. I would like us to reaffirm our common commitment to a new and better society.

Who knows, we may come to thank Kodwa for starting a revolution he never intended: one that will occur the day South Africans reconnect with their humanity through a new and caring relationship with their dogs.

Perhaps, because of Kodwa, we may yet declare 2008 'The Year of the Dog'. In December 2007, the ANC will hold its fifty-second national conference. It will be 'the first assembly of the ANC's highest decision-making body in the second decade of freedom'. Perhaps there, at what promises to be a crossroads conference, a resolution can be taken that the dog, so long denigrated, so long a symbol of abuse, should become a national symbol for the humanity of South Africans, as they celebrate qualities associated with this remarkable friend of humans: intelligence, empathy, loyalty, dependability, friendship, courage, protectiveness, sensitivity and caring.

Yes, let us declare 2008 'The Year of the Dog'.

Assembling the Broken Gourds:
an appreciation

Sometime in the 2004 academic year I presented a seminar reading in the Department of English Language and Literature at the University of Cape Town where I teach. In it I explored the intricacies and frustrations I encountered while editing a festschrift devoted to the South African intellectual elder Professor Es'kia Mphahlele, published in 2006 as *Es'kia: May You Grow as Big as an Elephant*. During question time, a colleague of mine, having noted the respect I conferred in my talk on Ntate Mphahlele, asked me who I thought had inherited his mettle as humanist public intellectual. I unhesitatingly responded that Professor Njabulo S Ndebele was the godson and that no one approximated Mphahlele's incisive intellectual engagement with the same degree of reflexivity as Ndebele.

My response was followed by an awkward silence during which the questioner smiled (I honestly cannot decide whether this was sympathetic or condescending) and, since there was no follow-up question, I did not elaborate. I am reminded of this occasion, however, and am very glad of the opportunity to follow up on my answer here, having been asked to write an appreciation of this collection of Ndebele's essays. This was an honour I had little expected, the culmination of a dream long harboured.

Readers who are interested in the mapping of African literatures and African history, along with African political, economic and cultural struggles, will not be surprised by this present collection. Beyond their obvious connection as writers who graduated from the University of Denver's Creative Writing Program, Mphahlele and Ndebele are deeply involved in the intellectual, social and political development of South Africans, first and foremost the previously oppressed and the previously advantaged, in the process of nation building and cultural *toenadering*.

While non-racialism remains the ideal towards which South African society is moving, it is the stations along the way that engage Ndebele so deeply. In a journey beginning with the publication of *Sarah, rings and I,* followed by the short-story collection *Fools and Other Stories,* then *Rediscovery of the Ordinary: Essays on South African Literature and Culture, Bonolo and the Peach Tree,* culminating in *The Cry of Winnie Mandela – A Novel* in 2003, Ndebele has been at the forefront of theorising about culture in South Africa. The 1991 collection of eight critical essays, *Rediscovery of the Ordinary,* contains material penned in the period between 1984 and 1989, and highlights many of the central concerns in his theory at just the time when apartheid's master narratives and shibboleths were being dismantled. It also occupied, however, a zone of uncertainty, of ambiguity and treacherous, porous surfaces as a result of interpellation into positions not of the subject's making, and in which all kinds of 'actors and interpreters' with different scripts to inaugurate the possible futures of South Africa stormed the central stage, which had recently been conceded with reluctance by the oppressors.

I am thinking here in particular of the now largely irrelevant ANC in-house seminar paper by Albie Sachs with its pyrrhic promise of democratic vistas resulting in the happy ending of the political settlement becoming conflated with that anticipated in cultural spheres. What the Sachs paper did was to demonstrate the veracity of Ndebele's observation that 'the death of apartheid [is] a social process, not an event' (see 'Innocence Lost, Opportunity Gained' in this collection). Ndebele's previous collection of essays was used as cannon fodder in a battle not of his choosing; he was reluctantly yoked to the Sachs position as the debate regarding cultural production in the New South Africa raged. He was in a particularly invidious position because his earlier critique of the protest aesthetic was read by many in the liberal establishment as making him their natural ally in declaring an official end to the liberation aesthetic itself, a process that has not ended. While he may have been against the literary and artistic value of the spectacular, Ndebele was not against the liberation aesthetic, as his preview of, say, what eventually came out as *The Return of the Amasi Bird: Black Poetry 1891–1981* (1982) shows. This is the disjuncture from which misrepresentations of his initial concerns emanate.

In the foreword to the re-publication of *Rediscovery of the Ordinary* in 2006, Michael Chapman comments:

To return to the essays so many years later is to realise that Ndebele's perceptions were not always fully grasped even by those who supported his critique of the politics of spectacle: his critique of the 'over-determined' South African social and cultural scene of the 1980s. The error was to interpret his concern with the spectacular as an implicit endorsement of its apparent opposite: the psychological mind-set of Western-style individualism. Ndebele's understandings, in consequence, were placed by several critics in dichotomous relationships: art versus politics; and the personal versus the public. But these were not Ndebele's dichotomies. His strenuous formulations still await the full justice of their possibilities.

While I do not wish to rehash the multifarious arguments and declarations of that particular debate, it needs be pointed out that the very harsh terms in which the old order was described are certainly, in a growing number of instances, relevant to the current political order: witness the uncompromising lyricism of the underground poet Lesego Rampolokeng. Ndebele's first collection of essays has been re-published *without any alterations*, pointing to the deeper truths that they explore, some of them a good twenty-two years after they were written. This re-publication affirms the longevity of his project then as now: to initiate a rupture in the epistemological structures of South African oppression. Such structures are dangerous and, as Ndebele comments in his essay 'Redefining Relevance', severely compromise resistance by dominating thinking itself.

The disparities of the past continue to assail the present and, if younger people wish to take up the craft of writing, painting, film-making and the like, they are desperately prevented from doing so if they are indigent. They are unable to study at centres that teach these art forms, where such centres exist, because their fees make them inaccessible. If one asks for the statistics regarding the number of black South Africans with an MA degree in creative writing, one arrives at the bathetic weakness of Sachs' 'cultural settlement'. The celebrated 'normalisation' of cultural output and creativity that was greeted with such fanfare in 1990 has worked precisely to perpetuate a stunting of talent.

Despite a broadening participation in cultural production, we have a situation in South Africa in which significantly fewer students come out of our institutions of higher learning with more than a passing appreciation of literature, let alone African literatures. So much for the celebrated Sachs closure, for we can now see how it marked and masked not the beginnings of societal transformation but its reformation. I agree with Graham Pechey when he observes in his essay on 'Post Apartheid Narratives' in *Colonial discourse/ Postcolonial theory*, that 'it takes anti-colonial struggles to produce neo-colonial conditions'.

I wish, further, to draw attention to the line emanating from Mphahlele to Ndebele precisely because part of the more significant body of academic criticism generated around Ndebele's writings fails dismally to make this connection. Quite a significant amount of energy in this criticism is expended on seeking to understand Ndebele's intellectual influences and thereby to neatly repackage him: he is variously described as a Black Consciousness proponent in the early years of his writings, as a 'reluctant' purveyor of non-racialism in the early 1990s and, unfairly, as a 'charlatan' and as a 'jester'. This sustained, almost obsessive and systemic need to 'unpack' Ndebele's intellectual influences is ripe for debunking.

If Ndebele is said to have learned so much about the Enlightenment project with its attendant shibboleths regarding the call for democracy, for rights, for knowledge, for speech and for constructive social discussion, does he not also take these very same concerns from, say, the universalising and optimistic vision of King Moshoeshoe? Did King Moshoeshoe not in fact usher in an age of democracy in his time as ruler of Lesotho, with all the equally attendant implications and respect for cultural and human rights? When we juxtapose the King Moshoeshoe who is able to speak to our troubled present with the one dismissively described by Brian Darrel and Richard Murray, in the inaugural edition of the four-page *Cape Argus* in January 1857, as 'a petty Kafir chieftain' we need to ask: who was the more visionary – the land-grabbing coloniser or the colonised?

Should Ndebele – who spent a significant part of his formative years in Lesotho – not have learnt something of the radical-democratic leanings apparent during King Moshoeshoe's reign? Or did he not later, at Oxford and in Denver, acquire the depth of the Mphahlele-nic genre? As a budding writer, did he not learn something of narrative strategies and stylistics from the likes of Thomas Mofolo, J J Machobane and others? Why does the shaping of the African intellect almost always have to emanate from

Europe? The insistence on the cosmopolitan intellectual system to explain the subaltern/native is tiresome precisely because in King Mosheoeshoe's very open kingdom lay the very prototype cosmopolitanism that is celebrated as having emanated from Europe. What is surprisingly lacking in any appraisal of Ndebele is the fact that he is certainly aware of these contradictions.

The critical perspective that ties some of Ndebele's intellectual influence to Black Consciousness ideology is absolutely correct, and it is fitting that he was the first intellectual to deliver the Steve Biko Memorial Lecture in September 2000 at the University of the Western Cape. But the question that is hardly ever asked, perhaps because it seems so self-evident to his interlocutors, is why he should not have chosen the ideology of Black Consciousness at the time his own consciousness became apparent, as reflected most decidedly in the essay on black development, published in *Black Viewpoint* in 1972. While this factor of attempting to uncouple him from the Black Consciousness's intellectual tradition is historically determined, what is almost always left unchallenged is the perception that he was expected to react in a conservative, obsequious manner in spite of his sensitive intellect. He was at this point the president of the Student Representative Council at Roma at the time when the South African Students' Organisation (SASO) was proving its intellectual worth and organisational dexterity. This fact is conveniently forgotten but does not take away from his formative years the constants that were to sustain his efflorescence.

In the relative safety of Lesotho, Ndebele had access to material banned in South Africa – and we know he is a voracious reader who acquired this habit quite early in his life in Charterston Location, Nigel. So how could he have reacted other than as a progressive thinker? This was an era in which the deflated self-concept of black people was being seriously challenged all over Africa, a time when Chinua Achebe, Mphahlele and other writers gave meaning to what it means to be African. A cursory look at any academic text of the time concerning identity politics, such as *Black Self-Concept: Implications for Education and Social Change* (1972), attests to the considerable and efflorescent engagement of black people in self-definition. Ndebele was bound to be affected by this ferment in an era renowned for the ebullience of Kwame Ture (Stokely Carmichael), the fiery energy of Malcolm X (Malcolm Little), the intellectual clarity of Patrice Lumumba, the launching and sustained progression of the Second Chimurenga, the liberation of Kenya as a result of the spectre of Mau Mau revolutionary activity, the wider dissemination of the lessons of Aime Césaire, Kwame Nkrumah, and Amilcar Cabral, the violent self-assertion of the Black Panther movement which gave direct impetus to the Black Consciousness movement.

Ndebele was also aware of the tradition of black radical intellectualism begun in the 1880s in the then Cape Colony. Surely he was aware of the erudition of fellow exile A P Mda? Why he is not seen as following this long line of intellection is a mystery to me. I see him as a natural successor and intellectual descendant of this radical black intellectual tradition precisely because he profoundly appreciates the critical interventions of the intellect in the remaking of the body politic. This is not merely fulsome assessment. The present collection fulfils some of the constants in that process: the preoccupations around what Ndebele characterises as 'committed leisure', the role of the arts in extending the limits of democratic participation, the promises of advancing knowledge, the deepening of insights in the creation of liberating, positive social values. Such preoccupations were constantly argued and reflected upon by the generation that either launched or managed indigenous newspapers such as *Umteteli wa Bantu*, *Ilanga lase Natal*, *Tsala ea Becoana*, *Leselinyana la Lesotho*, *Imvo Zabantundu*, *Inkundla ya Bantu* and *Abantu-Batho* and, later, *Bantu World*. To blithely ignore so momentous an influence on Ndebele's development, to ignore the decade of the 1960s in black politics, is to do Ndebele's intellectual development an enormous disservice in favour of 'packaging' his intellect. It comes across almost as an imperative to control.

❑

Some of the essays published here were written in the 1980s and are included precisely to show continuities in Ndebele's thinking. If he can be so scathing of the apartheid regime's fireworks display in 'A Brilliant Trick' and its lack of irony in 'Iph'indlela?', he can be just as scathing of the new order, as shown in the profoundly reflective essay 'Thabo Mbeki: comradeship, intrigue and betrayal'. What comes across in the period after 1994 is a society trying to remake itself. For that process to have any resonance, voices of reason are necessary, the question being only whether these are for or against normalisation.

As far back as 1972 at least, Ndebele sought to provide that voice of 'visionary optimism' in order to assert 'the right to determine our future with our minds and with our hands' as he comments in the essay, 'Cultural Planning,' in *Rediscovery of the Ordinary*. What, we may ask, is the role of the committed intellectual in the production and reproduction of social knowledge? Is it not, in fact, to encourage the broad masses to participate in the process of becoming active agents in the making of their own history, to (re)discover themselves in order to understand their historic mission in their exalted emancipation, thereby proving that 'the mainspring of cultural identity comes from below'? An argument he advanced in the essay 'Black Development', collected in *Black Viewpoint*. The distinction between a 'traditional intellectual' and an 'organic intellectual' serves my purpose here. The former are defined as '"traditional" professional intellectuals, literary, scientific and so on whose position in the interstices of society has a certain inter-class aura about it but derives ultimately from past and present class relations and conceals attachment to various historical class formations'. The latter, by contrast, are defined as 'the thinking and organising elements of a particular fundamental social class. These organic intellectuals are distinguished less by their profession, which may be any job characteristic of their class, than by their function in directing ideas and aspirations of the class to which they organically belong'.

When I place Ndebele in this schema, it is less for where he is situated than for his *identification* with the class origins of those with a history of three hundred and fifty years of colonialism and apartheid and what the evolution of South African society holds for them and the emerging privileged class within them. This does not exclude those communities who came here as settler minorities – rather, this vision places an onus on those communities to see the development of the majority as a priority that will enable everyone to flourish in a constitutional democracy. Anthony O'Brien captures this perception in Ndebele's essay on 'Cultural Planning' (*Rediscovery of the Ordinary*) where he makes the point that white South Africa '... must participate in the trying heroism of legitimate struggle'. Such a perception ties in neatly with the essay 'A Call to Fellow Citizens'. It is reminiscent of James Baldwin's call to the majority of his fellow Americans. In his book *Nobody Knows My Name* Baldwin concludes the essay 'In Search of a Majority' with these words:

I said that we couldn't talk about minorities until we have talked about majorities, and I also said that majorities had nothing to do with numbers or with power, but with influence, with moral influence, and I want to suggest this: that the majority for which everyone is seeking which must reassess and release us from our past and deal with the present and create standards worthy of what man may be – this majority is you.

·The present collection of essays charts the trajectory of Ndebele's intellectual engagement by arranging the material in loosely chronological order. I have noted that he grew up in an era where the intellectual tradition of the 'New African' movement grappled with African modernity, resulting in the work of the African National Congress and finally reaching closure in the 1994 multi-party elections. Ndebele experienced the woes of exile and the benefits of studying and mastering revolutionary and creative works in the relative comfort of Lesotho. With his contemporaries, he was able to look at ideas, perspectives and analyses of a decolonising Africa even as South Africa reverted to uncommon repression in the 1960s and 1970s. Ndebele's theorising of his own role is captured in his insistence on asking uncomfortable questions and, through these, his insistence that we need to critically engage with such questions in order to remake South Africa, and hence to read more, reflect more, write more on the issues of the time.

In this spirit of unfettered intellect I am reminded of Wole Soyinka's assessment of Walter Rodney's intellectual stance and independence of thought, when, in his introduction to *Walter Rodney's Intellectual and Political Thought,* he comments:

> In an intellectual world rendered increasingly turgid by ideological mouthers and phrase-mongers, Walter Rodney stood out for lucidity, relevance, a preference for actuality, its analysis and prescription over and above a slavish cant. He proceeded from attested facts to analysis, not like many others, commencing with worn and untested frameworks ... onto which the existing facts are stretched, pruned, tortured and distorted to obtain a purely theoretical semi-fit. Walter Rodney was not the latter kind.

Ndebele's complex independence of thought, his resistance to being incorporated into disparate constituencies' varied agendas is apparent in his writings, a roving spirit in pursuit of truth. As Lebamang Sebidi remarks in another context in *Es'kia*, such a free spirit reveals

> the venturing spirit of an authentic philosopher, who cares greatly about society and displays, at the same time, a total disregard for the party line. Because he cares so much about society, he continually dons the garb of a forlorn prophet who bemoans the misery and the squalor in which he sees his people living. He searches and pursues the truth because he believes profoundly in the ultimate validity of the dictum *verita liberavit vos* (truth will liberate you).

In similar manner, James Baldwin observed in *Nobody Knows My Name*: 'We do not trust educated people and rarely, alas, produce them, for we do not trust the independence of mind which alone makes genuine education possible.'

The link I draw here between Ndebele and Baldwin is crucial. Whereas Baldwin was an excellent novelist, he is best remembered for the bitterly clear essays collected in *Notes of a Native Son, Nobody Knows My Name: More Notes of a Native Son, The Fire Next Time, No Name in the Street, The Devil Finds Work, The Evidence of Things Not Seen* and *The Price of the Ticket: Collected Non-Fiction, 1948–1985*. Ndebele's essays are written with the same uncommon grace, the breadth of vision and objectivity that is as piercing as any James Baldwin essay. While both might now be constructed as essayists, what is generally forgotten is that a well-written essay is as powerful a delineator of the times in which it is written as any other art form. To be ignorant of this fact is to forget that essays do qualify as literature. This explains my relief that Ndebele, like Baldwin and Mphahlele, has rightly joined the ranks of the public intellectuals. With one crucial proviso: he joins this coterie with uncommon style, nuance, sustained logic, various registers and the discursive languages of a literary intellectual.

Whereas some public commentators-cum-intellectuals use the essay form more or less as a newspaper columnist might use his allotted space, or in the manner of a Baptist minister or pastor pounding his long-suffering pulpit to harangue and harrumph their congregants in blustery language,

Ndebele draws heavily on his training and skill as a literary academic, resulting in the luminous quality of his essays. Fred Khumalo writes in one of his
columns that Ndebele's thoughts are presented in such simmering prose
that they remain with readers long after they have moved on. Is it any wonder, therefore, that the earlier collection of essays, *Rediscovery of the
Ordinary*, still enjoys such currency? The present collection continues in this
direction by making the same kind of commitment to scholarship and education, using the intellect for a better society and South African intellectual
culture. It also broadens in scope to include issues that still assail learning
and higher education.

This should not come as a surprise as Ndebele is intimately involved in
the failures and successes of the higher education sector, beginning with
what Anthony O'Brien rightly calls one of his angriest pieces – 'Good
Morning, South Africa', written twenty years ago. Likewise, his address at the
then University of the North ('The University of the North in New Era')
reveals an exasperation with just how much the culture of political activism
had vitiated a once vibrant learning and teaching environment. This is
followed by his analysis in the essay, 'The "Black" Agenda and South Africa's
Universities', where he is adamant that the agenda of change at all universities should be 'black':

> The fact is both historically white and historically black institutions
> now have to react to the imperatives of a new political agency. None
> of them can continue to react in their old ways. If this understand-
> ing makes any sense, then all South Africa's universities are in the
> process of becoming 'black'. By 'black' I am again not referring to
> human colour coding, but to the historic centring of the majority
> interest in national life. And it is that interest that is the driver of a
> national transformation project that has to succeed. In doing so, it
> makes eminent sense to focus in the short to medium term on the
> legacy of available strengths rather than on a legacy of weaknesses.

Ndebele's most recent essay on higher education ('Higher Education and a
New World Order') places to the fore the seminal event of September 2001
and asks just how this sector, too, must re-position itself in an unsafe world.
The same theme came through when he delivered the keynote address

('Learning To Give Up Certitudes') at Wesleyan University in the United States: what does the younger generation bring overall to humanity that will not repeat the idiocies of the past? Towards the conclusion of this address he notes:

> One thing is certain: war and conquests in the twenty-first century suddenly look distressingly primitive as instruments for conducting the affairs of the world, no matter how advanced the weapons of war. We need a new value system for resolving world conflicts. In that value system the mechanisms for the resolution of conflicts and disputes would be founded on the principle that it is possible and even desirable to achieve mutually affirming solutions: to have mutually respectful victors and no losers.

The abiding thematic concern (as O'Brien indicates) is two pronged: to bring about a rupture with the canons of old and to introduce reconstitutive, reconstructive hope. We should not lose sight of the fact that addresses such as the above, while the result of deep reflection, do not always achieve their objectives – the transformation of the higher education sector has been one of the most protracted struggles in the new dispensation. What they do show is that Ndebele is not acquiescent to institutional mores and values, being, instead, what Cornel West sees as 'the Black intellectual [as] a critical, organic catalyst'.

❑

In April 2006, while attending a seminar in Stellenbosch, I was unwittingly forced out of my complacency concerning approaches to the arts. I made the 'unforgivable' comment that any African writer had to be the sensitive point of his society. A colleague vehemently opposed what he saw as 'prescriptive writing'. I pointed out that African literature could not be uncoupled from its community and history, past and present, whereupon I was told he was fine with such a view as long as it was strictly reserved for African literatures. I was mulling over this exchange when I had occasion to read Orhan Pamuk's incisive article in the *International Herald Tribune* of 31 July 2006, in which the writer is adamant that pretending to write for 'an ideal reader' is a myth, at best. Here are two divergent approaches to literature, one self-assured and individualistic and laced with ego, the other probing, communal and compassionate. I pondered this seeming dichotomy for months until the Ndebele project landed on my desk. In this, I thought, lay a possible answer to my disquiet.

To whom is a writer, even a public intellectual, answerable?

My reading of these essays convinces me, more than anything, that Ndebele is a communal writer in the tradition now recognisable within African literatures. Everything has to do with that initial and ongoing project discussed in a 1972 essay on 'Black Development' in all its dimensions and the possible ramifications. This does not preclude the fact that such development must happen within the context of a multiracial nation, currently under construction. The commitment of Walter Rodney to an immediate polity and the wider community of nations is apparent in Ndebele's essays. He makes that archaic abbreviation, PhD (*Philosophiae Doctor*) come alive. In numerous phrasings and rephrasings, he iterates and reiterates a constant when he describes himself as 'a speculative member of the public'. Is philosophy not, in fact, the love of wisdom, starting with speculation and arriving at incontrovertible truths, however undesirable or likely to end in grief and tragedy?

How, thus, is a society that is drawn on the premises and practices of violent repression, the denigration of multitudes of its majority, supposed to remake itself without understanding the processes operative then and now? To speculate, to think deeply and with integrity while interrogating apparently known facts seems to be the only way in which knowledge can be discerned and disseminated. And to arrive at a level at which the intellect guides conduct in all socio-political endeavours should be the highest form of civilisation. To be a visionary, as Mphahlele recognises, is to have the prophetic voice that Lebamang Sebidi refers to in his essay in *Es'kia*, 'Two Types of Writers and their Relation to Truth-Telling'. Mphahlele notes that the word 'prophet' is not used in the restrictive sense of being able to predict the future but, rather, in the sense of being

> [a]bout a man who sings, the prophet sings, and in what he sings he repeats a number of things …I am using the word 'sing' in the widest possible sense. When you sing you repeat a number of notes. Just like the blues. As you sing, it echoes and it goes forward and back again over what you have said before. A prophet does that.

Now before you can become a prophet, you have got to be discontented. No person gets up in the morning one day and decides to prophecy, just like that, without feeling a kind of ecstasy or rage – without a sense of compulsion. You have got to be driven by an inner compulsion.

What then are Ndebele's inner compulsions that allow him no rest? With what is he discontent? It is useful to remind ourselves of the exilic process that shaped him and his generation, together with an abiding interest in what was going on in South Africa. Ndebele honed his critical faculties in relation to his discipline of literature, with its strong moral imperatives. Coupled with this is an overriding concern for black development. Whereas Western literature is easily manipulated to suit the tenets of the Enlightenment almost as an ideologically free zone of human activity – a practice that ignores the philological role assigned to literature by various nations, not least the English – the subjectivity of the African comes from different processes. Ndebele's keynote address at the Conference on Writers from South Africa held at Northwestern University in Evanston in 1987 contains kernels of that compulsion.

In a single sentence Ndebele makes a claim that might seem self-evident unless one uses it to reach an understanding of what is now recognisable as a lifelong project driven by an inner compulsion reminiscent of Walter Rodney's own lifelong project: the awakening of a deep-seated hunger for knowledge, a hunger for speech; a hunger for constructive social discussion in an intellect blunted by racist practices designed to deny agency. They awakened, he says in *Rediscovery of the Ordinary,* our hunger for the ultimate right: *the right to determine the future with our minds and our hands* [emphasis added]'. The mind takes centrality. Further, Ndebele makes a case for just such a project in which the collective hunger is assuaged through recognising the necessity for 'committed leisure'. He notes that:

> Where before, reading was a mere function of social advancement; where it has been chiefly an indicator of acculturation; where it has been a functional activity to enable workers to read instructions and become better servants; where to read fiction has been to read industrially produced romance and superstition, then the more

creative, liberating, and positive values of reading have to be restored. Reading has to be seen as the deepening of insight; as the broadening of intellectual horizons in the serious search for solutions to problems thrown up, in the first instance, by our immediate environment; as a vehicle of vital information; and, no less importantly, as the enjoyment of, as well as reflection on, the miracle of human language. Politically, reading will be seen as an important extension of the democratic process itself. ('Towards Progressive Planning', in *Rediscovery of the Ordinary.*)

In respect of Ndebele's own use of English, it is perhaps germane to point out that he has, for some time, been subject to criticism regarding his views concerning this language and its future role in the new South Africa, a form of criticism apparent in Graham Pechey's essay on 'Post Apartheid Narratives'. But this is a tired formulation and argument. Through Ndebele's 1986 essay titled 'The English Language and Social Change in South Africa' and two essays in the present collection ('Whither English in the 21st Century?' and 'An Encounter with My Roots') extends his interest in 'dislodging' English from the claim of being *the* national language. Academics such as Pechey are insistent on who uses which language, whether that person can be duly regarded as 'post-native' or some such like nomenclature. Pechey's criticism is a theorising that occurs exclusively in the zone of Western universities as theoreticians grapple with, and make august pronouncements on, the post-colonial world; never the so-called First World. Such theoreticians need another (preferably white male) theoretician to repudiate their claims, in yet another tiresome process.

The combative strain in which Ndebele addresses such criticism reveals his growing frustrations at the initial crop of theoreticians' dismal failure to recognise that at the meeting point of languages a process of translation takes place, a process that they, being mono-lingual, fail to appreciate. They also fail to recognise the multicultural aspects of this momentous encounter, which Ndebele highlights in 'An Encounter With My Roots'. They fail to negotiate the crossings and re-crossings of linguistic thresholds that the black South African performs as a daily act; to such a subject, English becomes one amongst many linguistic registers by which the self, in Jan Assmann's words, is *translated* and *re-translated*.

To paraphrase Johan Jacobs in an essay on cross cultural exchanges, Ndebele, in his use of English, is acutely aware that South Africa is a polyglossic society and, thus, he is fully cognisant when he exploits English within its limits that he is reaching a select audience familiar with the language and its discursive fields. This does not mean that he has then to translate himself into eleven official languages at each turn! He is already *translated*! What Ndebele does, however, is to articulate his historical situatedness as a black person in an evolving world, now made more unsafe by George Bush's 'war on terror'. The perception that black intellectuals should constantly look behind their backs when using English shows a marked sense of condescension.

There are, alas, not many genuine public intellectuals in South Africa at present. As the society groans under massive socio-economic problems, and as the enervating succession debate continues to cause untold anxieties, the level of introspective articles has dropped to a cacophony of name calling. However, there are a number of social commentators who qualify for this tag, and it has gained significant currency recently, with the University of the Witwatersrand going so far as to set up the Public Intellectual Life Project with Xolela Mangcu as the incumbent intellectual. Among the more prominent members of this coterie of incisive thinkers are: Barney Pityana, Mamphela Ramphele, Steven Friedman, Judith February, and Adam Habib. A growing number of political commentators have also come to the fore, especially around the succession debate. This began when President Mbeki released his deputy-president, Jacob Zuma, in a well-measured statement delivered in a joint sitting of Parliament on 14 June 2005. The reason he provided was that Zuma was implicated in a case with Schabir Shaik, who was found guilty of fraud, and that both had 'a generally corrupt relationship'. This set in motion a protracted, bitter and divisive struggle within the ANC itself and the South African public in general. Matters were not helped when Zuma was four months later accused of raping a young woman who had visited his residence in Johannesburg. While he was eventually acquitted of this charge, during his court appearances all manner of conspiracy theories surfaced. It is for this reason that Ndebele wrote of Zuma's behaviour as the brutalising of the South African public.

To a degree, all these commentators, social or political, have had to contend with the debilitating criticism that comes from within the ruling party and its supporters. They have been variously labelled 'sell-outs', 'peacetime revolutionaries', 'ultra-leftists' (a tag that gained currency after the ANC Stellenbosch conference in 2001), 'coconuts', 'unpatriotic traitors' and – more recently by government mandarins – 'celebrity intellectuals'. The shouting down of the voices of reason and discernment is something that Ndebele does not countenance; hence his forays that display the mettle of 'the critic as interventionist'. The present collection of essays includes those written in the writ(h)ing throes of apartheid and, crucially, those that came after, up to the present. Though they take South Africa as their organising thematic concern, it is apparent that Ndebele is no longer to be regarded as a 'regional' writer. He expands the boundaries of his critical engagement to place South Africa at the centre of an ever-expanding world. His much sought-after keynote addresses to North American and English academies attest to this broadening world view. Together they result in the prophetic voice, the song Mphahlele writes of, which is revisited in various guises, each keynote akin to an étude but remaining part of the harmony.

The issues discussed in this collection include the transformation of South African institutions of higher education, leisure, the role of art in a democratic South Africa, social issues concerning the vulnerable, recognition of icons of our times, and the political domain. This is consistent with the form of articulation and discursive terrains Ndebele foresaw in his 1987 lecture at Northwestern University, leading him to assert that 'the textual authority of oppression [should be] replaced with the textual authority of liberation', even if such authorial re-textualisation can occasion painful moments of remembrance. Included here are rare pieces of debate, both within and outside of the academy. Take, for instance, the essay on the meaning of the late diva Brenda Fassie. While it begins with an autobiographical note in low key, it builds up and soars as Ndebele broadens our comprehension of what Fassie was all about: showmanship certainly, but also much, much more. Fassie was an artist who learned, untutored, to play the media, to make its fascination with her antics work to her advantage. But more than that, Fassie cast light in the volatile, seemingly hopeless climate of the 1980s, demonstrating the veracity of Ndebele's contention in his short story 'Uncle' in *Fools* that in the townships life was to be lived in the present with all its contradictions. We hardly think of Fassie as a provider of hope in the same way as the reggae music of Peter Tosh and Bob Marley, or the funky rhythms of groups such as Sankomota. And yet, Ndebele places her in that pantheon for, as he said in his Noma Award acceptance speech published in *Rediscovery of the Ordinary*: 'The task is to explore how and why people can survive under such harsh conditions. The mechanisms for survival and resistance that the people have devised are many and far from simple.'

Where the media may have missed the significance of Brenda Fassie, Ndebele asks for the deepening of perception and reality. And a perceptive reader can see linkages between the essay on Fassie and Ndebele's address to the South African Editors' Forum, included in the present collection under the title 'The State of Journalism and the Country'. In both we see Ndebele's engagement with epistemological shifts in the remaking of the old along with his often uncomfortable relationship with the media, signalled (in another essay, 'The Race Card') by his tussles with an editor who, thankfully, left his post but only after having inexplicably accused Ndebele of appropriating public funds. Proposing a newer, more counter-intuitive relationship with the media, Ndebele leaves the Editors' Forum with the challenges articulated in his closing paragraph:

> What is the capacity of the new journalism to unravel this situation through a new engagement with its society? For sure, we need a new public space that allows for new bona fides; that allows for vulnerabilities to be expressed, shared and addressed; that replaces the brazen heroism of old with the fragility of a bubble that can yet withstand huge atmospheric pressures. The comparison between a nation and a bubble is fundamentally counter-intuitive. But the power of the metaphor lies precisely there: in its seemingly improbable wisdom. We are capable of being an indestructible bubble: strong because we are sensitive, thoughtful, and resourceful. Some answers to our dilemmas seem to lie there. But we have yet to face that new space of promise. When will we return to the table to bare our souls once more? Who will take the lead?

The impression one retains from reading these essays is that of an intellectual at work: constantly shifting through aspects of his life, listening to impulses from interactions with the seemingly mundane and the profound, and reflecting on these experiences. The essays thus display a strong autobiographical sense of the philosopher-cum-writer/administrator, ranging from ordinary philosophical observations ('Elections, Mountains and One Voter') to the distinctly polemical ('The Year of the Dog'). Each is a critical engagement with phenomena, whether a tough topic such as HIV/AIDS or simply the lack of institutional transformation. Reading the collection leaves one with a Baldwinesque sense of criticism, recognisable as a shift in perspective from a creeping complacency to contemplation and reflection.

It is apparent that, from the moment he made his writings available to the reading public, Ndebele wrote with conviction and confidence and these qualities are apparent here. For, in mapping the various aspects of a liberated South Africa, Ndebele allows the distinct voice of authority to come to the fore, and always with the future in mind. His turning on its head the news of an alleged plot of a coup by Cyril Ramaphosa, Tokyo Sexwale and Matthews Phosa is a case in point. Instead of rushing forward to denounce and castigate either or both sides in this sorry saga, he notes ('Thabo Mbeki: comradeship, intrigue and betrayal') an important lesson: the further the nation moves from the promising vistas of 1994, the further it sheds its received 'specialness', and fails in the extraordinary effort to be noble. He demonstrates his concern with the loss of commitment to an optimistic, driving vision. And yet he does not mean this to occasion closure, for, as he writes:

> Yes, we are an ordinary people now, perhaps still reeling under the expectation that destiny owes us something. But when we became free, we lost our innocence. Yet we have to realise, too, that our new status does carry enormous opportunities. These opportunities suggest that a new kind of greatness will begin to be forged once we get down to mastering the new values and rules by which we have chosen to govern ourselves; to embrace the future boldly with a flexible, if somewhat pained, creative intelligence. That could be one of the many paths towards renaissance. ('Innocence Lost, Opportunities Gained')

Simply put, elegantly stated, profoundly direct: what the society has lost can only make it greater if it allows the rule of law to be consecrated in all its endeavours.

An undercurrent in the above extract is the humanistic impulse. And it is an impulse that imagines a radical democratic humanism taking root. This impulse underlies so many of the uncomfortable realities in these essays. We see it in the gentle chiding of an American president; the daring to ask the second most powerful leader in the country to spare the public his frankly unbecoming comicality of karaoke impersonations that feed the hunger for excesses in his supporters; the fatherly take on the madness of Zizi Kodwa, spokesperson for the ANC's Youth League and one of Jacob Zuma's most ardent supporters who had earlier called for Ndebele to be beaten up 'like a dog' for having had the temerity to write an article critical of Zuma's out-of-court antics. For Ndebele – as, it is increasingly apparent, for Barney Pityana and others such as Ferial Haffajee, Mathatha Tsedu and Mondli Makhanya – these are signs of moral decay that should be excised from the polity. Merged here is the understanding that mass action can never be a substitute for analytical reflection.

A modern capitalist state, Ndebele recognises, is much more complex than the general idiocies brought on by prancing about outside courthouses. And in such a recognition he draws on a readership of the like-minded, articulating what may be inchoate feelings of frustration and possible despondency as he searches for what Baldwin saw as 'the majority'. As he notes in his introduction to *Rediscovery of the Ordinary*, group excellence devoid of individual excellence is unlikely.

The sentiment reminds me of some wonderful lines from Mongane Serote's poem 'There Will Be A Better Time':

> if we be the most of us
> and the most of us is the will
> the will to say no!
> there will be a better time
> when time has run out for liars
> for those who take and take and take from others, take
> forever!
> and keep taking

for themselves alone
take and take and take
time has run out
when we say no!
no more –
no is not a word but an act, remember that – !

Sam Tlhalo Raditlhalo
Cape Town, 2007

NOTES

Quotations were taken from James Baldwin's *Nobody Knows My Name: More Notes of a Native Son* (Dell, New York, 1954); Njabulo Ndebele's *Rediscovery of the Ordinary: Essays on South African Literature and Culture* (University of Kwazulu-Natal Press, Scottville, 2006); *Es'kia: May you grow as big as an Elephant*, edited by Sam Raditlhalo and Taban lo Liyong (Stainbank & Associates, Rivonia, 2006); *Black Viewpoint*, edited by Steve Bantu Biko (SPRO-CAS, Durban, 1972) in which Ndebele's essay 'Black Development' first appeared; Anthony O'Brien's *Against Normalization: Writing Radical Democracy in South Africa* (Duke University Press, Durham & London, 2001); Graham Pechey's 'Post Apartheid Narratives in *Colonial discourse/Postcolonial theory*, edited by Francis Barker et al (University of Manchester Press, New York & Manchester, 1994); Johan Jacobs' 'Cross-cultural discourse in Es'kia Mphahlele's *Down Second Avenue* and *Afrika My Music*' in *Es'kia: May you grow as big as an Elephant*; Fred Khumalo's 'We are up to our stilettos in shallowness' (*Sunday Times*, 15 April 2007); Albie Sachs' 'Preparing Ourselves for Freedom' in *Spring is Rebellious: Arguments about cultural freedom by Albie Sachs and respondents*, edited by Ingrid de Kok & Karen Press (Buchu, Cape Town, 1990); Wole Soyinka's 'The Man Who Was Absent', an introduction to *Walter Rodney's Intellectual and Political Thought* by Rupert Charles Lewis (The Press University of the West Indies/Wayne University Press, Barbados/Detroit, 1998); and Wally Serote's *Selected Poems* (Ad Donker, Johannesburg, 1982).

Bibliography

Arnold, Millard (ed.), *Steve Biko: Black Consciousness in South Africa*. (Vintage Books, New York, 1979)

Asmal, Kadar; Chidester, David; James, Wilmot (eds.), *South Africa's Nobel Laureates*. (Jonathan Ball, Johannesburg & Cape Town, 2004)

Biko, Steve. (Aelred Stubbs CR ed.), *I Write What I Like*. (Bowerdean Press, London, 1978

Coetzee, J M, *White Writing*. (Yale University Press, New Haven 1988)

Eco, Umberto, *Serendipities: Language and Lunacy*. (Phoenix, London 1999)

Foucault, Michel, *Discipline and Punishment*. (Pantheon, New York, 1977)

Freire, Paolo, *Pedagogy of the Oppressed*. (Seabury Press, New York, 1968)

Gobodo-Madikizela, Pumla, *A Human Being Died That Night*. (Houghton Mifflin Books, New York, 2003)

Johns, Sheridan and Hunt-Davis, R, Jnr (eds.), *Mandela, Tambo and the African National Congress*. (Oxford University Press, New York, 1991)

Heywood, Christopher (ed), *Aspects of South African Literature*. (Heinemann, London, 1976)

Kuzwayo, Muzi, *Marketing Through Mud and Dust*. (Ink Inc, Cape Town, 2000)

Margolis, John D. (ed), *The Campus in the Modern World*, (Macmillan, Toronto, 1969)

Molete, Z B, *A Common Hunger to Sing*. (Kwela Books, Cape Town, 1997)

Philips, Howard, *The University of Cape Town 1881–1948*. (UCT Press, Cape Town, 1993)

Santos, B de Sousa, *Towards a New Common Sense: Law, Science and the Politics in the Paradigmatic Transition*. (Routledge, New York, 1995)

Sparks, Allister, *The Mind of South Africa*. (Heinemann, London, 1990)

Sparks, Allister, *Tomorrow is Another Country*. (Struik Book Distributors, Sandton, 1994)

Van Onselen, Charles, *The Seed is Mine: The Life of Kas Maine, a South African Sharecropper, 1894–1985*. (David Philip, Cape Town, 1996)

Note on titles

The original titles of some pieces in this collection have been changed. These are:

Good morning, South Africa (The University: Redefining Commitments)

Triumph of Narrative (Memory, Metaphor and the Triumph of Narrative)

African Renaissance (African Renaissance: a social quest)

The Lion and the Rabbit (The 'Languages' of Lions and Rabbits: thoughts on democracy and reconciliation)

Iph'indlela? (Iph'indlela? finding our way into the future)

An Encounter with My Roots (Multilingual Fiction: writing, language and identity)

The Ties that Bind (The Social Basis of South Africa: prospects and challenges)

Thabo Mbeki: comradeship, intrigue and betrayal (Thabo Mbeki: new opportunities for leadership?)

The 'Black' Agenda and South Africa's universities (The 'Black' Agenda and the Restructuring of Higher Education)

AIDS and the Making of Modern South Africa (The Dilemmas of Leadership: AIDS and state consolidation in South Africa)

Thinking of Brenda (Culture as Social Affirmation: thinking of Brenda)

Learning to Give Up Certitudes (Some Reflections on Giving up Certitudes)

Acts of Transgression (An Approach to Viable Futures)

Jacob Zuma and the Family (Jacob Zuma and the Transformation of the ANC)

Leadership Challenges (Perspectives on Leadership Challenges in South Africa)

The State of Journalism and the Country (Some Thoughts on the State of Journalism and the Country).

nny away the house was silent and empty. Sometimes he caught himself listening for the piano.

About mid-day on Saturday he went down to see how the building was progressing. He did not relish the idea of making his way through the Yard with the inimical eyes of the stallholders on him. They always watched him now and he often saw them nudge a customer and mutter something which he guessed was uncomplimentary.

But when he reached the Yard it was empty—deserted. There was not a stall in sight, not a box or a crate or even so much as an odd stick of celery to betray the fact that there had ever been a market there.

He sat at the wheel of his car staring, unable to take in what he saw. This was what he had always wanted. All his life he had wanted to see the Yard clear, swept clean, free of the contamination of the barrow people. This was how his mother had wanted it and it had taken all these years to bring it about, but the sight of it now made him feel completely and utterly beaten.

With a sudden sense of awakening he

him now. They'd have to see how it all worked out, but in future she would steer clear of running other people's lives and she would not be afraid any more.

Suddenly she realized she was not alone. Mrs. Tilley had lumbered in with Alfie, and Winnie and Glad Cheek were up at the bar getting the drinks. They all came over and joined her.

"Look who's here," they said, just as though they were the chorus in a play.

"I think we've got something to celebrate tonight," Melia said, and she told them of Florrie's conciliatory gesture.

At first they could scarcely believe her, but gradually they took the news in and became more and more elated. Alfie went home to fetch his father and Winnie Cheek was dispatched to fetch Princess Potter.

"She wouldn't say nothing, but Princess don't like it outside the bank," Mrs. Tilley confided. "Very draughty, she says it is, and she feels sort of on show, not like when she was tucked away so nicely in the Yard. Ah well, we'll see what we can make of Florrie's place."

All the same, their delight and relief were tinged with a certain sorrow. Florrie had been a raucous, obstreperous, outrageous woman but she had always put them on their mettle and roused their fighting spirit. They hated to think of her ill and dying. As Mrs. Tilley remarked sombrely it was good news but it made the beer taste flat.

But by the time they parted that evening the stallholders of Sparrow's Yard had made their plans and decided to depart to their new quarters with dignity. They meant to go quietly and at once.

21

CYRIL REDMAYNE ha[...] feeling uneasy for a long ti[...] at the back of his mind w[...] constant fear that someone might [...] the terms of his bargain with [...] Crockett. If the Press got hold of the [...] he shuddered to think what they w[...] make of it. He wished he could retract [...] condition and if he could have seen Me[...] in the Yard he would have spoken to h[...] about it. He could say he had been over[...] hasty, over-anxious, and he could appeal to her good sense as a parent. She would not be too stupid to see that a match between her daughter and his son was unsuitable. Perhaps, too, he ought to give that old man Wally Tagg something to compensate him for the loss of the stable.

Things had been going badly since they had come back to live at Villa Park and he had had such high hopes! Now the breach between himself and Helen was growing deeper and wider every day and with

knew that he wanted it as it had always been—he wanted the life and the colour and the confusion—he wanted the noise. He saw it for the first time as Johnny had seen it, all the poetry and the emotion and the music of it, and now it was too late. It had gone for ever, the old Sparrow's Yard that his father had created and he had destroyed.

A violent honking on a motor horn roused him and he realized he was blocking the road. A lorry load of girders was waiting to drive up to the Redmayne building, the cold, lifeless block of offices he had wished to see on the site of his old home.

The work was progressing rapidly. From the top you would be able to see all over Villa Park—it would be the highest building in the district. He wondered if he would ever be able to bring himself to go up there and look down.

Meanwhile all the Sparrow's Yard people were down at Florrie's place. Although it was a bad thing to lose the Saturday trade they had agreed to set about getting the new market place in order without delay and now they were all hard at it.

The shed proved to be larger than it appeared at first sight and when it was cleared, painted and repaired it would give good storage space.

The piece of land itself was as large as a tennis court, but it was overgrown with weeds which grew right up to the windows of Florrie's cottage and Alfie, Johnny, Wally and Uncle Harry were working at top speed to clear them away. Raymond lent a hand, too, but every now and again he would think of his mother and then he had to push his knuckles hard against his teeth and twist his nose into a sniff. Iris caught his eye once and she smiled at him. She was tugging at an enormous dockweed that defied all her efforts to move it so he went and gripped it in one hand and had it out in one mighty pull.

"You're strong," she said admiringly. "I was nearly falling over backwards."

"I could see you were," he said as he turned away.

"Raymond, are you really going to like us being here?" she asked.

"Why not? I've always thought fighting was a waste of time," he said.

"It was a wonderful idea of yours."

"Think nothing of it. It was Mum's idea, anyway."

"I wonder."

"Fifty-fifty, if you really want to know."

"I do."

"Well, that's it, then," he said as he began to attack more weeds.

Ascot had brought some tea and milk with her and half way through the morning she asked him if she could brew a pot of tea for them all. He took her into the kitchen and watched her while she pottered about setting out the things.

"Nothing like a nice cup of tea," she said in an effort to draw him out. "Here, you drink this, cock. It's a special cup—an Ascot special. Got a drop of whisky in it. We'll have this on our own, shall we?"

Raymond blinked and took it. He had a sip and looked over the rim of the cup at her.

"Nice," he said. "Warms you up like."

"Ah, that's what it's meant to do. You drink it down and don't you go worrying, my dear. We'll all rub along nicely. What about the coffee stall—do you think you'll keep it going?"

"I dunno. What do you think?" he asked.

"It's for you to say, my duck. I don't know but that I'd do it up smart and make it look all dinky. Wouldn't surprise me if it caught on. They're getting up to all sorts of old-fashioned things these days."

Johnny looked in at the window at that moment, mopping his brow and Ascot mentioned the coffee stall to him.

"Wizzo. A proper gimmick," he said. "If I hadn't to go back to Paris I'd help you with it."

A ghost of a smile crossed Raymond's face. "Maybe I'll do it up myself," he said.

Ascot encouraged the idea and they discussed it together. They were at ease with each other and she remembered how she had given him apples when he was a little urchin and he recalled that she had rumpled his hair and smiled at him when Mrs. Crockett wasn't looking. And now they were all to be together with him driving the van Mrs. Crockett was going to buy. Even Mrs. Crockett wasn't so bad once you got used to her. She had talked to him quite kind and sympathetic this morning and one day he was going round to Lantern Place again—she had asked him if he would and he was looking forward to it. From what he had seen it looked nice and cosy round there and so tidy and neat. Poor old Mum! He'd have to get the cottage tidied up, get it all decorated and made to look smashing. It would be quite a picture and Mrs. Crockett— she'd said he'd better call her Auntie Melia —had asked him if he'd like the market to be called Perks' Place. He thought that sounded very classy. Maybe in time it would be even better than Sparrow's Yard.

The work went on again next day. Better the day better the deed, as Camille said. Uncle Wally was not there because he had shaved his face, put on his best suit and gone down to the country to see Dook. He had done the same thing last Sunday and come back with an encouraging report.

"Just the same he is," he told them all delightedly. "I went to the gate of the paddock and called out, 'Come on then, Dook boy,' and he was over like a shot.

Might have been waiting for me. Looks younger, though—all of ten years."

"Seems you're going to make a habit of this, young Wally," Ascot said.

Wally grinned sheepishly. "Why not?" he asked. "I always did like to see a bit of green."

But he was home in time for the gathering at Camille's that evening because they were going to celebrate Iris and Johnny's engagement. Maurice was there too because Johnny was staying with him and he found an opportunity to confide some of his hopes to the family when the young people were out of the way.

"I'm almost scared to talk about it, but that young Johnny's got a real future in music," he said. "I've managed to talk him out of throwing up his job in the bank —don't want to go and be precipitate, you know—but the way he's shaping with Reub I can see another *Silver Staircase* on the way. Keep it under your hats, though."

Camille's eyes were dancing. She drew in a deep breath.

"Go on," said Maurice. "Tell me you knew all the time."

"I did too," she said. "I knew straight off. I can always pick them, you know I can, Maurice."

"It's a fact," he said. "Don't let it go to your head."

But it was impossible to prevent her mood of elation from infecting everyone else and that evening their sing-song was more jubilant than it had been for a long time.

Iris was the only quiet one. She felt like a winged creature that has been held prisoner under water and must wait for its wings to dry before spreading them and tasting the delights of untrammelled flight. She kept thinking she was still bound down and had to remind herself that now she was free, that now she could be in love without fear, she could marry and leave home knowing that Ma could manage without her help. She had not seen Ma look so carefree or so well for years.

It was time for Johnny to go. He was to fly back to Paris that night and Maurice said that Reub would be joining him there later in the week so Iris didn't have to worry about how he spent his evenings. Reub had a room with a piano and the minute Johnny left the bank every day it would be black coffee and work, black coffee and work, maybe even ice on his head.

"But can't he have time to eat?" she asked in dismay.

"Well maybe," conceded Maurice. "Just a snail or a frog's leg, perhaps."

"Urgh!" said Iris.

Later she took leave of Johnny in Lantern Place where the lamp was alight so that the scene was rather like it had been on that evening of wonder and fear when Cyril Redmayne had interrupted their first kiss. Only now it was almost summer and the air was mild and full of the smell of the lilac.

"Isn't everything wonderful?" she said. "Your music and Perks' Place and us!"

"Wonderful," he said. "And you're wonderful. I don't know what I ever did to deserve you, Iris, but I think I'm the happiest man alive."

"I'm happy too," she said.

It was a seeing happiness. She saw the shadows and she did not flinch from them —Tom, Cyril Redmayne, even poor Alfie Tilley. She could not cut them out of her life, they were an inescapable part of it but before she finally accepted this she asked: "Are we selfish? All this happiness for us! If only everyone could be happy, too."

"That would be heaven," Johnny said. "We're on earth and it isn't so bad. Let's make the most of it!"

When he left her she listened to his footsteps ringing away through the alley and she felt as though she would burst with joy—or was it sorrow? She stood for a moment longer under the lamp listening to the blackbird who seemed to be pitting his powers against the sound of the piano and the voices inside. Then she went in.

Uncle Wally's greasy old trilby was hanging on the hook and beside it was Maurice's new and expensive one. There was Uncle Harry's raincoat, too, shabby, but somehow undaunted.

They were all talking and she could distinguish their voices—Ascot's, Ma's, Camille's and Wally's gruff undertones. And then Maurice struck a chord and they all began to sing. "The Old Songs, the Sweet Songs." She stood scarcely breathing while the music poured out and the loved voices sang.

Tomorrow she would be going back to Abbeyfield, but she had Johnny's ring on her finger and none of the old fears in her heart. Just as the song ended she opened the door and slipped quietly back into Aunt Camille's sitting room.

THE END

GUIDE
TO THE COLOUR CODING
OF
ULVERSCROFT BOOKS

Many of our readers have written to us expressing their appreciation for the way in which our colour coding has assisted them in selecting the Ulverscroft books of their choice. To remind everyone of our colour coding—this is as follows:

BLACK COVERS
Mysteries

★

BLUE COVERS
Romances

★

RED COVERS
Adventure Suspense and General Fiction

★

ORANGE COVERS
Westerns

★

GREEN COVERS
Non-Fiction

ROMANCE TITLES
in the
Ulverscroft Large Print Series

The Smile of the Stranger	*Joan Aiken*
Busman's Holiday	*Lucilla Andrews*
Flowers From the Doctor	*Lucilla Andrews*
Nurse Errant	*Lucilla Andrews*
Silent Song	*Lucilla Andrews*
Merlin's Keep	*Madeleine Brent*
Tregaron's Daughter	*Madeleine Brent*
The Bend in the River	*Iris Bromige*
A Haunted Landscape	*Iris Bromige*
Laurian Vale	*Iris Bromige*
A Magic Place	*Iris Bromige*
The Quiet Hills	*Iris Bromige*
Rosevean	*Iris Bromige*
The Young Romantic	*Iris Bromige*
Lament for a Lost Lover	*Philippa Carr*
The Lion Triumphant	*Philippa Carr*
The Miracle at St. Bruno's	*Philippa Carr*
The Witch From the Sea	*Philippa Carr*
Isle of Pomegranates	*Iris Danbury*
For I Have Lived Today	*Alice Dwyer-Joyce*
The Gingerbread House	*Alice Dwyer-Joyce*
The Strolling Players	*Alice Dwyer-Joyce*
Afternoon for Lizards	*Dorothy Eden*
The Marriage Chest	*Dorothy Eden*